# THE CANADIAN SANSEI

With 66,000 members the Japanese-Canadian community is one of the smallest ethnic communities in Canada. Originally concentrated on the West Coast, their population was dispersed following the expulsion and internment of Japanese Canadians during the Second World War. In 1988 the redress of injustices to citizens interned during the war marked the end of a long fight that had united Japanese Canadians. The community has sensed a weakening of ties ever since.

The Nisei, or second generation of Japanese Canadians who lived through the war, suffered massive discrimination. Scattered across the nation, their children, the Sansei or third generation, have little contact with other Japanese Canadians and have been fully integrated into mainstream society. Tomoko Makabe discovered in her interviews with thirty-six men and twenty-eight women that, in general, the Sansei don't speak Japanese; they marry outside of the Japanese community; and they tend to be indifferent to their being Japanese Canadian. Many are upwardly mobile: they live in middle-class neighbourhoods, are well educated, and work as professionals. It's possible to speculate that the community will vanish with the fourth generation. But Makabe has some reservations. Ethnic identity can be sustained in more symbolic ways. With support and interest from the community at large, aspects of the structures, institutions, and identities of an ethnic group can become an integral part of the dominant culture.

*The Canadian Sansei* is much more than an account of third-generation Japanese Canadians. Makabe's explorations reflect on facets of history, culture, and identity in general as they relate to ethnic minorities in Canada and throughout the world.

TOMOKO MAKABE is a consultant, researcher, and writer based in Toronto. She is the author of *Picture Brides: Japanese Women in Canada*.

# The
# Canadian
# Sansei

*170201*

TOMOKO MAKABE

UNIVERSITY OF TORONTO PRESS
Toronto Buffalo London

© University of Toronto Press Incorporated 1998
Toronto  Buffalo  London
Printed in Canada

ISBN 0-8020-4179-5 (cloth)
ISBN 0-8020-8038-3 (paper)

Printed on acid-free paper

**Canadian Cataloguing in Publication Data**

Makabe, Tomoko, 1944–
The Canadian sansei

ISBN 0-8020-4179-5 (bound)      ISBN 0-8020-8038-3 (pbk.)

1. Japanese Canadians – Ethnic identity.   I. Title.

FC106.J3M335 1998      305.8956′071      C97-932120-4
F1035.J3M34 1998

University of Toronto Press acknowledges the financial assistance to its publishing
program of the Canada Council and the Ontario Arts Council.

The publication of this book was assisted by the National Association of
Japanese Canadians.

*For My Mother*

# Contents

PREFACE    ix

Introduction    3

1  The Japanese-Canadian Community: From Relocation
to Redress    16

2  Social Mobility: The Sansei Style    38

3  Sansei Socialization: The Way They Were Brought Up    60

4  Sansei Identity: Subjectively Defined    87

5  Sansei Behaviour: With a Focus on Intermarriage    111

6  Political Avoidance and Sansei Reaction to
the Redress Movement    139

7  Conclusion    163

APPENDIX 1: Myth of a 'Model Minority': Social Mobility and
Integration Achieved by Canadian Nisei in
a Metropolitan Community    181

APPENDIX 2: Interview Questions    195

NOTES    201

REFERENCES    205

INDEX    211

# Preface

It has been more than two decades since I first became acquainted with the Japanese-Canadian community as a graduate student from abroad. I got involved in the ethnic community in Metropolitan Toronto as part of my thesis work. It was my first 'research field' in a country largely new to me. At the same time, it was my first exposure to the 'Canadian' community, and thereby, in retrospect, my pursuit of understanding the Canadian society had begun.

When my graduate studies came to an end, I said to myself that I would get back to the field some day – to the Japanese-Canadian community, hopefully from coast to coast, beyond the boundaries of Metropolitan Toronto. This book is the outcome of my wishes, which were sustained and materialized twenty years later.

A grant from the Japanese Canadian Redress Foundation has allowed me to conduct a field survey, travelling to over twenty different cities and towns in six provinces and regions from Montreal to Vancouver. The grant also enabled me to devote my full time to drafting the manuscript over six months, with no other commitment. Editing the manuscript was made possible by a grant from the Special Projects Fund offered by the National Association of Japanese Canadians. I would also like to express my appreciation for the support and assistance offered by the Toronto Chapter of the NAJC towards the publication of this book.

I am grateful to Virgil Duff, exectutive editor of the University of Toronto Press, for choosing the manuscript as publishable material for the Press. The anonymous readers of the Press not only read the manuscript, but gave me feedback in a constructive and supportive manner. Without their help this book could not have turned out as it has.

I am indebted to Kathlyn Horibe and Shirley Yamada for their editing of the early drafts of the manuscript. Kate Baltais and John St James, of University of Toronto Press, contributed their professional editorial skills. The final manuscript has been significantly improved by their editing and suggestions.

Lastly, this book would not have been possible, of course, without the participation and cooperation of the sixty-four respondents and the many other 'informers' and supporters whom I met during the course of interviewing. The respondents always talked to me with such willingness and openness. To most of them I was a total stranger-researcher, but they were friendly, sociable, and cooperative, with an 'I'll help you' attitude. Personally, it was a great pleasure to get to know so many Sansei, the '100% Canadians,' and to become friends with them. My understanding of the Japanese-Canadian community has been substantially expanded and deepened. It now seems almost complete.

TOMOKO MAKABE
Toronto, Summer 1997

# THE CANADIAN SANSEI

# Introduction

This book is about Sansei, or third-generation Japanese Canadians, and the forms by which, and degree to which, they identify with their ethnicity as Canadians of Japanese descent. The research on which the work is based is derived from sixty-four Sansei who reside in various regions across Canada, from Montreal to Vancouver. I personally visited with each of them to talk about their ethnicity and what it means to be a Sansei in the post-redress era of the 1990s.

Since the arrival of the first Japanese immigrants on the Canadian shore in the 1870s, the ethnic community of Japanese had been thriving along the West Coast, at least until it was completely dismantled in 1942 by the Second World War. For five decades since the expulsion, after being forced to scatter across the country, the Japanese-Canadian community has nonetheless persisted as a social-cultural community. In the meantime the movement to redress the injustice its members experienced came into being, and enjoyed a successful ending in 1988. Now, it seems, a lingering voice is heard here and there: Is this tiny ethnic community eventually going to disappear?

Over the past two decades, I have done a number of studies on the Japanese-Canadian community, mostly in Metropolitan Toronto (Makabe 1976, 1982, 1990, 1995). I have been a resident of this metropolitan community ever since I first came to live in Canada as a student in the early 1970s. One of the studies I got involved with in the mid-1970s as part of my doctoral-thesis work examined the ethnic-group identity of Canadian-born Japanese. The principal source of information for the study was a series of intensive, qualitative interviews with one hundred Nisei, second-generation Japanese Canadians, and twenty Sansei, the children of the Nisei respondents.[1] The sample size of twenty individuals in a large metropolitan community was too small to provide a systematic survey of the facts of Sansei life. The findings, although only tentative, nonetheless were of particular value, I argued, in predicting the future trends of the community in light of the fact that this small ethnic community would be largely patterned on the characteristics of the third generation, the largest in number, if not influence.

When my graduate studies came to an end, I said to myself that I would some day get back to the field to follow up on the Sansei group. If and when such an occasion arose, I would seek to have a sample group beyond the boundaries of Metropolitan Toronto, locating Sansei in different provinces and regions of the country. This book is the outcome of my intent, which was sustained and materialized twenty years later.

Having examined the two generational groups in my earlier research for a comparison of ethnic identity, the notion that the Sansei are distinctively different from their Nisei parents has remained with me ever since. The gap in terms of their basic perceptions of the ethnic community and the ways in which they view themselves as a racial minority seems so fundamental and ingrained that the Sansei appear to be a totally different social animal from the Nisei. They are free of the old ties and community feelings that have so characterized their parents. To some, the Japanese community, wherever it exists, is only a relic of the past; there is little sense of even relating to it, let alone belonging to it. The socialization of Sansei occurred in the post-war Anglo-Canadian culture, outside ethnic institutions and free from the burden of racism and discrimination, at least in their perception.

Whenever I talk casually with my Nisei friends and acquaintances about the Sansei, the remarks I most frequently hear, after acknowledgments that vast differences exist between the two generations, is that the Sansei are 'completely assimilated' or '100 per cent Canadianized.' From the perspective of some Nisei parents their children have retained very little of their ethnic identity. They are Canadian, pure and simple. 'They think, speak, and act like *hakujin*,'[2] says a Nisei father, detaching himself from his own offspring. This father further admits that with the *hakujin* he still does not feel at ease and comfortable. This may therefore mean that he is not completely at ease with his own *hakujin*-like children, and does not interact with them as freely and equally as he does with his fellow Nisei.

Other Nisei criticize by saying, 'The Sansei think they are *hakujin*,' implying that the Sansei are naive, for they lack awareness of the full impact of prejudice and discrimination in society and have delusions about not being racially defined as Japanese. Often, to me, these parents' remarks make them sound as if their own children belong to a different race or are a different kind of being from them altogether.

The rift between the Nisei and the Sansei may not be as notable or as serious as that which occurred between the Japanese immigrant (called Issei among the Japanese in North America) and the Nisei when they were coming of age on the West Coast, as described by Nisei writer Ken Adachi (1976), for instance. For the Issei remained essentially Japanese in terms of their personality traits, attitudes, and ideals. With no common language, the two generations had difficulty in communicating and in understanding each other. Members of the second- and third-generation groups use the same language – English – yet their way of thinking, their style of communicating and interacting with others, their fears and desires often appear to be too disparate to share with each other. The Sansei's personality traits, attitudes, and ideals seem as distinguishable from those of their parents as those of the Nisei are from their parents'.

Sansei indeed live very different lives from the lives their parents led decades ago. The education and professions of the Sansei move them all over the world. They do not perceive discrimination as a problem and thus do not conceive their ethnic background as having ever been an obstacle in their life. Consequently, the vast majority marry people who are not of Japanese descent. The dif-

ference in experiences between the two Canadian-born generations have been drastic, and even dramatic, in light of the fact that
the process of assimilation and integration[3] in this visible-minority
group has been accomplished in just one generation. Have the
Sansei, however, really been assimilated to the point that they have
become *hakujin*, as some Nisei parents claim? Does being a Japanese Canadian really have little relevance to most of the Sansei?
These questions have intrigued me for some time, long after I left
my work as a researcher in the field of ethnic-community studies.
In the meantime, however, I have never ceased to be an observer
and participant in the community of which I am a part.

Back in 1975, the twenty Sansei I encountered in my fieldwork in
the Toronto area consisted of fifteen men and five women, with an
average age of twenty-seven years. Half of them were already
employed, as a lawyer, a city planner, an engineer, a merchandizing
manager, an architect, a computer operator, a data analyst, a fashion
designer, a teacher, and a 'casual labourer.' With modest incomes,
they were still in the early stages of their careers, with their career
plans somewhat uncertain or, for some, in flux. The rest of the
sample members were students attending either university or community college, seeking professional or vocational training.

In 1993, eighteen years later, the education and training process
was over for the majority of the Sansei population. They had
attained mature-adult status, as had all of the sixty-four individuals
who appear in this study. As the Sansei battle to achieve higher
social status was approaching its zenith, it was indeed the 'right
time' for me to catch up with them, to see how they were doing in
general terms in their struggle for 'success,' occupationally and
otherwise. The timing was also beneficial for me in grasping the
essence of a Japanese-Canadian community in transition and
determining whatever part the Sansei, as mature adults, play in it.
As they grow older and become firmly established in their socio-
ethnic status in the larger society, what changes have occurred in
their ethnic awareness and in their involvement with the community? Has ethnicity become increasingly peripheral to the lives of
many Sansei?

A series of more specific questions was formulated to deal with the broadly stated issues raised above in order to form the content and direction of the present investigation. Some of them were similar to those raised in my earlier study (Makabe 1976), but they have all been reformulated in accordance with changes I witnessed from the mid-1970s to the early 1990s.

In planning and designing research for this study, I was not primarily concerned with testing one or a few closely related hypotheses, seeking statistically relevant evidence for 'the theory.' My goal was not to generalize the findings in a systematic way, but to describe in detail and analyse in depth the nature and forms of ethnicity revealed by the Canadian Sansei. In the analysis of the gathered data I have placed the emphasis on description, using some relevant concepts as analytical tools, not creating a structure or theoretical framework as such. At the end of the analysis, in the concluding chapter, I will discuss the implications of some research findings for the theory of persistence of ethnicity, in an attempt to provide some answers to the following questions: How and why has such a small community of Japanese in Canada managed to maintain its identity? Is this ethnic community eventually going to disappear nonetheless? The tendencies and generalizations found in the Canadian Sansei, I believe, could further be probed and compared in other contexts, using different ethnic groups or third-generation groups.

The inquiry begins with describing the meaning of Sansei identity: what does it mean to be a Japanese Canadian for the Sansei?[4] What constitutes the basis for identification as a Japanese Canadian for them? How do they define and interpret the ethnic heritage passed on to them? How does each Sansei express his or her ethnic identity and how is that expression manifested in terms of behaviour in his or her life?

Individuals can share a similar perspective and identify with each other for a number of different reasons. We are going to search for the content and the nature of ethnic identity among the Sansei, more specifically, for the reasons why they think they are ethnic-group members. The shared perspective can be based on a sense of common ancestry and history, knowledge of a traditional Japanese culture, a sharing of a similar Japanese-Canadian outlook, or simply the common use of ethnic labels and symbols. Since they are a racially defined minority group, the impact of physical distinctiveness that society continues to associate with ethnic identity, and which the Sansei must bear, cannot be underestimated. They cannot get away from definitions imposed by others, regardless of their subjectively defined identity. What are the characteristics of those Sansei who have either a strong or a weak feeling for group identity? How do social and geographic mobility affect ethnic identity and ethnic-group persistence? Do differences in the size of the ethnic communities where the Sansei grew up or currently reside have any impact on defining and shaping their individual group identity?

Second, the present investigation concerns the effects of the Nisei parents' quest for achievement and assimilation on their children's socialization and ethnic identity. Sansei are the sons and daughters of a generation that was too busy rebuilding shattered lives after the post-war resettlement and often worked too hard to be fully accepted by society at large. Some argue that these parents were too ashamed after the humiliation of the forced evacuation and internment to provide much content to the ethnic identity of their offspring. To the extent that Sansei know little about the historical heritage of the community, and even of their own family's background, lack of information and of communication has been a noted 'problem.' These concerns have been expressed and debated previously by some members in the community. Some of them insist that the internment-camp experience the parents went through has robbed the children of their ethnic identity, a sense of history, and a connectedness to the community. My task here is to probe in depth the nature of 'the problem' and the resulting effects from the Sansei perspective.

In probing, an attempt is made to test whether the Sansei perceive the internment experience as significant and unique enough to distinguish Japanese Canadians from other ethnic groups in Canada; whether or not among the Sansei the experience forms a component of a distinctive Japanese-Canadian identity.

The movement to redress the injustice experienced by the internment victims went on throughout the 1980s. It was an important event, a challenge to Japanese Canadians who were forced to re-examine the incident of internment itself and to redefine the legacy of it in comprehensive ways so that the issue could appeal to the younger members of the community as well as to the general public. The movement was also momentous for and crucial to the direction and reconstruction of the ethnic community, wherein history could be changed thereafter. How did the Sansei react to the challenge? How did they deal with the issue? What did redress mean to them? To what extent were the Sansei involved in this historical process that was so significant for this minority group? These are the questions raised in the course of this investigation.

Third, consideration must be given to the dimension of ethnic identity manifested by the Sansei in terms of behaviour in their social life. Some may be actively involved in ethnic churches or other groups, while others may have found a spot in the larger community where they find a more meaningful outlet. By investigating the pattern of involvement and participation of Sansei in social activities within and outside the ethnic community, and their patterns of interpersonal relationships, an attempt is made to examine the kinds of ties to the ethnic group the members have. The argument is that commitment to an ethnic group can be expressed partially, if not wholly, through membership in ethnic churches, the enrolment of children in language classes, and the maintaining of intimate relationships with other members of the group. Can we determine the extent of identity maintained by the Sansei by examining their patterns of involvement and participation in social activities within the ethnic community and their interpersonal relationships?

Sansei are increasingly marrying non-Japanese throughout Canada. The significance of interpersonal and marital relations, as revealed by a very high ratio of interracial marriage among the Sansei, is scrutinized in depth in searching for the reasons and consequences of intermarriage on ethnic community participation.

Lastly, my inquiry forecasts the future of the Japanese-Canadian group and its community in Canada. Whether the community is relatively large with a concentrated population, such as those in Metropolitan Toronto and Greater Vancouver, or a fragmented small centre in northern Ontario or in southern Alberta, the future of the Japanese-Canadian community everywhere in this country will largely be determined by whether the Sansei, with a 'full Canadian upbringing' and cultural orientation, get fully involved in the community, and whether or not they will do so soon enough. Exploration of the Sansei's ethnic identity can provide a clue to the survival of a small ethnic community such as the Japanese-Canadian community. Does a 'Japanese-Canadian community' of Sansei exist? How do the Sansei themselves define their community? The survival of the community itself will largely be determined by the attitudes and commitment of the Sansei towards it. Do they prefer doing things for the community collectively or see the need to keep up existing organizations? As responsible adults, do they accept the responsibility to support and maintain ethnic institutions such as the Nisei home for the aged or the Japanese-Canadian heritage centre? Or is it already too late?

All those questions are important as there are practical implications, I believe, and these ought to be dealt with immediately. Currently undergoing a considerable transformation after redress for the unjust actions of the Canadian government during and after the Second World War, the Japanese-Canadian community is changing in its demographic-organizational structure, with an increased interest in new programs and development plans for the future. Information obtained from this study, therefore, would be valuable for Japanese-Canadian institutions and organizations in planning for their future.

A total of sixty-four Sansei respondents, thirty-six men and twenty-eight women, constitute the sample group for the study presented here. These individuals are located in such areas as Montreal, Ottawa, Kingston, Hamilton, London, Chatham, Ancaster, St Catharines, Metropolitan Toronto, Guelph, Waterloo, Thunder Bay, Geraldton, Winnipeg, Lethbridge, Calgary, Kelowna, Vernon, and Vancouver. Close to half, twenty-nine Sansei, reside in Metropolitan Toronto, the major population centre of the Japanese in Canada. The balance of the respondents reside either in small centres such as Thunder Bay, with only a couple of hundred Japanese Canadians, or in isolated communities 'away from the centre,' with less than a dozen or so Japanese families. Not all of the respondents who resided in Toronto at the time of the interviews are necessarily 'Torontonians' who were born and bred in the metropolitan area. Two-thirds come from Toronto or its vicinity, while the remaining one-third are originally from northern Ontario, Quebec, British Columbia, Manitoba, and Alberta.

With a range from 25 to 52 years, the mean age of the sample group is 38.5. Most of these people were born in the ten-year period after the end of concentration-camp life for their parents. A large majority are in the midst of forming families and raising children; 41 out of 64 are married with or without children; three are in common-law arrangements; 15 are single, and of these, four are divorced or separated and one is widowed.

The principal source of information for this book is a series of intensive qualitative interviews conducted with these sixty-four respondents between March 1992 and October 1993. It is within the context of their lives that the question of Sansei identity is to be probed – their words form the basis of the present book.

The Sansei are defined or commonly understood as the native-born children of native-born parents. Included in the group for this study are those whose parents were born and raised in this country as well as a few whose mother or father came to Canada in their early childhood. Some respondents' parents spent their formative years attending school in Japan, and a few have Nisei parents who went to Japan under the Canadian government's repatriation scheme during and after the war and returned to Canada as sponsored immigrants in the 1950s. Two respondents have a parent who is non-Japanese.

The 'snowballing' method of sampling, which I was familiar with from my earlier study, was again used in locating the respondents. This sampling method was the only possible way to locate respondents when even the churches and other ethnic organizations were not sources of population filing. In many regions, no Japanese organization or group substantive enough to be called one exists, while in the large centres like Toronto, with a variety of churches and other types of community organizations, only a very limited segment of the Sansei population actually hold membership in those organizations.

For some time before the start of my fieldwork, therefore, I tried to meet as many 'informants' as possible, mostly in the Toronto area, and asked them for the names of adult Sansei whom they knew, whether children of the informants, their cousins, distant nieces or nephews, family friends, or 'the kids I went to school with' – as long as the individuals were residing in Canada. Once I started interviewing, the respondents were asked to provide names of Sansei whom they knew, other than their siblings. I also had a fair number of names that seemed to be Sansei that I had picked up from ethnic-community newspapers and other publications over the years. Snowballing in this manner in order to draw up the sample group continued until the fieldwork came to an end.

The sixty-four respondents were randomly drawn from all the available names given to me or gathered by myself, which in the end was well over six hundred. This sample is different from the sort one would select as a sample group to study the stratification of the Japanese-Canadian community or the Sansei community as such. No claim is made about the 'representativeness' of the sample. The list of six hundred or so names was still too limited as a proportionate representation of the entire generation group, which is scattered across this vast land. Nevertheless, randomness was used as consistently as possible in selecting the individuals so that representativeness of the sample group would be increased at the highest level. Age and gender were the main factors considered in selecting possible respondents for the sample group.

Because of the snowballing approach, the refusal ratio was very low, a pleasant surprise, and actually a blessing to me. The Sansei members I contacted were a different lot altogether from the Nisei, when they were approached for the earlier studies. Over 90 per cent of them responded, when asked if they would like to partake in my interview, by saying: 'Sure, I would.' Less than a dozen of the individuals approached by telephone refused an

interview because they were not interested or were just 'too busy.'
A few could not make time for the interview after a few attempts
were made to set up an appointment. In the end, drawing up the
sample group was a much, much easier task for me and less time-
consuming than on previous occasions. The fact that they were
told the reference source when they were first approached, and
that they had been referred by their relatives or friends, may have
affected their positive response to being interviewed. For the
majority, however, it did not seem to matter very much. No one
refused to allow the interview to be tape-recorded either. Consequently, each one of the interviews was recorded.

Not only were the respondents willing to be interviewed and
very cooperative, they were also very open and sociable, and eager
to discuss the questions. Overall, they were relaxed and confident.
In their complete openness towards me, a stranger-researcher, and
towards the project as I briefly outlined it, I sensed a deep 'difference' between the two generations of Japanese Canadians that I
have discussed earlier. In contrast to the spontaneity and willingness of the Sansei to take part in this work, the Nisei were preoccu-
pied with various notions of themselves and their families within
the community. They had a hundred reasons for not being willing
to participate in the study: 'I'm not the kind of Nisei you expect.'
'My life is dull and simple, and I have very little to contribute to
your study.' 'I want to help you, but I shouldn't be part of your
study.' 'I have to be careful, because people can identify you from
what you say.' 'I cannot talk well and can be misunderstood.' And
so on, just to quote a few remarks as I remember them. In addition, there is, of course, the usual excuse: 'I'm too busy.' The tension that I sometimes felt so strongly with some Nisei in attempting
to get their acceptance and consent was completely absent from
the Sansei members wherever I visited them.

The interviews were largely unstructured, but the choice of
questions was predetermined (all the interview questions are in
appendix 2). I always started by asking about the respondent's family history, about whatever they knew about the background and
experiences of their grandparents, the original immigrants, and
then of their parents, followed by their own experience of growing

up. Encouraged to elaborate on the responses, no one refused to answer any question. Some respondents had difficulty in providing their family history or in understanding and answering the question on, for example, whether the Japanese in Canada can or should maintain their group identity in the future, and if they can/should, then how. As those individuals had never been confronted with these questions before, or had never thought of them before, some of them found it difficult to put their answers into words and to be articulate and consistent. The interviews normally took one and a half to two hours to complete, and were conducted, in most cases, in the homes of the respondents or in either their office or mine (in the case of respondents residing in Toronto). As none of the respondents spoke but a few words of Japanese, all of the interviews were conducted in English.

Following this introductory section, this book is organized into seven chapters. In the first chapter, in an attempt to arrive at an understanding of the changing structure of this ethnic community and the present state of the group, the historical background of the Japanese group in Canada is discussed, with a focus of the postwar period from relocation to redress.

In the second chapter, an attempt is made to give a profile of the Sansei as represented by the sixty-four men and women involved in this study. The chapter focuses on educational and occupational spheres of the Sansei experience and offers an explanation as to how progress has been achieved by members of the sample group.

Chapter 3 deals with the socialization experience of the Canadian Sansei. The central themes explored in this chapter are: (1) the Nisei refusal to acknowledge the historical heritage of the Japanese-Canadian group, and in particular its negative aspect – the legacy of racial victimization and persecution; and (2) the consequences of this refusal upon the socialization of the Sansei.

Chapter 4 examines what it means to be a Canadian of Japanese descent. What does being a Japanese Canadian mean to each individual Sansei? What constitutes the basis for identification or consciousness as a person of Japanese descent? How does each individual Sansei express his or her ethnic identification? How important in one's everyday life are the meanings attached to one's ethnicity? This subjective aspect of Sansei identity is documented in the respondents' own words.

Chapter 5 investigates the behavioural aspect of the Sansei identity. How is ethnic identity manifested by the Sansei in terms of their everyday behaviour? Can we somehow determine the extent of their identity by examining their behaviour? The focus is placed on the patterns of involvement and participation in social activities, both formally and informally, within as well as outside the ethnic community. The issue of intermarriage – the reasons for and consequences of it – is also discussed in this chapter.

Chapter 6, the last chapter of data analysis, deals with the political arena of Sansei life. It reports on the political attitudes and participation patterns of the Sansei as well as their response to the issue of redress for the Second World War incarceration.

Finally, the concluding chapter 7 discusses the implications of these findings for theories of ethnicity – particularly, the persistence of ethnicity. The role of external factors in determining the continuity of generations and the persistence of ethnic-group cohesion is discussed and articulated, based on research findings.

At the end of the book (appendix 1) is appended a report entitled 'Myth of a "Model Minority?": Social Mobility and Integration Achieved by Canadian Nisei in a Metropolitan Community.' It discusses the Nisei experience of social mobility and integration. Based on two sets of data collected in Toronto, this report was written as a research report before the present project started, and provides information on the Nisei and a summary of their experience. Because these are the most comprehensive, quantitative data on Nisei experience, I have appended the report to this book. Its findings are used as references throughout the course of the discussion wherever it is relevant to do so.

## Chapter One

# The Japanese-Canadian Community: From Relocation to Redress

*... Everything was done [to give the Japanese an opportunity to return to their homeland], ... officially, unofficially, at all levels and the message to disappear worked its way deep into the Nisei heart and into the bone marrow.*

Joy Kogawa (1983, 184)

The Japanese-Canadian community is one of the smallest ethnic communities in Canada. In 1991 the members numbered about 66,000, or roughly 0.2 per cent of Canada's population.

The definition of ethnicity in the 1991 Census of Canada was derived by modifying the question used in 1986: 'In which ethnic/cultural group(s) do you or did your ancestors belong?' In 1991, respondents were asked: 'To which ethnic or cultural group(s) did this person's ancestors belong?' The phrase 'do you' was removed to clarify the intent of the question, which was to measure the origins of the respondents. When the respondent provided only one origin, the response was considered a single definition. For example, 48,595 gave Japanese as their only ethnic origin. Multiple identification occurred when the respondent provided more than one origin. Some 17,085 Canadians gave a response that included Japanese and one or more other ethnic or cultural origins. The total response is the sum of the single and the multiple identifications for the group, which is nearly 66,000. Of these, 80 per cent were residing in twelve Census Metropolitan Areas of five Cana-

TABLE 1.1
Japanese-Canadian population* by province and major
Census Metropolitan Areas, 1991

| Provinces/CMA | | Population |
|---|---|---|
| Newfoundland | | 30 |
| Prince Edward Island | | 55 |
| Nova Scotia | | 310 |
| New Brunswick | | 140 |
| Quebec | | 2,680 |
| Montreal | 2,360 | |
| Ontario | | 24,380 |
| Toronto | 17,060 | |
| Hamilton | 1,485 | |
| Ottawa-Hull | 1,280 | |
| London | 620 | |
| Kitchener | 575 | |
| Thunder Bay | 405 | |
| Manitoba | | 1,455 |
| Winnipeg | 1,380 | |
| Saskatchewan | | 670 |
| Alberta | | 8,745 |
| Calgary | 2,755 | |
| Edmonton | 1,820 | |
| British Columbia | | 27,145 |
| Vancouver | 19,845 | |
| Victoria | 1,240 | |
| Total | | 65,680 |

Source: Statistics Canada, 1991 Census of Canada, Ethnic
Origin (catalogue 93–315), tables 2A and 2B
* The population number is the sum of single and multiple
identification for the group.

dian provinces (table 1.1). This is quite a different picture from
that going into the Second World War.

Before 1942, over 95 per cent of the Japanese in Canada (a total
of some 23,000 persons) were living in the province of British
Columbia, with more than three-quarters of them clustered within
seventy-five miles of the city of Vancouver. Today, as the figures in
the table indicate, more than half of the entire population of Japanese Canadians is concentrated in relatively large population centres, such as Metropolitan Toronto and Greater Vancouver, or

widely scattered throughout numerous other cities and towns
across Canada. The concentration is not large enough in any one
place to characterize it as a Japanese-Canadian district or residential area. In no one single area in Vancouver or Toronto are Japanese Canadians readily observable in large numbers as one walks
down the street, although certain areas, typically the tourist section
of Vancouver, have a larger proportion of Japanese-owned com-
mercial enterprises than do other parts of the city. An analysis of
the population distribution by census tracts in Metropolitan Toronto based on the 1986 counting, for instance, indicated that
there was not a single census tract giving the Japanese more than
2 per cent proportionally out of 424 tracts in the entire area (Makabe 1990). The geographic dispersion was quite notable both
within the city of Toronto as well as in surrounding cities and
towns. The completeness of dispersal applied to other areas, wherever Japanese were located. The demographic distribution patterns illustrated by these figures resulted from a series of events
that occurred half a century ago – the forced internment and
resettlement of Canadians of Japanese ancestry, an event that took
place during and after the Second World War.

The Japanese-Canadian community is largely fragmented
because of both its small number and its physical dispersion. It has
remained small indeed, with only a minimum rate of growth,
partly because of the extremely modest Japanese immigration in
the post-war decades.[1] Since the Second World War some 18,000
Japanese have immigrated to Canada, about 380 a year (*Immigration Statistics*, 1992). Placed in the entire context of Canadian
immigration, the flow from Japan has been so slight as to be almost
negligible. Also, about 10 per cent of those 18,000 were actually
Canadian citizens 'repatriated' to Japan during and after the war
and allowed to return as immigrants (Kobayashi 1989). No mention, therefore, can possibly be made of this ethnic community as
we see it today without touching its physical features and demographic patterns, which were largely created as a result of the federal government's wartime policy regarding the Japanese in
Canada.

The central theme of the resettlement policy was to force Japanese Canadians to disperse as widely as possible across Canada and to discourage them from living together in the same geographic area. In response, people did indeed disperse themselves as they were ordered. This particular policy turned out to be quite effective and successful, perhaps the most effective public policy ever administered by a government to deal with an ethnic-minority group in this country. It not only removed members of the community by physically dispersing them, but it also destroyed their organized communities by breaking up their closely integrated institutions and associations. Historically speaking, only rarely has a Canadian community ever been so completely broken up and thoroughly disrupted in its normal development. Without some understanding of the historical events and background surrounding formulation of this policy it is virtually impossible to adequately assess this particular ethnic community. This chapter will therefore provide a historical account of the formulation and implementation of the government policy to forcibly resettle the Japanese Canadians across Canada, the central part of their history in this country.

The first documented immigrant from Japan arrived at the Canadian shore in the late 1870s. The Japanese immigrants were attracted to Canada, and British Columbia in particular, for two major reasons: (1) they could expect to find immediate work in the fishing and lumbering industries of the province, and (2) they could also live in a region where the climate and geography resembled that of their homeland.

From the very beginning, however, there was hostility in British Columbia on the part of white Canadians towards Orientals, based on an irrational fear of the 'yellow peril,' a fear that British Columbia would be inundated by a group of people who differed racially and culturally from them, and who, to their minds, posed a threat to their standard of living. The Japanese could not be assimilated, they believed, and their geographic concentration within one area – in a fishing village in Steveston, or in a part of Vancouver known as Japan town – and their visibility further spurred anti-Oriental sentiment.

In the early years, the Japanese were employed mainly as cheap labour in such major industries as lumbering, fishing, mining, and railroading. As they gained skill and knowledge, and acquired capital, they were able to move out of these industries and buy farms, fishing boats and equipment, stores, and homes. This shift occurred mainly in the 1920s, as general expansion in the province came to an end. In the years approaching 1941, Japanese Canadians had become established economically. Though their employment involved only six occupations in 1893, four decades later, this number had surpassed sixty (Young 1938).

In addition to the usual difficulties experienced by all immigrants, the history of Japanese immigrants and their families in settling in Canada was by and large one of upward struggle in which they faced constant discrimination. The discrimination practised against them, either by law or by custom, was prevalent, persistent, and effective. As early as 1902, a measure disenfranchising British subjects of Asiatic origin had been passed in the Legislature of British Columbia. Japanese born in Canada, as well as Japanese nationals, ceased to have the right to vote in the province (Adachi 1976; Ward 1978).

Disenfranchisement also meant exclusion from a whole series of activities in the political and economic life of the province. Their exclusion from the voting lists banned the Japanese from all licensed professions and occupations, and as the number of licences issued to them was gradually cut back, many workers were forced out of the fishing and lumbering industries. These occupational barriers also affected their Canadian-born children, who were educated, highly skilled, and acculturated to Canadian society, but were now unable to obtain jobs outside the Japanese community. It became virtually impossible for the second-generation Japanese Canadians to penetrate or achieve mobility within the dominant economic institutions of the province.

British Columbia was an area of recent settlement in need of population for the exploitation of its rich resources. The gold rush of 1858 brought an influx of settlers, more predominantly from Britain, into the vast emptiness of the colony. They were highly self-conscious of their British origin and wished to have the colony remain an area populated by British immigrants (Adachi 1976, 37–8). Other settlers, many from abroad, had started coming in large numbers around the turn of the century, which was revealed by the high proportion of the foreign-born, compared to the Canadian-born, population. In the 1911 census more than half of the total population residing in the province were foreign-born subjects, and 50 per cent were still so in 1921, the largest proportions of all the provinces. The balance of power thus was constantly changing in correspondence to the number and the place of origin of the newcomers. The province itself – the newest member of the Dominion after joining it in 1871 – was also geographically and psychologically isolated from the economic and political development of the rest of the country, and had sustained a desire to maintain its own status with the Dominion, independent from the authority of the federal government.

The nadir of the history of hostility and discrimination against the Japanese Canadians came with the bombing of Pearl Harbor in December 1941. 'As a matter of military interest in the Pacific situation and deemed necessary to the safeguarding of national security' (Canada 1947, 24), all enemy aliens – most of whom were persons of the Japanese race (Japanese nationals as well as Canadian-born children of Japanese parents and Japanese immigrants naturalized as British subjects) were removed from the so-called defence zone in British Columbia to internment camps in the interior of the province. Thereafter, all the policies implemented and actions taken by the government for evacuation and internment were mobilized under the banner of 'national security,' although no attempt was made by Ottawa to define publicly what was meant by 'national security' or 'military interest' and what the 'defence of Canada' involved (Adachi 1976, 219). On the part of the government the mass removal of Japanese Canadians would, speculated Ken Adachi (211), 'greatly simplify the task of defending the coastline against possible invasion, of removing the source of widespread apprehension among the white population,' which might become the focus for riots. Under the government's repeated statement that 'national security' was the overriding consideration, the issue of evacuation was questioned by practically no one in the country. The evacuation from Vancouver Island, the mainland of British Columbia, the Fraser Valley, and other areas where the Japanese lived meant uprooting communities, disbanding numerous businesses, breaking up families and home life, and the substantial loss of personal possessions and properties.

At the time this government order of removal was issued in 1942 under the authority of the War Measures Act, only 25 per cent of all Japanese in Canada had retained their Japanese citizenship; the rest were Canadian citizens, about 60 per cent of whom had been born in Canada. Japanese were removed either to roadwork, farming, or industrial projects organized by the government, or to various internment camps. As a result of the evacuation, 11,500 persons spent the war years in 'ghost town' camps in the interior of British Columbia, 2500 were in sugar-beet fields in Alberta, 1000 were in the farming area of Manitoba, and the rest were engaged in self-supporting projects in British Columbia or in road projects or industries in Eastern Canada (La Violette 1948, 96). Various wartime restrictions were also imposed. All the Japanese, with the exception of those few who were well-off enough to move on their own to the interior, lost all freedom of movement and therefore the ability to earn anything more than a subsistence livelihood for more than four years. Homes, land, businesses, equipment, and other property owned by the evacuated Japanese were 'sold' over the protests of their owners at prices that could scarcely be called adequate. As Davis and Krauter (1971, 58) have stated, the experience of the Japanese during the war is 'probably the worst single example of the oppression of a Canadian minority group by the combined forces of public opinion and government policy in the entire history of this country.'

Japanese Canadians had already been relocated to various internment camps and projects for over two years when the basic principle of the government policy for removing them from the West Coast was formally announced in a statement made by Prime Minister Mackenzie King to the House of Commons in August 1944. The major policy statement on the Japanese since the expulsion of 1942 (Canada, House of Commons 1944, 5917), this statement was momentous in determining the future of the Japanese and their community with far-reaching consequences: '[I]t must be accepted as a basic factor that it would be unwise and undesirable ... to allow the Japanese population to be concentrated in that province [British Columbia] after war ... The sound policy and the best policy for the Japanese Canadians themselves is to distribute their members as widely as possible throughout the country where they will not create feelings of racial hostility.'

Thus, it became clear to the Japanese that returning to their homes in the coastal areas of British Columbia was out of the question in the foreseeable future, and that the dispersal and relocation were permanent. The Japanese were to be distributed more equitably throughout the provinces and throughout the nation. It was assumed, as the statement further implies, that if the Japanese had not been concentrated in one province, as they were previously, the hostile attitudes and the racial discrimination against them would never have developed. The notion was that resettlement was the solution to what King called 'the Japanese problem,' as resettlement would lead to the economic and social integration of the Japanese population into the larger community. In King's view the Japanese themselves were to be blamed for their 'problem,' and thus the solution was for the Japanese to voluntarily disperse themselves across the country and rapidly assimilate into the Anglo-Canadian society.

Dispersal was synonymous with assimilation. That was the notion prevailing in society then, and was basic to the minds of policy makers and the liberal-minded public (Sunahara 1981, 132). It was commonly accepted that minorities – visible or otherwise – could and should be assimilated; at the same time, the stigma of being unable to assimilate was fairly strongly attached to them. In order to be assimilated, however, they must become less visible, and thus they must be geographically dispersed. The dispersal would only be of benefit to the minorities, the argument went, because it would reduce racial discrimination, and as a consequence, economic mobility would become possible and eventually attainable for them.

In 1945, a year after King's policy statement was made, the government launched a program to segregate the 'loyal' members of the Japanese community from the 'disloyal' and to 'repatriate' to Japan those deemed disloyal as part of the permanent post-war dispersal of the Japanese in Canada. Thus, the strategy to attain the goal of assimilation became twofold: (1) disperse to east of the Rockies those Japanese who were willing to remain in Canada, and (2) repatriate to Japan those who refused to move east and thus were considered to be 'disloyal.' To solve the 'Japanese problem' once and for all, the dispersal policy added an additional element that was meant to work towards deporting or repatriating as many Japanese as possible, as soon as that was physically possible.

The scheme ended up with the eventual repatriation of 4000 Japanese to Japan. More than half of them were Canadian-born and two-thirds were Canadian citizens. Many were children accompanying their parents. Those returning were doing so because they were too old or too sick to begin again (many of the repatriates, however, returned to Canada in the 1950s as sponsored immigrants when the Canadian immigration policy permitted this).

It cannot be overemphasized that Japanese Canadians were actively urged by the government to 'return' to Japan. Arrangements were made so that they would return 'voluntarily.' For example, travel expenses for adults and children alike were carried by the government. The actions of the government were inducements for Japanese Canadians to desire to go to Japan, rather than remain in Canada. The government's encouragement of repatriation was indeed a success – for a time, nearly 10,000 Japanese signed applications to be repatriated (La Violette 1948).

Government policy towards Japanese in the United States, both during and after the war, was similar to that of the Canadian government in many respects. Public opinion, too, was similar in the two countries. Nevertheless, on the whole, the Canadian policy tended to be more severe than the American (Sunahara 1981; Makabe 1980). Internment began earlier and ended later in Canada. The Canadian government's post-war strategy of mass deportation had no counterpart in the United States. As the war against Japan drew to an end, the United States permitted Japanese Americans to return to their homes in the coastal area; in Canada, Japanese Canadians were not allowed to return to the coast until 1949.

And the Canadian government rejected Nisei for military service until near the very end of the war, while in the United States, from early 1943 Nisei could enlist.

Under the 'loyal' versus 'disloyal' scheme, every Japanese Canadian aged 16 years and over was required to choose between the two resettlement options. This was a choice that most Japanese in the United States were not required to make and one that no other group in Canada had to make ever, with the possible exception of the Acadians two hundred years ago. Many Japanese Canadians, especially the Nisei, had not the slightest desire to 'return' to Japan, which to them was a foreign country. Nor did Canada say that they were accepted unconditionally as Canadians. Through dispersion – which was imposed and compulsory, not voluntary – they had to show evidence of their loyalty to Canada.

With the overwhelming majority of Japanese Canadians being loyal citizens of this country, the wartime policy of the Canadian government brought two issues into sharp focus. First, the dominant element that led to the evacuation and internment was racial prejudice, and not a need for 'national security.' Second, under this policy, these ethnic persons called Japanese Canadians were in fact Japanese – at least they had to be either Canadians or Japanese and they could not be both.

As the assimilationist view became a dominating force in formulating and in enforcing the policy, many Japanese Canadians had come to agree with the federal government that dispersion was necessary. The leadership in the community, represented by the *New Canadian*, the community newspaper, took the initiative in the movement for 'cooperating with the government.'

*New Canadian* was started in Vancouver by a group of concerned Nisei in 1938. It was the only community organ that was allowed by the government to continue publishing when war with Japan broke out in 1941. The bi-weekly paper, the only means of communication for many Japanese, connected the evacuated communities, linking scattered individuals and families. Through its editorials it endorsed King's policy. For example, in the editorial of 12 August 1944 we read: 'It will be sensible and patriotic for us to accept and cooperate in the situation with good grace.' To obtain the government's objective of geographical dispersal, it was contended that cooperation was both necessary and desirable. The need for the Japanese to disperse themselves across Canada was one of the themes debated in *New Canadian* before the evacuation, and thus was 'a familiar topic' long before the war. The newspaper had repeatedly published discussions on desegregation and integration encouraging the Japanese Canadians, especially the Nisei, to move to Central and Eastern Canada, where discrimination would be less severe.

At an early stage in implementing the dispersal policy, the federal government hoped to place one Japanese person, but not more than one Japanese family, in each eastern town and village. A number of Japanese thought likewise, and some of them actually became anxious when it was not done (La Violette 1948, 150). However, many others were reluctant to respond to the policy until the war with Japan was actually over.

Toronto became the destination for those who opted to resettle in the East. By 1948 the Japanese-Canadian population in that city was approximately 3800, and Japanese Canadians were reported to be living on at least 293 different streets, according to documents located in various archives (Oikawa 1986).[2] Concerned about the possibility of the Japanese congregating in certain areas, the federal officer in charge of relocating the evacuees recommended that the government discontinue its policy of paying the travel fares of those moving from British Columbia (Oikawa 1986, 98). *New Canadian* kept reminding its readers to avoid forming any segregated community life, and articles often appeared that emphasized the importance of avoiding 'a very natural tendency' to live on the same streets and to work at the same places, as the early arrivals had tended to do in Montreal and Toronto.

Although no official assurance was given by the government that Japanese Canadians were now permanent residents of Canada, one of those 'pioneers' courageous enough to opt for the 'unknown territory' of Eastern Canada was Ed Kitagawa, who came with his family to resettle in Toronto directly from Vancouver as early as June 1942. They were one of the few families who decided to become 'self-supporting' to avoid the internment. Kitagawa accepted dispersal, although he knew it was not right for the government to make it an order for the Japanese to obey; for Ed Kitagawa, speaking in his nineties in the early 1990s in coversations with me, '[d]ispersal was not a matter of conscious choice, rather it was a matter of natural course out of necessity.'

The published collection of writings of his late wife, Muriel Kitagawa (1985), gives vivid voice to those who lived through the war years and at long last describes the events from the perspective of Japanese Canadians themselves. During and after the war Muriel Kitagawa was one of very few Nisei who kept protesting against the wartime policies by writing letters directly to the government. Nonetheless the overall attitude towards resettlement, as expressed in her writings, reveals that the Japanese were willing to start all over again in the East, and were eager to become permanently resettled away from their unhappy experiences in British Columbia.

An empirical study I did in Toronto in the mid-1970s (Makabe 1976) provides evidence of the conscious efforts made by the Japanese to disperse and become less visible once resettled in the city. The one hundred Nisei respondents interviewed for that study more or less admitted that they consciously or subconsciously avoided living in any one section of the city. At first, when their financial situations were more stringent, they settled in the immigrant reception area of downtown Toronto, particularly around Spadina Avenue, close to the garment factories. As they secured better employment, they left the old central city for new, higher-status areas. In general, it was a two- or three-step residential movement towards the suburbs for the Toronto Nisei.

What did the federal government's policy of dispersal mean to the individual Nisei while 'on the move' all those years? The following is a good summary of the comments made by the Toronto respondents:

> The dispersal policy was not necessary, but it was a good thing. I didn't deliberately try to stay away from other Japanese, but I knew in the back of my mind that it was a good thing. I've always been aware of this because of [what] happened to us before on the coast. (Makabe 1976, 110)

Regardless of their awareness or lack of awareness of the government policy, Nisei did not try to become less visible, nor did they move their residences to purposely disperse themselves because they were told to do so; they nonetheless admitted that dispersal was necessary and that 'it was not any good for Japanese to congregate again.' If racial discrimination was to be reduced, the Nisei recognized that dispersal would benefit both the Japanese community as a whole as well as the individual. Acceptance by the larger society became possible only as a consequence of the dispersal of the population and by their becoming invisible, as their rather brief experience in Toronto verified. As they dispersed, as many personally witnessed, the discrimination disappeared. Thus, dispersal became 'a natural course of action' for many Nisei, who internalized as good the notion of dispersal.

Many indeed wanted to be as inconspicuous as possible. Whenever they moved to a 'better location,' they did so in the hope of not only improving their social status but also ridding themselves, in one fell swoop, of their visibility and their 'Japanese-ness.' Racism, the uprooting and resettlement, the loss of all goods and properties, and the stripping of their citizenship provided a strong subconscious determination for them to disperse first and foremost as sparsely and thinly as possible. This mind-set seemed to stay with the Nisei for a fairly prolonged period, as depicted at the beginning of this chapter by Joy Kogawa in her novel *Obasan* (1983), much longer than they themselves knew.

Another pioneer family, the Nakamuras, a farming family originally from Mission, British Columbia, moved to Montreal in 1943 after spending one year on a sugar-beet farm in Alberta. Before too long, they permanently relocated to a small farming community in southwestern Ontario to re-establish themselves as independent farmers (Makabe 1995). Forty years later, in an interview, the older Issei couple spoke of their attitude towards integration and their willingness to be part of the local white community. During the period of evacuation, the BC Security Commission had required each person seeking relocation permission to submit evidence that he or she would be accepted in the community where residence was planned, that there would be housing, and that work could be obtained. Even though the regulation became invalid by the time they came to southern Ontario, the couple faithfully followed the steps of the procedure. They talked to every one of the residents in the neighbourhood before they purchased the farm to explain their situation, and told them what they intended to do. Immediately upon settling in the area, the Issei couple mingled with the white community and joined the local church group in an effort to integrate.

Dispersion also became 'a stronger framework of thought and action' for those Japanese Canadians who opted to resettle in Montreal (Oiwa 1986, 23). As early as 1944, Oiwa noted, 'the tendency of dispersion' already existed among the five hundred or so settlers, although the majority were still temporarily residing in the downtown reception area. A few years later, with the population at a little over a thousand, the need to disperse was further intensified. In Montreal the Japanese more or less tried not to create a ghetto or the economic interdependence that had existed in the pre-war communities, although most did not avoid interacting with their fellow Japanese. They temporarily lived and worked together and helped each other out, but when it came to buying their homes, the resettlers dispersed themselves consciously and conscientiously. When dispersed, they were invisible and, in Oiwa's terms (1986, 27), 'seem to have preferred it that way.'

Many people who came to Montreal in the earlier years had been refused entry to Toronto. As more and more Japanese had moved into Toronto, the city's Board of Control made it a closed city. June Tanaka, her four young children, and her aged mother came to Montreal in 1944 from an internment camp to join her husband, who had ended up in Montreal after being refused entry to Toronto. Mrs Tanaka, in occasional conversations with me, spoke of her first week in Montreal looking for a place to rent that could accommodate a family of seven. She also had a notion, 'somewhere in the back of my mind,' that dispersal 'must be a good thing to do.' She finally found a flat in a predominantly working-class and French section of the city, in an area that happened to be away from other Japanese families. With physical survival at stake, the Tanakas ventured to live among French Canadians, 'total strangers' to them for at least the initial period of resettlement. To their surprise, in the French-Canadian neighbourhood nobody seemed to care who the Japanese were or where they came from.

Because of the strategy of mass deportation, which was concluded in 1947, and the stringent conditions imposed on movement and relocation in Eastern Canada, the whole resettlement process lasted substantially longer in Canada than in the United States, despite the fact that internment began earlier in Canada. There were restrictions on travel and ownership or leasing of homes and businesses, and trade licences were withheld for a long time, mostly in response to constant political and public pressure from the province of British Columbia (Adachi 1976). Consequently, the evacuees could not return to their homes even after the war against Japan was over; in fact, they were not allowed to return until 1949. Had the dispersal been voluntary and had the evacuees been allowed to return to their coastal homes as early as 1945, as most Japanese Americans chose to do, the state of the present Japanese-Canadian community and the lives of its members would be quite different today. The Japanese-American communities quickly re-established themselves in the coastal areas, whereas the 'right' opportunity for Japanese Canadians seemed missed and there was insufficient energy left for them to rebuild a normal community life.

In the spring of 1949, seven years after they had been uprooted from the West Coast, the last wartime restrictions on Japanese Canadians were removed. They were finally able to freely move about the country and return to British Columbia if they wished. However, there was no large-scale rush back to British Columbia. As Muriel Kitagawa wrote in 1947, there still existed an ongoing fear on the part of some of the public of seeing an influx of evacuees returning to the coastal area. There were also many other barriers that prevented many Japanese from returning to the West Coast. It was not a matter of 'going home,' in Kitagawa's words (1985, 237): 'Our former homes are gone ... Our stores, our businesses, our boats, our farms and other small savings are gone the same way.' Those who had by then resettled in the East found themselves better off, even though they had had to start from scratch.

The first to go back to the West Coast were the Nisei fishermen, followed by their families and some other evacuees. Even to the present day, most Japanese Canadians – especially those living in Ontario and Quebec – have not shown a keen interest in returning. British Columbia has remained a symbol of all that was evil in terms of racist behaviour and a hostile attitude towards 'easterners.' Only recently have some Nisei found it hard to resist returning to the coast, to their 'roots,' in part because of the better climate.

The Japanese population in British Columbia, therefore, has never reached its pre-war level. Nor has the community, as it existed before the war, been reconstructed. The intent of the dispersal – the destruction of the ethnic community – has been fully achieved. The evacuation and relocation process destroyed the organized communities, separated family units, broke up the closely integrated institutions, and disrupted various associational groups and friendship ties. What has developed since 1949 is a community very different from its counterpart in pre-war British Columbia, a community formed of individuals and families of very different backgrounds – people from cities, farms, isolated fishing villages, and logging camps – resettled in Winnipeg, Montreal, or wherever else Japanese chose to relocate.

It may be said, in sum, that the net effect of the forced evacuation and resettlement was to disperse Japanese Canadians beyond the physical bounds of British Columbia into areas of wider opportunity, not only physically but occupationally and socially as well. Those who moved East spread out into various parts of the country and into a variety of jobs, businesses, and professions – unprecedented for the Japanese. They were able to build new and better lives after the war, as some Japanese Canadians claim, with the evacuation producing benefits far outweighing the harm documented by Adachi (1976, 362), though others think otherwise. As a Sansei student puts it, the group has done fairly well *despite* (not because of) government policy, which was unjustifiably racist and 'fundamentally coercive in nature' (Oikawa 1986, 1).

For almost five decades since the expulsion, the Japanese-Canadian community has nonetheless somehow persisted as a social-cultural community in the sense of the ethos of interacting social groups. At present, in either Toronto or Vancouver, one can easily count fifty or so religious and secular organizations and associations in each Japanese community. Even in Montreal, with a Japanese population of only two thousand or so, the names of at least ten groups regularly appear in the community's monthly newsletter, which has continued publishing for all those years.

At the outset of resettlement, anti-organizational sentiment was fairly strong among the Japanese, particularly among the Nisei in Eastern Canada. Their strategy for a smooth adjustment to their new life was to maintain a low profile in every sense, with the Japanese organizations viewed as a 'social crutch' retarding assimilation. The group in Montreal, for instance, turned down a proposal to form a Nisei organization because 'it would attract undue and unfavourable attention, give rise to misunderstanding and actually hinder the process of assimilation' (*New Canadian*, 13 March 1944). There still existed a fear of building up any community life by congregating in organizational settings and thus making 'those very same mistakes as we made in Vancouver.'

Largely out of necessity – to deal with critical issues facing the community as a result of resettlement – the Japanese Canadian Citizens' Association (JCCA), an extension of the Toronto-based Japanese Canadian Committee for Democracy, was formed in 1947. The first national Japanese-Canadian organization to be formed after the war, it worked on linking the various communities scattered all over the country by combatting enforced deportation and pursuing the property-claims issue, matters that needed to be dealt with immediately by a unified force for the good of the entire group. The association thus functioned as a self-protective organization for many years, taking an active part in the struggle to achieve legal equality and to improve the social welfare of Japanese Canadians, who supported the local as well as the national chapters of the association as important instruments with continuous fund-raising campaigns. After achieving its goal, however, the JCCA lost much of the reason for its existence, and for a time, as anti-Japanese discrimination diminished substantially, many people lost interest in maintaining the organization.

After the formation of the JCCA, religious groups of both Christian and Buddhist denominations were the next organizations to be revived in most cities and towns where the Japanese resettled. The Issei needed to have a place to gather together, and as the Nisei were unable to find the social outlets they needed in the larger society, church groups filled that vacancy. Within each denomination, various social groups were organized along sex and generational lines.

It took the Japanese community in Toronto two decades to erect their community centre, the Japanese Canadian Cultural Centre in Don Mills, which was completed in 1962. Something more than a community centre exclusively for the Japanese Canadian, the Centre's guiding philosophy and purpose is to provide a meeting place between Japanese Canadians and other Canadians in the Metropolitan Toronto community. This philosophy appealed to the Nisei members of the community, who had been steadily climbing the ladder of success in their efforts to be fully 'Canadian.' The preservation of a sense of ethnic community seems to be the main task of the centre, with the centre serving as a symbol of Japanese identification to both Japanese Canadians and to other Canadians.

In the early 1970s, a decade after Toronto, the community in Vancouver witnessed serious attempts by groups and individuals to recreate a Japanese community. Young people were 'coming back' to Powell Street, the centre of the thriving community before the expulsion. Dozens of Issei, who tended to be impoverished and alone, had also come back to settle in Vancouver, and a community volunteer group, *Tonari-gumi*, was formed by younger members to provide the services needed by these elderly seniors.

A culturally oriented group of individuals had started the Powell Street Festival in the mid-1970s. Attracting the attention of the general public, after nearly twenty years, the annual event has become almost institutionalized. As Toronto's Japanese Canadian Cultural Centre does, Vancouver's summer festival serves as a symbol of Japanese identification for its community.

The importance of these religious and cultural institutions, as cited above, seems to be derived from the contribution the institutions make through their members in establishing and developing social relationships with other Japanese, and in maintaining old friendship ties among the members themselves. This seems to be the principal contribution of the social-cultural and recreational clubs and groups, whether they are formed in smaller centres such as Calgary or Thunder Bay or in Toronto or Vancouver. Picnics, dances, bazaars, annual dinner-meetings, wine-and-cheese parties, and sports tournaments are sponsored by the community-wide organizations and open to the public. But apart from these activities, the focus is on small groups organized around various interests and hobbies within each organization or, independently, as private social circles. Therefore, if a sense of 'groupness' is still maintained by Japanese Canadians, at the core of this 'groupness' there is a network of interpersonal ties, more private and intimate than the large-scale community-wide ties.

An increase in income, an adaptation to middle-class lifestyles, and geographical dispersion have noticeably lessened the visibility and frequency of formal and informal ethnic association by Japanese Canadians. Yet the Japanese community – a tightly knit network of informal, personal relationships among people who are psychologically contiguous more than anything else – has persisted. As mentioned at the outset of this chapter, there indeed no longer exists a visible and distinctive Japanese-Canadian community as such anywhere in Canada except for the personal community within each city, of which the main participants are the Nisei. Even support for existing ethnic institutions and organizations seems largely the fruit of Nisei 'sentiments' and a sense of obligation towards the old community, which once occupied so important a place in their daily life and in the lives of their parents.

For Japanese Canadians in Canada 1977 had a special meaning, as the year was celebrated as their centennial year, commemorating the first documented arrival in 1877 of a Japanese immigrant in Canada. It was celebrated across the country with various joint events organized to link the widely scattered communities. Around that time, some individuals in the community started expressing interest in seeking redress for the wrongs that the government had perpetuated against Japanese Canadians (see chapter 6 for further discussion on redress). 'A sense of incompleteness gnaws at me,' a

Nisei writer in Toronto noted. 'I need to feel right about my country. I need this to happen while I am still around to appreciate it' (Moritsugu 1991). This emerging awareness was gradually mobilized into a unified force within the community by its younger members, by those who were not old enough to have experienced incarceration during the war. Their need to endorse the cause was born out of their desire to use their knowledge of the past to deal with a community wounded by the internment. Redress became 'a dream of justice in our time' for the group engaged in the movement. 'We wanted to tell our story, the story of Japanese Canadians, and we wanted it told from the inside as a necessary act of liberation,' as one of the activists expressed (Miki 1992).

The need for a nationally organized and unified body was recognized as the voice to seek redress. The JCCA was reorganized in 1982 with a new name, the National Association of Japanese Canadians (NAJC), and formed local chapters in areas where a sufficient number of Japanese resided. The NAJC engaged in years of intense activity both in public-relations work in the community and in lobbying the larger community. The campaign came to a successful conclusion in September 1988 – rather to everyone's great surprise – when an agreement was reached between the federal government and the NAJC, which included official acknowledgment from the government of the injustices inflicted on Canadians of Japanese ancestry during the 1940s and individual monetary compensation for the 'survivors.' Chiefly responsible for this achievement were a handful of dedicated supporters in each city who fought for redress, while the majority of the community remained indifferent and silent throughout the years – the apolitical behaviour generally typical of the reticent Japanese Canadian.

The campaign for redress brought back to the community some survivors who were expending most of their attention and energies on their careers and social life in mainstream Canadian society. Since the 1988 settlement for redress, various activities and conferences have been organized on a national scale for the first time since the 1942 expulsion, funded by the compensation fund granted as a part of the redress settlement to rebuild the community both nationally and locally. Thus, the movement led by the

NAJC made the community more 'visible' once more to both the Japanese and the general public.

Fifty years after the evacuation and uprooting of the community, the Nisei have been busy organizing and participating in reunions of groups from home towns, 'ghost towns,' and road camps where they spent the war years together, the Japanese-language schools they attended, and the sports leagues in which they played. As a result of the redress movement, for a time, pilgrimages to internment camps in the interior of British Columbia became an event that attracted some former evacuees as well as those 'who were not yet born.' These reunions seem to help bring Japanese Canadians back together, and the Nisei sentiments seem to be re-enforced by the sharing of memories and the renewal of old friendships.

Thus, the Japanese-Canadian community in the post-war era was initially reborn as a social-cultural community for the Issei, then for the Nisei, and against heavy odds it has somehow persisted. In most of the social groups, the Nisei are the active participants as well as the supporters. Because of their extremely small numbers, the influence of the immigrants from Japan in the post-war decades has remained insignificant. Like their predecessors, those who have remained (many of the post-war immigrants from Japan opted to return to Japan after some years in Canada) are incorporating into society at large. Such institutions as the Japanese Canadian Cultural Centre in Toronto and the National Nikkei Heritage Centre in Vancouver (to be constructed in the near future) may continue to exist for years to come, attracting some Nisei and possibly immigrants from Japan. And the Sansei and the Yonsei as well?

To what extent do the Japanese community organizations provide a means of community interaction for the Sansei? No doubt the Sansei are more actively involved in community-wide institutions than in ones in the Japanese-Canadian community. Are they then willing to take on the responsibility of maintaining such ethnic institutions as the Japanese Canadian Cultural Centre or the NAJC? In the post-redress era, is the Japanese-Canadian community as a whole becoming stronger as some members claim? With this task now largely up to the younger generations, it remains to be seen whether or not that is so.

These questions will be examined in forthcoming chapters of this book, with the focus on the Sansei, the third generation and largest group in the present Japanese-Canadian community. Before that, however, in the next chapter, we will trace the background of the Sansei, the focus group of the study, to see how well they have done in establishing themselves occupationally as well as socially. As the Sansei's battle to achieve higher social status approaches its zenith, we shall see whether 'Japanese-Canadian values' helped – if they did at all – to motivate the Sansei to achieve mobility.

## Chapter Two

# Social Mobility: The Sansei Style

*When I was very young, I was afraid of being Japanese Canadian because we were still considered to be enemies of Canada ... My determination to excel at school was driven by a combination of fear and the naive sense that the academic world offered a level playing field, an opportunity to succeed in spite of race or ethnic background.*

Bruce Kuwabara (1994)

The sixty-four individuals, altogether thirty-six men and twenty-eight women, who are introduced in this chapter are all Sansei, third-generation Japanese Canadians. Born in Canada, they all went to school and grew up in the Canadian community. They live in predominantly Caucasian neighbourhoods of large to medium-sized areas, with 84 per cent residing in homes owned by themselves.

The sample group are all gainfully employed in full-time jobs and include a few 'professional mothers.' One young Sansei woman with 'no occupational title' was just 'taking a break from employment' when she was interviewed. No students were included in the sample group. Considering the ongoing economic recession, with an unemployment rate of 11 per cent or so at the time of the interviews, the group as a whole was more fully em-ployed than the general population.

Well established occupationally as well as socially, all in the group identified themselves as 'middle class,' although a few insisted on relegating themselves to the 'lower side of middle class.' Many are still striving to attain a higher social status than they have already achieved, but they tend to do so in a rather relaxed manner, 'in my own terms and pace.' They are employed as accountants, architects, artist-technicians, auto mechanics, business managers, dentists, engineers, graphic designers, lawyers, office secretaries, realtors, and sales clerks, as well as farmers, nurses, and schoolteachers, but there are no fishermen, plumbers, carpenters, welders, gardeners, or factory workers – occupations held by many of their fathers. The majority of the individuals are in their thirties and forties, generally holding middle-ranking management positions and making in-roads in mainstream society. It may be fair to say that the Sansei in this group occupy relatively secure economic positions in comparison with the Canadian population at large, and doubtlessly hold more favourable positions than did their parents decades ago when they were the same age.

The Sansei form an extremely well-educated group. The average number of years of education completed by the present sample was 16.2, which is equivalent to obtaining a university degree. They have by far surpassed their parents' level of educational attainment, which averaged twelve years for the Toronto Nisei (see the report in appendix 1). Thus, it can be said, the education that the Nisei could not afford for themselves has been made available to their children. Almost seven of ten respondents have a university or postgraduate degree, with 14 per cent having a diploma in a specific professional or vocational field, while 19 per cent are high school graduates.

In terms of gender and age, there are no significant variations observed in the level of education attained. Both the men and the women, whether relatively older (close to their fiftiess) or younger (still in their twenties) are alike in their educational pursuits. Among the respondents in Quebec and southern Ontario, there is a slightly higher average educational level achieved, whereas in smaller centres such as Winnipeg, Thunder Bay, and the interior of British Columbia, the individuals are less likely to be university educated. These less-educated Sansei are typical 'home town natives' who were born and have lived in the same area throughout their life (with the exception possibly of going away for a few years), unlike their fellow Sansei who left their home town forever when they entered university. Those who are residing in other smaller centres such as Ottawa, London, and Kingston, Ontario, moved to these areas from other regions of the country for occupational-professional reasons; these individuals are the best educated of all members in the sample group.

Japanese Canadians are, on average, among the most highly educated of all groups in Canada (next or almost parallel to the Jewish group), with the Sansei generation the highest educated of all subcategories within the Japanese group. There have been many documented cases, in both the United States and various parts of Canada, to support the thesis that the Sansei are at the forefront of a trend in which a population is almost universally college-educated. Our data conform with this generalization.

If the Nisei vigorously pursued higher education, but in the end barely managed to complete high school, the Sansei have done so as a matter of course: 'Going to university was expected.' 'There was no question about it [going to university] in my family.' Whereas 19 per cent of the Nisei in Metropolitan Toronto managed to get some post–high school education, nearly 70 per cent of the present Sansei respondents were able to complete their college education or more.

The Japanese Canadians' belief that self-advancement was achieved by education is doubtlessly the chief factor that contributed to achieving the level of education reported here by this Sansei group. In discussing the values that the Nisei parents attempted to inculcate in their children, the emphasis placed on education and schooling was the one most often mentioned. Some respondents sensed, in spite of their fully 'Canadian' upbringing, that they were brought up somewhat differently from their non-Japanese peers because of this 'particularly strong and persistent' value, and the other 'Japanese-Canadian values' connected to education, namely the long-standing virtues of a strong work ethic and achievement. In the course of growing up, those values seem to have been passed on in the Japanese-Canadian home from the

Nisei parents to the Sansei children, largely through role model-
ling and reinforcement. Close to two-thirds of the respondents
affirmed one way or the other the significant impact of the value
placed on attaining a higher education.

The strong need to achieve a higher education by taking full
advantage of educational opportunities is not particularly unique to
Japanese Canadians or distinguishable from those of society at
large. In general, it has been a value of great importance for immi-
grant-ethnic groups in North America. During the 1950s and 1960s,
when most of the respondents were at school, academic compe-
tence became the more important goal for many sections of both
the middle and working classes in North America, particularly those
members of the working class made up of urban ethnic minorities
(Elkin and Handel 1989, 134). Thus, in a newly developing subdivision in the north end of Metro Toronto, one respondent observed
that the children from predominantly working-class backgrounds,
including himself, were all 'moving up.' From early on this Sansei
man was encouraged by his parents to get ahead and to go to university; therefore, he encouraged all his friends to come along with
him. While the school milieu also tended to place an increased
emphasis on academic achievement, the Japanese-Canadian family
appeared to be a most eager partner to attain this goal.

In examining comparatively educational achievement among
major ethnic groups in Canada in the period between 1941 and
1981, research recently conducted in Canada (Shamai 1992) concluded that Asians were the only group that managed to break
away from their position as 'underachievers' in schooling to become 'overachievers.' In the researcher's interpretation, this is
because of the Asian family and its ethnic values, which are its
members' most important sources of socialization. Hirschman and
Wong, in their American study (1986), verified a desperate faith in
education among Asian Americans to be historical. Their research
indicated that native-born Chinese and Japanese Americans had
reached educational parity with majority whites already in the pre–
Second World War era. In the early decades of this century,
Hirschman and Wong have argued (1986, 16), societal discrimination and racism, although quite extensive, 'did not diminish the

ability of Japanese- and Chinese-American families to support the
education of their American-born children at levels comparable
to or above that of the majority population.' The authors agreed
with the notion of ethnic economy established earlier by Bonacich
and Mondell (1980) in explaining the extraordinary educational
achievement of Asian groups. Being so-called middleman minorities, immigrant parents hoped to secure a means for their children
to enter the ranks of the 'independent professions, the pinnacle of
the petit bourgeois world, or to take over the family business or
farms' (Bonacich and Modell 1980, 152) by providing the children
with the highest possible education attainable.

The Japanese in Canada were indeed not an exception in retaining this faith in education, which was noted to be 'historical' or 'traditional' by some respondents in this study, in the sense that the
veneration accorded to education, having originated in Japanese
society, was further reinforced in North America by the Issei with
the Nisei, and then with the Sansei, perhaps a little bit more firmly
and insistently than it had been emphasized in other groups. The
traditional value of obtaining the highest possible education seems
to be one of the cultural elements that was the last to change, probably next to diet, commented a few respondents. Their parents gave
up the Japanese language or their religious practices rather quickly
and easily. Instead, they focused on pushing their children to get an
education. Thus, going to university was 'the natural thing to do,' a
mutually understood and accepted course of action by both parents
and children. A thirty-nine-year-old Sansei research chemist, who
grew up in a large working-class family in Winnipeg, stated:

> All of the nine children in my family went to university at least for one
> degree; two of us are PhDs. My parents always saved money for each
> of us, i.e., the family allowance money they received. They always put
> it into the bank. There was some money available when we went to
> university. They seemed to have expected that all of us would go to
> university. We knew somehow we had to go to university. We did fairly
> well at school from grade school on.

A Sansei mother of five who grew up in the 1950s and 1960s in

Scarborough, a Toronto suburb, spoke of 'the traditional value' she observed in her extended family. Both her parents, now in their eighties, completed high school – an exception rather than the norm in their time – and had 'a natural expectation' that their three children would go to university. However, university was not for one of the children, the son, who barely completed high school, and therefore became a major disappointment to the father: 'Schooling and education were primary, the most important focus for us when we were growing up. Even my grandfather's whole focus was for all his ten children to get an education. Education to him was a ticket for bettering themselves. My father completed high school, which was rather unusual for his age group at that time. To get higher education was thus a family tradition. My sister and I went to university almost naturally, so did almost all of my cousins.' Both the Issei grandparents and the Nisei parents were alike in their hope for a better way of life for their children. Since very few other options existed, they very likely saw schooling as the only means left for their children to achieve upward mobility.

A Sansei man who became a professor grew up in the 1950s in a small isolated community in the interior of British Columbia, where most of the children did not go beyond grade 8. The professor, who currently teaches at one of Ontario's universities, noted that he and his sister were the first ones from that community to go to high school and then on to university. His parents, older Nisei from a fishing background, had little education, and had lost all their worldly possessions during the war, when they were uprooted from their home in British Columbia. The whole process of uprooting, losing all their goods and properties and being stripped of their citizenship, as the son saw it, provided a strong subconscious lack of attachment on the part of his parents to material possessions. 'Education was the most important. I don't remember how many times my Mom and Dad said to us: "If you get good education, nobody can take it away from you." Material things can be taken away from you, but education is always within you.' Education was the only way to make good in this world. My grandparents came to North America to try to make a better living for their families with that belief in education intact. That value would have been passed on to my parents and they certainly accepted that.'

A young Sansei woman, also from a working-class background, who grew up in the 1960s in the newly developing suburb of Mississauga, Ontario, maintains that although a college education was not possible for her parents, who are relatively young Nisei, they made sure that all four of their children received one: 'The push to do well at school from our parents was always there when we were children. "In order to get a good job, you need to have a good education," was their message. They encouraged us to get education as far as we could go. We were not allowed to play sports or have a part-time job until we maintained certain grades at school. That message was very strong and persistent.'

Nisei parents believed in education so strongly because they wanted to give their children the opportunities that were denied them. 'There was more than the usual emphasis on attaining education,' recalled a forty-five-year-old Sansei industrial designer who grew up in Toronto's inner city. He was told by his parents not only to excel in schoolwork, but to be 'a good student' by conforming to rules and regulations because he was Japanese. 'I had to perform well all the time according to my parents, on behalf of the entire Japanese community.' The message from his parents was that 'one must be a credit to one's family and to the community.' (The community here means the Japanese-Canadian community, which had been completely wiped out during the internment and relocation; the Toronto community was barely on the verge of reviving itself in the 1950s when the Sansei designer was going to school.) His parents grew up in a pre-war Japanese community on the West Coast – a small, yet very strong and cohesive farming community where kinship networks often overlapped with friendship networks to reinforce each other. These strong family and community networks, characteristic of the Nisei, thus served to enforce social control and to reinforce the desired behaviour, that is, getting an education and achieving success in whatever pursuits they engaged in. These needs further facilitated mobility among the members who grew up in the community in subsequent generations. This unusual emphasis placed by the parents on education always stayed with the child 'as a focus of my growing up.'

These expectations and demands by the parents produced stress and anxiety in their children. Not a few respondents mentioned the implied pressure placed on them. The younger ones got the message that they had to go to university because their older siblings and cousins all had. Therefore there was no choice, according to a thirty-seven-year-old Sansei engineer from a small community in northern British Columbia. One of those Sansei who thought he was 'basically white' while growing up in a town with two other Japanese families, his codes of behaviour or outlook were not a bit different from those of other kids, yet he insisted that he was brought up somewhat differently: 'There were a lot of expectations that were placed on us in our family; unspoken, but most of them pretty well laid out for us. I knew I was expected to go to university. All of us [three children] did. Those of my friends who went to university did so by choice. They weren't expected to. It wasn't a planned course, but I knew somehow from the early years on that it was for me. I didn't resent it at all, though. It was a natural expectation in our family.'

Not everyone made it, however, partly because of the unusual amount of pressure. It was a firmly accepted expectation to obtain a higher education, not only from the individual's family but also from the entire Japanese-Canadian community. In the case of the industrial designer mentioned above, he did quite well 'up to a point,' then in high school he became very depressed. He would 'never be a student.' He became lost, not knowing what to do with his life, and it took a good number of years to 'discover my inner strength, trying to keep some of the earlier pressure at a distance.' In the meantime, he changed his major area of schooling more than a few times until he finally settled on designing as his trade. According to the designer, the entire Sansei generation experienced the pressure and stress, to some extent at least.

Education is an important determinant of one's initial position in the job market and affects one's subsequent opportunities as well. The members in this Sansei group, with prerequisite educational qualifications and an upgrading of skills behind them, have achieved mobility within the dominant economic institutions, and on average have settled into fifteen-year career tracks. The largest proportion of the respondents, exactly half of them, are currently employed in some sort of profession, and 28 per cent are in managerial/administrative jobs at the middle level in either corporations or government agencies, or are owner-managers of small businesses. Those respondents who did not go on to university after completing high school entered white-collar fields or skilled trades, but none of them is engaged in so-called unskilled blue-collar occupations. According to census information (Kobayashi 1989), Quebec and Ontario tend to show a higher per centage of the Japanese-Canadian workforce in professional-managerial categories and the lowest in blue-collar positions, as compared with the western provinces. (In British Columbia, for instance, the highest percentage of the Japanese workforce are in blue-collar positions.) The present sample, as it deals only with members of the third generation, is too small and limited in its size and scope to confirm the regional patterns observed in the national census data.

Twelve of the sixty-four Sansei subjects, all of whom happen to be men, are self-employed: running an orchard, or small firms of architecture, graphic design, engineering, or general building contracting, with or without partners. Others own and run small businesses such as a coffee shop, a screen-print shop, and a photography shop. Traditionally, the occupational goal of many Japanese Canadians was self-employment: either to be independent land-owning or -leasing farmers or to own and run a small business for economic independence. This was certainly the highest position that the Issei immigrants could achieve within Canada's economic institutions in the pre-war period, and the Nisei (at least those who were old enough to start their occupational pursuits in this period) were forced to work in ethnic enterprises, typically family-owned small businesses, because of widespread discrimination in mainstream occupations. The Sansei who have been relatively less mobile and those who are 'stuck' in the areas where they were born and raised tend to end up self-employed. All of the self-employed professionals, as well as their businesses, serve the gen-

TABLE 2.1
Occupational strata between generations (N = 60)

| Nisei father* | Sansei | | | | |
|---|---|---|---|---|---|
| | Professional | Managerial | White-collar | Blue-collar | Total |
| Professional | 4 | 1 | 2 | – | 7 |
| Managerial | 7 | 6 | 1 | 1 | 15 |
| White-collar | 2 | 1 | 2 | 1 | 6 |
| Blue-collar | 17 | 9 | 4 | 2 | 32 |
| Total | 30 | 17 | 9 | 4 | 60 |

\* The Nisei father's occupation is the main occupation, reported by the respondent, that the father was engaged in when the Sansei child was growing up.

eral public; none of them depend on the Japanese or other Asian communities for their services and livelihood.

Almost all of the respondents' fathers had retired from active employment by the early 1990s. According to their Sansei children, Nisei fathers were typically employed as tradesmen, such as printers, electricians, welders, machinists, mechanics, carpenters, and jewellery/watch repairmen. The younger Nisei fathers achieved considerable occupational-economic mobility as a result of employment as a system analyst, a professor of computer studies, a research scientist, a producer of TV programs, the owner-presidents of small manufacturing firms, and executives and senior managers in various establishments. As a whole, the group's Nisei fathers had substantially achieved enough economic mobility within the dominant economic institutions to gain 'success' – to take on the ways of the Canadian middle class consistent with the evidence reported earlier in the field.

In documenting intergenerational mobility between the Nisei fathers and their children (table 2.1), each generation has been divided into four broad occupational categories: professional, managerial-administrative, white-collar, and blue-collar. Professionals are those individuals employed in some sort of profession. The managerial category includes proprietors of small businesses, as well as managers employed by corporations and government agencies. The blue-collar category includes all men and women either working in the skilled trades or employed in factory-type or farm-labour-type jobs. As the figures in table 2.1 indicate, only a few Sansei men in the present sample appear in the blue-collar category; none of the women are blue-collar workers.

Table 2.1 presents stratum turnover from one generation to the next, from Nisei fathers to their Sansei children. It can be observed along the diagonal that about 23 per cent of the Sansei children occupy the same job status as their fathers. We see, however, only very few individuals who experienced 'downward mobility,' that is, Sansei white-collar and blue-collar workers whose fathers were in the professional or managerial-administrative categories. Instead, more than half have in fact 'moved up.' Upward movement has largely been from the blue-collar sector to the professional or managerial sector. Over half of the respondents' Nisei fathers had careers as skilled workers and ended up in the blue-collar sector. This figure is about 10 per cent higher than the Toronto Nisei samples surveyed earlier (see appendix 1). On the other hand, almost the same proportion of Sansei are employed in some sort of profession.

The high rate of upward mobility among the Sansei reflects, in part, the intergenerational shifts in the occupational structure of society at large that took place in the 1970s and the 1980s. It is also to a large extent the result of the very high educational levels obtained by the Sansei, owing to the virtue of education and the importance of hard work 'unusually emphasized' by the Nisei parents, as discussed earlier in this chapter.

There is a general feeling of contentment concerning their careers and their economic positions among the Sansei. Most of them consider their careers to be satisfactory and feel secure and confident about themselves, having climbed the social ladder to the same level that others of their age group have, and higher than their fathers did; although exceeding whatever their fathers attained 'has never been intentional' or 'an important goal to attain,' some members noted.

For those respondents employed in professional and management fields, work offers not only the basis of a decent material life but also a great deal of self-esteem. Concerning their career pursuits, these individuals emphasized the importance of advancing themselves as far as possible – one of the important, if not the most important, goals in life for them. But in the midst of a lingering economic recession and slow growth, when jobs are lost so quickly and unexpectedly, some have 'learned to live and move with the slow pace in business,' and not to place unrealistically high expectations on career advancement.

With regard to their attitudes and aspirations, the Sansei are oriented towards independence or self-employment, in addition to getting ahead as far as they can in their professional and management careers. The Sansei women who were interviewed, many of whom were either schoolteachers or health-care providers, did not express the same level of concern or aspiration as the men did concerning career advancement. For the men, the goal is to establish themselves independently in their professions or to own and expand a business of their own. They regard self-employment as the ideal goal because they value the freedom and autonomy inherent in self-employment more highly than they value mere economic security.

Among all the individuals interviewed only a few explicitly expressed an urge to strive for economic 'success' or a desire to 'make good.' While the Nisei talked of the importance of hard work and the need to achieve security and success (documented in my earlier investigation in Toronto), it is not as important for the majority of the succeeding generation to make good, 'to impress others,' or to become materially successful. In assessing their accomplishments in occupational or material pursuits, only a few respondents reminded me of the Nisei in having to prove themselves, their abilities, their sense of endurance, and their competitiveness.

My overwhelming impression is that the preoccupations of the Sansei remain modest. Their work is mostly, if not only, a means of achieving a satisfactory life, a lifestyle. Many values that they aspire to are familistic, within their control, and sought for the good of their family, with personal advancement in their careers viewed as including, not alienating, the family. Both the men and women with families are unanimous in attesting: 'My family comes first.'

Those who are single and unencumbered with family responsibilities prefer 'to do what I want,' or 'to have a job I enjoy doing,' with sufficient time left over to spend free from work responsibilities.

For some respondents, it is still possible and probable that they will change their jobs once or twice, or even 'do something completely different' from what they have been doing in the past years. This philosophy is in stark contrast to that expressed by their fathers, who were obsessed with seeking security and 'making it.' The Sansei do not consider success as such as 'the prime focus of my life.' They seek to derive satisfaction first from the jobs they do, but more from their family and friends and from their leisure-time pursuits. The tension created by the fear of marginality and the success-oriented attitude, characteristic of the Nisei, served to generate the Nisei's intense drive for success; a decline in this tension seems to have diminished ambition in their children.

The Sansei's economic security, and relaxed and confident attitudes, are further enhanced by a lack of fear of discrimination and the concomitant insecurity. Few respondents indicated that they had been handicapped by their ethnic-racial background – at least once they had become adults.

The stigma of discrimination, close to the form of discrimination Henry (1994) termed as everyday racism, is still felt by some Sansei in their psyche and mentality largely because of their childhood experiences. Every individual had indeed come across incidents at certain points of their growing up that can or cannot be considered discrimination, and been confronted with discriminatory acts and racist remarks, either overt or subtle. For some, it was obvious they had suffered from discrimination, while others were not bothered seriously about it. More women than men tended to report an incident of being treated 'badly and hurtfully.' They talked about the experiences, using concrete citations and recalling the hurt feelings they had had to endure as children. Men were inclined to say that they did not remember any particular incident worth mentioning, or to insist that another child's acts of name-calling or taunting were 'minor things.' In retrospect, they tended to refuse to consider such acts discrimination. Included are some of those who 'often got into trouble' and fought against racist remarks and name-calling.

There were a few, such as Bruce Kuwabara, a Toronto architect quoted at the outset of this chapter, who still remembered their childhood fear of being Japanese Canadian because they were considered to be enemies of Canada. But even those who were hurt by and suffered from racial remarks and attacks when they were young agreed that in adulthood they have experienced no personal discrimination, nor have they detected much prejudice or discrimination against Japanese Canadians today. None of this generation has encountered – or to put it more accurately, perceive themselves to have encountered – employment, housing, or any other form of discrimination, although all expressed the belief that racism is a serious problem in Canada and that discrimination and racism 'exist everywhere in society.' It is rarely a problem for them personally, however. This is a view shared by the majority of Canadians surveyed in a recent public-opinion poll undertaken by Decima Research in 1993 for the Canadian Council of Christians and Jews.

Our respondents were also convinced that being Japanese seldom limited their opportunities for advancement or restricted them in pursing anything they wanted to do, nor did they feel it would hinder them much in the future. Responding to the questions 'Do you think your ethnic background was an obstacle at one time in the past?' and 'Do you think it may be an obstacle to your future somehow?' the reply was overwhelmingly 'No.' According to the results from the 1990 survey of the Toronto Nisei, their response was not largely dissimilar; only about one out of five Nisei respondents (19 per cent) stated that they experienced difficulty in getting a job or in other employment situations because they were of Japanese descent (see appendix 1).

A young engineer employed in a large bureaucracy in Toronto maintained that, as far as he was concerned, social exclusion of the Japanese as such is non-existent, both in the formal and informal spheres of society, and that it was even difficult for him to conceive such a notion. According to this engineer, an individual's experience of being badly treated or discriminated against is that individual's perception. This comment pretty well reflects the majority view of the Sansei on this issue.

> You can say that you're discriminated against all your life, which might not be the case. I don't think I've ever been discriminated against because of my racial background. This is my perception. I applied for a lot of jobs when I was looking for one after I graduated from university, and I got rejections. A lot of them. I accepted them. I didn't look for excuses why I didn't get a job, most certainly not in terms of my racial background.

For a Sansei sales manager employed by an Ontario automobile-parts manufacturing company, business is tough these days. In business, if a customer says no and shuts the door, said this manager, you never know why. It is possible that the customer does so 'because he doesn't like you because you are non-white.' But the forty-four-year-old ambitious manager, for whom getting ahead was still fairly important, bluntly rejected the notion that prejudice directed against a visible minority might affect his chance of 'success in getting business' or 'getting to the top' in his organization. 'I never go through any of my days and moments thinking that I lose business because the customer doesn't like to have a non-white to deal with.'

A public-school teacher, a thirty-four-year-old woman from Calgary, Alberta, who is upgrading her education to a PhD while on leave from her teaching position, is typical in her perception and attitude of the female Sansei professionals:

> I don't think there is discrimination against Japanese in the workplace today. I don't believe I ever miss getting a job because I'm Japanese. I don't think that would ever happen. My Japanese background sometimes works to my advantage. I'm well remembered because I'm visible and my name is different.

The teacher kept her maiden name after she got married to a non-Japanese because she wants to be regarded as Japanese rather than something else. She insisted that, in any public situation other than the field of education, she does not encounter discrimination, nor is she treated in any way differently – at least she does not sense it. Being Japanese therefore has not held her back from getting ahead in her career or getting another promotion with the board of education where she has been employed for nine years. If the system is working against her because she is of Japanese descent, in this Sansei woman's view, it is too subtle for her to recognize it.

Being a woman is often the barrier, insisted the female Sansei professionals in the group. Rather than being a person of Japanese descent, the women in the group feel that their gender, and possibly their personality or their unaggressive style of presentation, might be holding them back. They are inclined to downgrade the impact of racial prejudice and discrimination as a factor affecting them and their chances for promotion or advancement as teachers, nurses, or therapists at their place of work. In the upper strata of school boards, hospitals, or other bureaucracies, although it is very obvious that there are still too few women holding the top positions, these women do not see any reason for not getting ahead, however high one may wish to advance, provided they are willing and ambitious and aggressive enough. Being a woman and a visible minority is perceived these days to be an asset, they said, rather than a liability, because of the laws and the hiring and promotion practices in place.

A thirty-year-old female Sansei writer, temporarily managing a bookstore in downtown Toronto, believes that the choice of careers for Sansei women is almost unlimited; from kindergarten teachers to lawyers to television reporters with a national network, they find little difficulty landing jobs, provided they are willing. But for herself, the writer-manager maintained that being female has been much more salient a problem than being visible as Japanese or Oriental. She would be more sensitive in her writing, if ever, with the feminist rather than the racial perspective, said the writer. 'I don't experience discrimination personally. I never have. I have much more of a problem being female than being a visible minority. I think the hierarchy goes: female at the bottom, a visible male, then a white male. In my youthful days, much of my energy went into a sense of feminist rage than it went into the sense that I was being discriminated against as an Asian.'

During the course of the interviews, many of the Sansei men and women in the group often incidentally remarked that their Japanese background has been an advantage rather than a disadvantage, either by merely having a Japanese name, as with the Calgary teacher cited above, or because of the reputation Japanese Canadians have earned as good, honest workers. Japanese Canadians have established themselves as being very reliable and dependable people, not only in their places of work but also in their respective communities. Reputations can be mere stereotypes with no validity, argued a self-employed graphic designer, but he did not deny that the Japanese stereotype – good design sense and good honest work – is an advantage for him and for his business partner. Many other members agreed that this reputation has no doubt benefited them; however, whether one takes one's background as an advantage or a disadvantage is a matter of personal choice. A Sansei man who is vice-president of a small manufacturing firm in an industrial section outside Metropolitan Toronto insisted: 'I'd be genuinely offended, if I am hired or am promoted to VP at this firm because they think that Japanese are hard-working, dedicated, reliable, loyal, etc. They have to hire me and promote me for my ability, not for my race of people. I don't take my Japanese background as an advantage.'

A Sansei artist who resides in a city in Western Canada saw a tendency towards reverse discrimination in the art community. 'You may get a certain favour or sympathy, if you are non-white.' People recognize him as Japanese from his name alone. He might be treated favourably, first, because he is a visible minority and, second, because people feel some affinity towards Japanese artists. Reverse discrimination was not always appreciated by this young artist-technician, although he had recently joined a group of 'Artists of Colour' to be on the alert for issues of racism and human rights. He would nonetheless like to be treated equally by all, judged 'solely on my ability and talent.' Many others joined him in expressing their reservations concerning the employment-equity program endorsed by the government and society at large, because it legislates differential treatment for some and thus is 'a mixed blessing.'

Not all of the sixty-four individuals were convinced that being a small visible minority has never limited their opportunities for advancement or restricted them in their career pursuits. A thirty-one-year-old Toronto accountant, a head-office manager-to-be in the finance department of a large retail firm, expects it will be tough to move up to the senior managerial levels in this particular organization, where the top positions have been traditionally occupied by white people with an Anglo or Jewish background. He realizes that he does not have 'that family connection.' His ethnic background can become an obstacle, an even greater barrier for him as he climbs up the ladder towards the company's senior level of management. In his assessment, society is not yet ready to accept a visible-minority member at the top of this corporation.

A thirty-nine-year-old Toronto architect, who grew up in a working-class family, runs a small firm on his own. He established his business fifteen years ago as he had wanted to be independent right from the very beginning. In the past few years, he has been fighting to survive largely because of the slow pace of business, and because he felt he had 'problems of social status and social contact.' One cannot enter the business of architecture and 'make good' with education and qualifications alone. It requires patrons or clients, he said, and these people come from the well-to-do class, and very rarely from the class and ethnic background from which he comes. It was his belief that because he did not grow up in that class, he was at a disadvantage in a business such as independent architecture, that many jobs are never offered to him because he does not operate and move in the right circles.

A forty-five-year-old female lawyer, practising in Vancouver for thirteen years, also admitted that her ethnic background has been an obstacle and can definitely become more of one in her future career advancement, although being 'successful' as a lawyer per se is no longer important for her. There is an assumption that Asian women are, to use her words, 'softer, kinder, more submissive' and 'would be easier to deal with.' This assumption extends into the legal field as well. She strives to obliterate this stereotype, but in the process she sometimes feels that 'we are losing more than we are gaining.' The employment-equity program is often ineffective in tackling such stereotypes, which exist in every sphere of society, she said. 'The white male ha[s] practised employment equity for

years and years. It's about time to even out the playing field. I work
in the male-dominated world with the double criteria, my gender
and ethnicity, curbed out against me. I know this is a long-lasting
struggle. Some changes are taking place. Changes don't come easily though.'

In the 1990s, after two decades of praise as 'the model minority'
because of the upward mobility they have achieved in comparison
to other racial minority groups, are the Japanese in North America
really no longer the victims of white racism, albeit insidiously subtle in form? The overall answer to this question from the respondents from the present Canadian Sansei group is one of assent,
with a small minority (the three individuals cited above out of the
sixty-four, to be precise) questioning or dissenting. The majority of
them bluntly refuse to accept the notion that they are the victims
of any form of discrimination. Rightfully so? As long as they
remain 'yellow' in the eyes of the majority, as long as racism and
social exclusion remain an integral part of Canadian culture and
society, the answer to this question perhaps should be 'No.'
    An earlier study conducted by Suzuki (1977) of Asian Americans
– Chinese and Japanese, the two largest comnponents of the Asian
group in the United States – concluded that their upward mobility
has been limited by the effects of racism, even though they had
attained a relatively high level of education. The empirical part of
Suzuki's investigation, which relied on data from the 1970 American census (and is therefore outdated), demonstrated that a basic
contradiction existed between the educational attainments of
Asian Americans and their incomes. The education attained obvi-
ously did not garner nearly as much earning power for Asian males
as it did for white males by comparison. On the whole, Asian males
thus were, Suzuki meant to say, underemployed, underpaid, or
both. They really had not achieved middle-class status, as measured
by the economic indices. Since their status was a good measure of
the relative status of Asian Americans as a group, Suzuki concluded
that the 'celebration of their phenomenal "success" as the "model
minority" was at best premature, and at worst, a devious deception'
(Suzuki 1977, 41). In her investigation of the income earned and

detailed occupational status occupied by the Asian American group as a whole, Lee (1989), like Suzuki, argued that earnings returns from higher-than-average educational level achieved remain consistently lower for Asians.

However, a decade after Suzuki's work, one of the findings from Jiobu's analysis (1988) of the 1980 census data for the state of California indicated that (1) Japanese have the highest earnings of all the groups analysed, including Mexican Americans, blacks, and the five major Asian American groups, and (2) the levels of earnings of Japanese do not differ significantly from the white population. Jiobu (1988, 212) concluded that California's Japanese Americans are 'very near or exceed whites on socioeconomic measures.'

Likewise, Lieberson and Waters (1988, 152–3), in their investigation of the earnings of native-born members of racial minorities in the United States, noted that earnings for those of Asian (but not South Asian) origins were the highest of all the racial minorities. The Asians were also the only group that was not at a disadvantage relative to whites in earnings. While the authors emphasized that the division between whites and visible minorities remains strong, the diversity among different racial groups is significant.

In Canada, a similar indication, not in earnings but in occupational status, has been revealed from a recent social-trend report by Statistics Canada (1995). It is recognized here that visible minorities (native-born as well as immigrants) with a university education were, as a whole, not as likely as whites with the same level of education to be in the higher-paying professional or managerial occupations. Underemployment among visible minorities is thus a reality, the report noted. However, the same government report pointed out that university-educated Japanese aged twenty-five to forty-four, who were employed in the eighteen months before the 1991 census, were most likely, of all groups compared, to be in professional managerial occupations (65 per cent); this proportion is closest to the figure obtained for white adults (70 per cent).[1] Thus, it is probably safe to state that as far as the Sansei are concerned, both in Canada and the United States, they are the generation that has attained the highest level of education in recent decades, and most of them have been channelled into professions and jobs, as well as earnings, appropriate to their prolonged schooling and training.

Further questions have to be raised, however. In keeping with their education and qualifications, have the Sansei attained positions as executives or top administrators in the corporate world or in big bureaucracies? Have they been passed over for promotion to these high positions by whites in the system? These are important and intriguing questions that can only be answered by qualitative, in-depth research.[2]

This chapter has provided evidence of the social mobility attained so far by the Canadian Sansei. It focused on the educational and occupational spheres and offered an explanation of how progress was made by the individual. The Japanese-Canadian value of attaining education helped to motivate the Nisei and to achieve mobility, which has been firmly transmitted by the parents to their Sansei children, as the group as a whole have proved to be almost all college-educated.

Following the Second World War and the internment of this ethnic group, most discriminatory barriers against them were removed, and the Nisei and Sansei capitalized on new occupational opportunities to build middle-class lives. The Sansei as a whole are 'middle class' enough, as they claim, to choose their occupation in a variety of professions or businesses, and to live in a variety of locations and communities.

The Sansei have been called the generation of security, and the testimonies given by the respondents reported here confirm this perception. Being a Japanese Canadian has not limited their advancements, and for quite a few it actually helped with their occupational and social pursuits. This sense of security is associated with their belief and conviction that they have been little handicapped by racist and discriminatory practices and the prejudice prevalent in society. Accepting the prevalence of discrimination and racism 'everywhere in society' today, which is a 'serious problem,' the Sansei do not perceive it as a relevant problem to them personally. That this seemingly inconsistent view is not contradictory in the minds of the Sansei may well be an indication, on the one hand, that they have indeed become *hakujin*, however unconscious the notion may be and however naive it may sound, and it can be a proof, on the other hand, that the Sansei are taking on the ways of the Canadian middle class and employing themselves in mainstream society. The paradoxical attitude of the Sansei will further reveal itself, taking somewhat different shape in their expressions of ethnic and self identity, which will be dealt with in depth in later chapters.

## Chapter Three

# Sansei Socialization:
# The Way They Were Brought Up

*When I was growing up, my parents simply did not call attention to them-*
*selves as Japanese. Neither my mother nor my father ever said to us, 'We*
*take off our shoes at the door because we're Japanese.' They never told us*
*that the reason we ate rice almost every meal – even with roast beef or meat*
*loaf – was that we were Japanese. They never taught us that the Japanese*
*words for rice and for meal are the same:* gohan.

David Mura (1991, 308)

Learning to become ethnically Japanese, like any other socialization process, is a complex acquisition of attitudes, values, status,
and roles, and involves absorbing the various elements of culture
and distinctive historical heritage of the ethnic group (Elkin and
Handel 1989). To define the Japanese-Canadian culture as such,
which makes up the content of Sansei socialization, is therefore a
complex task, as it varies within this generational group according
to such factors as socio-economic status, age, occupation, region of
the country, and type of community in which the particular Sansei
grew up.

In the preceding chapter, we have seen that because of the
strong desire of their Nisei parents to assimilate in the post-war
period, the Sansei incorporated themselves into Canada's middle
class and seemed to fit into mainstream society very well. The Nisei
strove for material gains and vigorously pursued acceptance as
assimilated members of Canadian society – and they succeeded.

For most of the Sansei, the process of growing up with full 'Canadian content' turned out to be fairly normal, easy, and smooth – no matter in what region of the country they resided.

Reference was also made in the previous chapter to the expressed Sansei feeling that they were somewhat differently brought up. As children growing up in the fully integrated community among dominant-group members, they were experiencing different feelings about themselves – not just a mere recognition that they looked different, but the awareness of certain things differentiating them from others, that is, the importance of education and getting ahead that was unusually emphasized within their family. A Sansei man's recognition that he was told by his parents over and over again that he must work hard to excel in school and that he must be a good student because he is Japanese was an illustration of this difference. The Nisei value placed on higher education had a significant bearing upon what the Sansei went through in terms of extended schooling and the consequent course of career selection and pursuit.

In this chapter two themes characteristic of Sansei socialization will be explored: (1) the Japanese-Canadian legacy of victimization, racism, and persecution; and (2) the consequences of the Nisei refusal to discuss the subject of their internment. Before proceeding to the analysis and discussion, however, four Sansei descriptions of their socialization experiences will be presented: Kathy, who grew up in Hamilton, Brian in Montreal, James in Toronto, and Brenda in Vancouver (all of the names have been changed). The descriptions portray both the 'Canadian upbringing' of these Sansei as well as various ethnic element of socialization involved in the process.

*Kathy: Hamilton, Ontario*

I was born in Hamilton in 1955 and grew up on the Mountain. I've lived all my life in the area. We had two Japanese families that went to my school, but none on my street that I played with. So I didn't have Japanese friends to play and grow up with. My mother, being the youngest of a large family, doesn't speak Japanese well, so the language was not spoken at home at all when I was a child. I didn't go to the Japanese language school. My parents didn't encourage me to go to the language school, and I really didn't have an interest in going.

In my family it was rather discouraged from trying, if anything, Japanese things. My parents wanted me to fit in rather than to be different. On Saturday morning, I went to ballet lessons with my friends, instead of to the Japanese language school. At one point I remember expressing my interest in learning Japanese dance, but I was told 'no,' so I continued ballet. On Sunday, I went to the Sunday school in the local Anglican church, with my friends.

I was brought up differently to the extent that some of the traditions that I hear about as being Japanese – the feeling of not letting your family down, that feeling of duty – were probably more in my family than in my friends' families, and they are quite inbred in me. I always knew I was Japanese. By the time I was in Grade 1 I was aware of it, partly as a result of discrimination. There were some children who weren't allowed to play with me. I don't recall any teachers in school who were discriminatory. I was always a well-behaved student with good marks.

My parents' Japanese-Canadian network consisted of relatives between the two fairly large families and friends. Even now their best friends are all Japanese Canadians. They've kept in close contact with them over those years. They've other friends, but they are not as close as their Japanese friends.

I remember going to annual community picnics in summer, the church picnics, bazaars, and Christmas parties. There was a Japanese community in Hamilton in that sense. I don't know that many Japanese Canadians personally, but I know of them through my relatives and their friends. We seem to have known most of the people, if not all of them, in the city.

I joined the Sansei Club when I was sixteen. I was encouraged to join in case I might meet a Sansei boy there. My brother joined the JC [Japanese-Canadian] ski club in Toronto where he met his wife, a Japanese Canadian. There was more pressure [to marry a Japanese] on my brother than on me. The preference on my parents' side was well understood, although never said in words. Out of the Sansei Club in Hamilton a few couples were born, given the thirty to forty teenagers there. We did a lot of social things together, and I had a great time. The group is not active any more though. Fourteen years ago, Hamilton's Japanese Cultural Centre was founded, and my parents have been involved in it. They attend most of its activities, but are not actively running it.

I was aware that my parents weren't very comfortable with their ethnic background. From early on, I was always told that I was different from others, so that I had to try harder; I had to perform better than others to get the same acceptance level. Right up to when I went to university I was told the same thing over and over again. So I don't think they were completely comfortable with their heritage themselves.

## Brian: Montreal, Quebec

I was born in Montreal in 1954. We lived in the east end of Montreal, a predominantly French neighbourhood, hardly any Orientals there, and no Japanese. The kids I grew up with were all French Canadian. That's why I speak fairly good French. I went to a private English school instead of the local French school. French is my second language, and I can get by with it without much difficulty.

Growing up was difficult at times. You look different and kids play on that. My son, age seven, today does not get as much verbal stuff, name calling, as I used to. When I was growing up, it bothered me being called Chinese, to the point that I really didn't like Chinese. I didn't like being mistaken as Chinese. I was small but surrounded by big boys, so nobody could bother me. I was lucky. You learn how to survive one way or the other. I always knew that I was different.

My folks are Buddhists. My grandfather was one of the people who started the church in Montreal after he came to live in the city from the camp. I went to church every Sunday and grew up around it. The main source of social contact with Japanese families was the Buddhist church for my family. My parents' social contact was almost exclusively with the people from the Buddhist church. They got along with the neighbours alright, but never became friends with them such as visiting each other's home.

I was involved in the church too and played the organ for them. There was a language class run by the minister, and I used to go every Saturday morning. At home Japanese was spoken all the time, because my grandparents, my father's parents, used to live with us, and my father got an elementary-school education in Japan, so he is still more comfortable speaking in Japanese. For myself, I can understand and speak a fair amount.

Until the end of high school, most of my close friends were people from the church. I still associate with some of them – those who are still around. It was a very small, closely knit group. There were a lot of children of my age group. We were the only youth group organized within the church, with about twenty members.

I got to know my wife through the church. We used to go to Sunday school together. I did date a lot and all of my girlfriends were white, mostly English-speaking. It was never said to me that I was to marry Japanese, but my parents were very glad to know that I married Japanese. When I brought my white girlfriends home, they never said anything about that. They're more open than I thought they would be.

### James: Toronto, Ontario

I was born in Toronto in 1950, the eldest of four children in the family, and we grew up in Rexdale, a part of Etobicoke. The neighbourhood was typically suburban, mostly Caucasian residents, and there were no other Japanese. The only other Japanese family we used to see was our cousins' family. Most of my friends I grew up with were Caucasians.

Japanese Canadians tried not to congregate in specific areas like many other groups did. I don't know that it was a conscious effort for my parents to live in a neighbourhood without other Japanese families around. It was the thing to do for Japanese at that time. Whether they really discussed it with their friends or whether they just did it on their own initiative, I don't know. I have to believe something like that was done at the conscious level. I think the war, the way they were treated, had everything to do with it.

We were raised in the local United Church, and went to Sunday school there. It was a typical Canadian upbringing with the exception being that we ate a lot of Japanese food.

I'm the oldest in the family. My mother attempted to teach me

Japanese when I was a teenager, but it was much too late. By then I was too Canadianized and had other priorities than learning Japanese. My brothers and sister followed in my steps. My mother then gave up on us all. The language was seldom spoken at home. We never went to the language school. Most of my friends didn't think that I was Japanese. In my late teens, one of my friends came over to our house and saw my father for the first time. He asked me, 'Your father is Japanese?' There was very little that would distinguish me, my brothers, and sister from other kids in the neighbourhood, other than the fact that we looked different. But it really didn't matter to my friends.

I had that awareness of my identity and heritage, but it wasn't strong enough to know what they really meant. When the Japanese Canadian Cultural Centre was opened, my mother pressed me to go there to meet other Japanese kids and girls to do certain social things, judo, etc. I was too busy growing up with my own friends. I never went.

My mother had a lot of Japanese things around the house. She's a very craft-creative person, and I find that more inherent within me. I'm a graphic designer by profession, and my designing sense also comes from something inherent, and influence from my mother and my folk's cultural background, I guess. Two of us in the family went to the Ontario College of Art and entered the field of designing.

We were brought up in the ethnic culture like any other ethnic groups, like the Hungarian kids in my class were. Behind the closed doors at their home I'm sure that they were doing things slightly differently. So were we.

My parents were not involved in any Japanese organizations actively or formally. They're mostly participants. My father was active with the local church for a while. He was involved in Boy Scouts and other neighbourhood groups when we were young, doing things most parents were required to do. They had non-Japanese people to associate with through their involvement in those activities, but their closest friends were all Nisei; they still are.

*Brenda: Vancouver, British Columbia*
I was born in 1960 in Vancouver, and grew up in the east end of the

city. There are two older brothers in the family. The neighbourhood in the east end was and is still predominantly working class, ethnically mixed, with a lot of members from European backgrounds in the 1960s. There were some Chinese kids in the pubic school I went to and a few Japanese. At the high school there were eight Japanese kids. We formed a close group and socialized a lot. Japanese families didn't live in the same neighbourhood, but somehow used to know each other, loosely connected to each other. People moved out of the east-end area, one by one, as time went by, but my parents have remained there.

At home, when my grandmother was alive and living with us, the Japanese language was always spoken between her and my mother. Mother was sent back to Japan before the war and spent eight years there. Japanese holidays were celebrated – we had the good-luck noodles on New Year's Eve almost religiously every year; *mochi*, other Japanese food all the time. We had boys' day and girls' day celebrations with special foods, too.

I didn't get exposed to any Japanese organization or group when I was growing up. I was one of the few who didn't among the kids I used to associate with. I didn't go to the language school; didn't go to the Japanese church either. Instead I went to the local church. I tried to learn the language later at university, but couldn't pick it up. We went to JC picnics, *bon-odori* (folk dances), concerts, etc., where we met many other Japanese.

I knew I was different from other kids, not so much because I was Japanese. I always wanted to be considered the same as all my peers. When I got called names or it was mentioned somewhere that I was different, I felt insecure. Consequently I was very shy. I had problems of shyness. I turned inside, and didn't come out of the shell for a long, long time.

I feel a little bit different from other Sansei, maybe because I've never been involved in the community. I always felt out of place with other Japanese Canadians. One of my friends was active in organizing the Powell Street Festival, and I wanted to help her. I somehow felt I didn't fit into the group. They went to the Japanese language school and have a better command of the language.

My parents didn't belong to any group in the community; didn't associate with any Japanese Canadians either. Only recently they've joined the group formed by the people from my mother's old home town in Japan. Their friends in my childhood were non-Japanese. They seemed a bit different from other Japanese in the area. They're always busy; couldn't afford to do anything extra. Life was very hard for them, even before I was born.

My father had a drinking problem. He's an alcoholic. Our family was dysfunctional at times because of his problem. My parents didn't avoid the association with other Japanese intentionally, but didn't get involved in anything because of my father's drinking, I think. My parents suffered from hardships, and this was partly the cause of his problem, but that may very well be a result of the internment that he went through. He was a fisherman before the family was evacuated and tried to be a fisherman again in the 1950s when they were allowed to get back to the industry. He failed in whatever he tried and has kept minority feelings within him.

I think they tried to assimilate to Canadian culture and society very hard. Despite the hardship, my parents stuck it out together. The family was very important for them, and they emphasized the family values very strongly, the very values I always carry with me.

Their upbringing, as it is represented by the four Sansei here, can be described as fairly 'Canadian' or 'North American.' Their Nisei parents were trying to be more Canadian and to raise their children to be as Canadian as possible. Sansei children were sent to standardized schools in the local community, they mixed with children of different ethnic groups, and they participated in sports and other recreational activities. A Toronto Sansei lawyer recalled in an article in the *Globe and Mail* (Omura, 1993): 'We went on family camping trips and had barbecues with our neighbours. We joined community hockey, soccer, and baseball teams. We were Scouts and Girl Guides. We belonged to the Anglican Church. We lived in well-kept, middle-class neighbourhoods.'

The core values emphasized by their Nisei parents were identical to the North American ones: individualism, independence, materialism, human decency, and the work ethic. 'Our life at home was not so different from the Cleavers on *Leave It to Beaver*, commented a thirty-eight-year-old Sansei man. Indeed, most Sansei found themselves growing up in 'well-kept, middle-class neighbour-hoods,' often with no other Japanese families around. Nisei parents chose to live in communities in which ideally they would be the only Japanese family, and thus, they thought, less conspicuous. 'It was the thing to do for Japanese at that time,' said James, who was born in Toronto in 1950 and grew up in Rexdale, a Metro Toronto suburb.

'My parents did not try to group together with other Japanese, and they didn't want to live next door to the Japanese,' noted a young Toronto-born Sansei accountant, who grew up in Scarborough, another Metro suburb. His parents, starting their own family, set out as a policy not to group together with other Japanese. They emphasized to their children the importance of being inconspicuous in society. Twenty and some years later, when the time came for this accountant to buy a house for the first time, with his newly wed wife, he chose to live in a subdivision of a small town north of Metro, where not a single Oriental yet lived. It was a conscious effort made by the son as 'the thing to do for the Japanese-Canadian family.'

The message that dispersal – the result of government-imposed constraints – was 'a good thing to do' came from their parents, acknowledged their Sansei children, no matter whether they grew up in Montreal, Chatham, Lethbridge, or elsewhere. Therefore, one cannot discuss the ethnic socialization of the Canadian Sansei without reference to the fact that it has occurred for most of them completely outside the boundaries and the influence of the ethnic community, physically or otherwise. Within the context of the 'voluntary mind-set' of the Nisei dispersing themselves and disappearing, the post-internment Japanese-Canadian families were formed, and it was there that Sansei socialization took place.

Dispersal meant assimilation. The Nisei parents were determined to be assimilated to the fullest extent into the larger society and culture in which they were raising their offspring, said virtually all of the sixty-four respondents. The essence of this determination was expressed by some Sansei respondents as a 'natural outgrowth' or a 'natural course of action' that was inevitable under the circumstances: others assessed it and concluded that 'there was little more to it than [it was] simply natural or unintentional.' The efforts made by the Nisei were deliberate and did not happen naturally or by chance. 'It was wholesale rejection of everything Japanese to fit into the mainstream,' commented a thirty-one-year-old Sansei artist, who grew up completely outside the ethnic community in an Ontario city in the southwestern part of the province.

A lot of Nisei, if not all of them, purposely avoided joining any Japanese group or association. They did not speak the language, they did not send their children to Japanese language school, they did not even use chopsticks, and most gave their children Anglo-Saxon names. Rejecting and abandoning their ethnicity meant Anglo conformity (Gordon 1964) on the part of the Japanese Canadians, who completely renounced the immigrants' ancestral culture in favour of the behaviour and values of the Anglo-Canadian core group. As Brenda recalled, she felt 'shut out' from both her Japanese friends and the opportunity to learn the language, so years later at university she took courses to learn Japanese on her own initiative. The same happened with Kathy, James, and many others. A thirty-year-old Toronto woman, who grew up in North York, observed that there was nothing culturally Japanese in her family; her parents spoke 'not a single word of Japanese' to their children; what they had was 'all North American and very middle-class oriented.' The four children in the respondent's family didn't go to the Japanese Canadian Cultural Centre, nor to the Japanese church. David Mura, an American Sansei writer, who grew up in suburban Chicago, depicted his Nisei parents' attitudes towards assimilation in a very similar manner in his memoir *Turing Japanese* (1991), as quoted at the top of this chapter.

For a fifty-two-year-old woman, one of the oldest respondents in this study, who has lived in a northern city in Ontario almost all her life, the true reason for assimilation only became understandable to her much later in her adulthood. While on a quest for her roots, it came as quite a revelation to her to learn that the need for assimilation after the war by both individual Japanese Canadians like her parents and the collective community was sensed with such a level of urgency and intensity. Before coming across this explanation, it was her understanding that the third generation had no knowledge of their historical heritage because the Nisei had lost all their belongings and possessions while struggling to survive. This Sansei mother of four said: 'My parents never explained to me why they tried so hard to be assimilated. It was a conscious effort on their part, no doubt. Assimilation – to be accepted – was the only way for Japanese after the war when they were resettled in this area. This theory explained to me why I knew so little about my family background and my cultural-historical heritage. Our parents had no choice but to assimilate to the society at large, forgetting that they were Japanese.' While this respondent, a part-time nurse, was raising her own children, she realized that there was nothing culturally Japanese instilled within her, nothing tangible, let alone the language or the religion to pass on to her children. The Japanese community in the northern Ontario city was thriving in the very early years of resettlement, but was long dismantled by the time her children were growing up. 'Everything's gone by then. You can regain certain material things, but not your heritage.'

Socialization experiences described by the four Sansei cited earlier illustrate the fact that certain common elements of culture – language, religion, customs, and other visible aspects of heritage – are involved 'as things to observe and learn' in the course of growing up in the ethnic family. Brian learned 'the Japanese way of life' by observing 'a lot of Buddhist practices.' especially while his grandparents were living with his family. 'Behind the closed doors,' in James's description, his family were doing 'things slightly differently,' like other ethnic families of his friends were. The sketches also suggest that the Nisei parents were 'teaching' the children to be aware of their cultural background and their ethnic identity by various means: by telling them stories and legends as well as by providing such ethnically defined activities of everyday life as holidays, ceremonies, songs and dances, and the like.

The stories told by the Nisei parents could have included the legacy of racism and discrimination that the Japanese Canadians endured in this country, with special reference to their 'wartime experiences.' The internment represents a significant historical and personal event in the lives of the Nisei, although not every parent of the Sansei respondents actually experienced the internment or incarceration. The incidents that occurred during and after the war, and which were personally experienced and suffered by a large majority of the Sansei's parents, could have been told in the form of storytelling, while looking over the family photo albums or while visiting the family's old residential sites on the West Coast. In the process, the legacy was to be transmitted between the generations. Uniquely involved in the internment experiences are minority feelings and sentiments that the Nisei parents seemed to have held throughout the years, explicitly or implicitly, as detected, for instance, by Kathy and Brenda. We can thus see that a Sansei as a child was taught that he or she was 'different' and could not expect the same privileges as many other people, unless he or she were to 'try harder' or 'perform better than others.' Like any other children in a visible-minority group, the Sansei learned about racial differences and the special meaning of them as they grew older, indirectly from their parents or informally from their peers; they therefore absorbed the popular beliefs of the community.

One of the findings from my 1976 study on the ethnic identity of Toronto Nisei proved empirically that the basic process of Nisei socialization was rooted in ethnic culture and community. By living in Japanese neighbourhoods that involved daily association with Japanese playmates and friends (67 per cent of the Nisei respondents lived in so-called Japanese districts or communities, and 56 per cent of their peer-group friends were mostly Japanese), and regularly attending language schools (90 per cent attended language school for some period of time), the Nisei experienced a relatively high degree of group association and solidarity that had been preserved from childhood.

About one-third of the Sansei in the sample group studied here reported that although their childhood friends had included one or a few Japanese, most had been non-Japanese. The remaining two-thirds, which include Kathy and James, had no Japanese children to grow up with or to play with. For these Sansei, interaction with Japanese people was limited to their relatives within the family circle. 'The only other Japanese family we used to see was our cousins' family,' James recalled.

Yet some parents at least tried to make their children aware of the fact that they were Japanese. A large majority of the Nisei parents, even those who were strong advocates of assimilation and integration, such as the parents of Kathy and James, encouraged their sons and daughters to go out to meet Japanese and make friends with them. When Toronto's Japanese Canadian Cultural Centre was opened, James's mother pressed him to go there to meet other Japanese children – especially girls, but he refused to go. His younger siblings followed the footsteps of their older brother and did not go either. Kathy was also encouraged by her parents to join the Sansei Club in Hamilton's Cultural Centre in case she might meet a Sansei boy there. She actually joined it and had 'a great time' at the club. If it was a feasible and workable thing to do, the parents sponsored and sent the children to such activities as language classes, church programs or summer camps, community picnics, and parties. Two out of ten respondents in the sample group reported that, at one time or another in their childhoods, they were exposed to Japanese language school or Japanese lessons, either for a very brief period for some or for more than a few years for the others. One of five were raised in the Buddhist church, while only half that number (9 per cent of the total sample group) were involved in Japanese Christian church groups. Some fortunate ones joined youth clubs or various sports clubs and leagues within the ethnic community, where they associated with other Sansei and learned the culture or, as one Sansei man said, 'got the feeling of the Japanese culture.'

Over half of the respondents in the sample stated, on the other hand, that they had no chance to join any of the community associations because they lived in areas where there was no group to join or their parents, like Brenda's, chose to stay away from Japanese organizations.

Variations among the individuals in terms of their degree of exposure to ethnic culture and/or ethnic group activities seemed substantial. The respondents who grew up in the Toronto area were the ones most likely to have been exposed to either the language school, the church, the sports club, or some of the social activities organized at the Japanese Canadian Cultural Centre. Those who grew up in Greater Vancouver were similarly exposed, perhaps to a lesser extent than in Toronto, although without a proportionate number of subjects drawn from the area, it has not been empirically proved in this study.

A forty-five-year-old Sansei woman coming from a working-class background described growing up in inner-city Toronto in the 1960s: 'I went to the Buddhist church. The whole family did. My parents made sure that we went to Sunday school. I went to the Japanese language school for two years. We took Japanese dance lessons privately with a teacher too. My mother wanted us to know how to cook Japanese food, so we took cooking lessons from her.' She noted that perhaps her parents were more 'Japanese-ish' than the average Nisei she knew, partly because her father had spent most of his formative years in Japan. At her home, daily meals were basically Japanese – always served with rice – and at an early age, the children were taught how to eat properly with chopsticks.

Another Toronto resident, a thirty-six-year-old Sansei man who was extraordinarily athletic, was heavily involved in sports while growing up in East York (Toronto). He also participated in a lot of other activities going on in the Japanese community.

> My father sent us to the language school. I attended it for seven years from age eight to fifteen. My father made us go. I must have liked the school; I had friends there. My father was a black-belt judo player. He was taking me to the *dojyo*. Judo players there were exclusively Japanese then, now they may have more *hakujin* players than Japanese.
>
> My folks are Buddhists and are active members of the church. I was taken to the church from a very early age. There was a very large youth group within the church, my age group when I was a teenager. We socialized for many years as a group of friends, but broke apart when we started university. I joined the JC tennis club later and was a member of the JC hockey league, too. Some of us from the league went to Japan for three weeks to play with Japanese teams in 1983.

This Sansei man has managed to keep contact with his Japanese associates for a long time, even after he left the community groups physically, largely because he has never left Toronto. At the time of the interview, however, he and his family were about ready to move to Boston for his new job.

A forty-eight-year-old Sansei nurse and mother of two teenagers pointed out that, even in such a small, isolated place as Geraldton in northern Ontario, in the 1950s there was quite an active life in the Japanese community, with twenty some families involved. The Nisei Club organized picnics, cultural festivals, and Christmas parties. 'Everybody participated in everything, and I used to know practically every Japanese family and every Japanese kid in Geraldton.' Her childhood friends were of various mixed nationalities, including a few Sansei who moved away at the end of high school. The respondent herself left home for the south to study nursing, and by the time she came back, the Sansei in the town were just ready to leave. The ethnic community in the small town then disappeared with them leaving the town one by one.

The cultural influence of their parents and the community was not substantial enough or persistent enough to have a sustained bearing on the way the characters of the Sansei were formed or in shaping what they are today ethnically, insists a thirty-four-year-old Sansei industrial consultant from Raymond, a farming community in southern Alberta. Although the farm was physically isolated, his family was surrounded by numerous elements of ethnic culture and constant interfacing with other Japanese – while his generation stayed around.

> The Japanese community in Raymond was small but a tightly knit community when I was growing up there. The centre of the action was the Buddhist church. I attended Sunday school and the language class taught by the minister. My parents were active supporters of the church; Dad was president of the church association for some years. My friends were both Japanese and other kids in the community who were from diverse backgrounds. At home, there was a Buddhist altar, and festivals and holidays were celebrated with special feasts. My sisters were dressed up in traditional kimono on such special occasions as religious holidays and weddings at the Buddhist church.

Decades later, since he left home in Alberta and had made Toronto his permanent home with his own family, the consultant insisted there was 'little impact' in his daily life from 'the ethnic community' that he grew up with, or from the ethnic culture as he was familiar with it in his childhood.

While Nisei parents set out to teach, or to help teach their children certain aspects of their ethnic culture and identity, at the same time they deliberately set out to suppress certain other aspects of their ethnicity. One of the elements of the uniquely Japanese-Canadian heritage is their internment during the Second World War. How has this been dealt with and passed on in the Japanese-Canadian family? What were children told about this legacy, and what have they learned from the personal experiences of the parents and the elders of their family who had gone through the internment?

A survey recently conducted by an American researcher (Nagata 1990, 1993) investigated the cross-generational impact of the Japanese-American internment upon the children of those who were incarcerated. Close to six hundred Sansei were involved, responding to a mailed questionnaire. One of the major results of the survey indicated, interestingly enough – and this was consistent with the findings obtained from the Canadian Sansei reported here – that strikingly little communication occurred between the Sansei and their parents regarding the internment. Virtually all the respondents in our sample group reported that their parents maintained a silence about their experiences in the camps, about the years spent after being uprooted from their homes, and about their expulsion from the West Coast of Canada. 'There's an unwritten rule in my family that the internment camps, and even the days before the war, were not to be talked out,' stated a respondent. My earlier Toronto study also documented evidence that the majority of Nisei did not communicate a great deal about the internment to their Sansei children (Makabe 1976, 1980).

The data from the American survey have quantitatively confirmed the extent of this silence and the degree to which the Nisei's internment experience has influenced the lives of their offspring. Silence and concealment were taking place alongside the socialization that was directed at the goal to be accomplished – complete assimilation and integration – and were the strategy adopted for the goal's attainment. To supplement the data provided by the Nagata questionnaire survey, and to elaborate upon the nature of communication and the subtle background of silence maintained for decades in the Nisei family, direct quotations from the respondents in our study are presented as a baseline of our discussion. They represent the responses of the total sample group fairly well.

The respondents were asked to elaborate in terms of how much they knew about the internment as a historical event, and in particular about the personal experiences that the elders of the family went through. They were also asked who were their sources of information concerning the camps, and the degree of communication they had with their parents or other people about the internment. The following quotations are portions of statements made by the respondents that are most relevant to the topic under discussion.

In Toronto, an owner and manager of a photography shop: 'I don't know a lot about JC history including the internment. My parents didn't talk about their background or their past experiences at all. I think they didn't want their kids to be confused and disturbed when they were growing up. They just tried to provide a stable home, a normal family life, without referring to anything that had occurred in their past at all.'

In Toronto, a language teacher: 'Nobody talked to me about the internment until I began questioning when I was in high school. I questioned my mother and my relatives [father deceased by then]. I felt angry because of the fact that I had been denied my heritage because they kept silent. I think a lot of Nisei purposely avoided the subject matter altogether.'

In Toronto, a civil servant: 'I think they had long forgiven [that they were interned]. They had seen the benefit of moving out of, away from a concentrated ghetto. And they saw their children doing reasonably well – [being] accepted. My parents never talked about it until I asked them when I was in my 20s. There was a lingering bitterness. It wasn't strong, but there was a lingering bitterness, and I've carried that as well. It was silent when I was growing up.'

In Montreal, a 'production worker' in a family-owned screen-print shop: 'My parents never discussed their personal experiences. It never occurred to us to ask our parents. No curiosity when I was growing up, and they never volunteered. I have to admit that I know only so little about the internment, too.'

In Calgary, an executive secretary: 'My Dad never wanted to talk about what went on during and after the war. He avoided the subject completely [mother not interned]. He might answer questions if we really prodded him. He doesn't talk in detail about what happened to him and his family. I'm sure he will never forget about what happened. He preferred for us to read for ourselves on what has happened to Japanese Canadians. I learned about it mostly from reading books and the mass media.'

A visual artist who grew up in London, Ontario, but currently lives in Calgary: 'To a certain extent my parents didn't want to talk about the past. I asked questions sometimes and then they talked a little bit. Otherwise they didn't necessarily want to talk about it. They are more willing to talk about it now after redress. When I was young, I simply didn't ask questions. In our family you have to ask questions.'

In Vancouver, Brenda, a community-development worker: 'When I did my assignment for a social studies project in Grade 10, I asked my father his experiences at the internment camp. He never talked about before that. He doesn't bring it up voluntarily even now. I found out that my grandmother was buried in Revelstoke, but that was never told us. My parents didn't give us information systematically, just telling stories and making casual remarks.'

As a matter of fact, as Brenda did, a few respondents attempted 'interviewing' their parents with a set of questions either for social-studies projects or history assignments to learn about their experiences at the internment camps. 'It was uncomfortable for him to talk to me,' Brenda found out, and it was equally uncomfortable for her to ask her father. He was rather shy throughout the interviews, said Brenda, not opening up, which was very strange, because her father is a very outgoing man in other respects. In one such interview, a respondent from Steveston (currently residing in

Toronto), found out that her father was in the prisoners' camp in Angler, Ontario, but he refused to talk about that part of his life at all. The daughter now has a fairly good understanding from the library research that she has done why her father ended up in a prisoners' camp and spent years there.

'My father could not respond to my inquiry,' a Sansei woman in Beeton, a small Ontario town, reported. It was too difficult a thing to talk about the internment for her father. He was angry and refused to ever go back to Vancouver even for a visit. He always reacted with anger to the subject matter whenever she asked him questions. Thus, in one way or another, the children learned that their parents' past experiences were not to be a topic of conversation at their home.

The quotations so far illustrate clearly and consistently the points highlighted in the findings from Nagata's survey. They document the very high degree of silence and concealment that has surrounded the subject of internment within most Japanese-Canadian families. Communication tended to be quite limited in both frequency and length, with little substance. Consequently, the Sansei's knowledge about the event is, generally speaking, limited and fragmented. It was common for the respondents to be unaware of even the most basic facts about their elders' internment experience – when, how, and why the government's order of mass evacuation was issued, and the names and locations of the internment camps. They had little information or understanding of 'the intimate details' concerning the four long years of incarceration, the hard decisions that had to be made by some fathers regarding military service or, for others, repatriation to Japan, and the reasons why some chose to resettle east of the Rockies. The quotations continue.

In Thunder Bay, a sales clerk: 'Our parents tried to shelter us from hardships that they had by not talking about the past. They came to the town and wanted to become a part of the larger community here. They didn't want to make a lot of waves by saying and telling their children what had happened. We didn't grow up upset because of this. My father didn't want to talk about the past. He just talked about good, funny things. No sense in talking about the past, I guess. I know he was incarcerated in the prisoner-of-war camp for a couple of years.'

In Calgary, a school teacher: 'My parents don't talk about the war years freely. Sometimes some stories come down incidentally. Sometimes I have to ask, then push and push. It's not things that they dwell on. There is some hesitance from them to share that part of their history. I started asking them when I became a teenager. The conversations were brief and limited.'

In Chatham, an insurance broker: 'My parents hid their feelings very well. Father is a guy who always tells all kinds of stories, but about the internment he likes to tell only funny stories about something odd, always something funny, hiding negative sides of the experience at the camp, etc.'

In Ottawa, a research chemist: 'My parents came to live in Winnipeg from the amp. I don't know why because that was something that they didn't talk about much when we were younger. Mother only incidentally brought up something; such and such a thing happened in Slocan or something like that. It was just a story about something and it wasn't specifically regarding the fact that she was there or how she got there. Mother talked more than Father did. I was not really interested in knowing the details. That wasn't something that I really felt like prying about.'

In London, an industrial designer: 'My parents talked to each other about their experiences, but not to me. They recalled certain things about the internment, and shared the past with their friends. They didn't talk for my benefit. I sensed their feelings about being victims of discrimination, not being fully accepted, and that they were told to leave the Coast by force. But the actual history I knew little when I was a child.'

In Montreal, Brian, manager of a family-owned manufacturing firm: 'I heard stories of the wartime events. They came out in bits and pieces here and there, but only in the past five or so years since the redress issue came up. At home we never really sat down and had discussions about the internment, i.e., how they felt about it. My parents never showed any emotions about the loss or anything else they might have suffered. They lost the chance to go back to school. My father is a very private person and completely

silent about the internment. He doesn't show his emotion. We
have to pry to get him to open up. My information came from my
mother and the older Nisei at the church.'

Forty per cent of the American Sansei in Nagata's survey indicated that their information about the internment came primarily
through overhearing conversations or from outside sources such as
books and films, and not directly from their parents. When the
Nisei parents talked about the subject, it was to each other or with
their friends rather than with their children. The internment was a
casual, infrequently mentioned, incidental topic of conversation in
which the stories were often funny, odd, or insignificant, with reference only to the positive aspects of the event. The Sansei children
had to piece together bits of fragmented stories to get a picture of
their parents' experiences.

Unwilling to discuss their camp experiences with anyone, even
members of their own family, the Nisei had perhaps feared that
other people, including their own children, would not understand.
It took forty years for some of them to begin to talk among themselves, and this occurred only after redress became a public issue
in the early 1980s (see chapter 6 for further discussion). By then
most of the Sansei were out of school and some of them had left
home. 'Memories for them were not pleasant. It is something that
they are ashamed of, not for something that they did, but for something that they had to endure,' commented James. Another
respondent said that his father has long forgotten about the
internment. But according to the son, the father wants to go
back to Japan to be buried there, partly because he spent some
childhood years there and still has uneasy feelings towards this
country. Repression, denial, or rationalization in the form of non-
communication and concealment may have been a necessary reaction not only for their own survival (Mass 1991), but also for the
protection of their offspring, as hinted by a few respondents.

In Toronto, a youth counsellor: 'My parents had feelings of frustration and embarrassment, and they disliked being Japanese
Canadian. The whole picture was to wipe out the past altogether,
not to mention it. Thinking of the evacuation and internment
bring bad feelings, and they didn't want to deal with it. My knowl-

edge about the event was extremely limited until very recently. And still is.'

In Toronto, a lawyer: 'My parents never spoke. The whole thing was *shikataganai* (it cannot be helped) to them. They don't gain anything by telling everybody about it. "It's over and done with it, so forget about it." There are a lot of losses, I know. They lost a big house they built in Steveston, a fishing boat and fishing licences, but you cannot make up those losses, so you just move on. That's what they did.'

In Toronto, James, a graphic designer: 'I don't know intimate details of what happened to my parents and to the Japanese in Canada during the war. I've seen some family pictures taken at the camp, but I don't know what it was actually like because my parents didn't really talk about it. They rarely talked about it until fairly recently. When I was at school, internment never came to me. I was not interested in investigating the details of the event.'

In both the United States and Canada, Sansei observed similar differences between their fathers and mothers. Both groups of children maintained that their mothers were more likely than their fathers to initiate a conversation about the internment camps and that they are more likely to know their mother's side of the history and her views about the event. The Canadian fathers tended to be, in the children's views, more unemotional, unwilling, private, evasive, cryptic, and uncomfortable than their mothers in discussing the internment. Her father always reacted to the subject of internment with anger and bitterness, a female respondent commented, whereas her mother did not have the bitterness her father did. The mother never portrayed the internment as being a terrible experience.

According to Nagata, women are more likely than men to communicate on topics that are emotional or affect-laden, or, she speculates, the internment was more difficult to go through for Nisei men than for the women. Thus, after so many years, the men were the ones who still had a fair amount of pain, bitterness, and anger. A forty-four-year-old Sansei sales manager with a manufacturing firm in Mississauga said that his mother would sit for hours talking about her childhood life. His mother grew up in Marpole, Vancouver, in the tightly knit Japanese community, and has a strong sense of community. The manager's mother had a 'fun time' in the internment camp. His father, in contrast to the mother, 'talks only very infrequently about the past,' and the son knows almost nothing about the father's side of the history. His father 'doesn't open up' because, so the son thinks, the internment was more difficult for him. In addition, the men talk less because they had to endure racist comments much more than the women did. The quotations continue.

In Toronto, a writer–bookstore manager: 'For my father it was very hard to speak about the camp. He was only about ten. My mother was even younger, and had nothing to lose, so it was easy for her to speak. We learned the Japanese-Canadian history at school. I would ask my father about what I learned at school, but he wouldn't respond. He would say nothing, and just leave. He just wouldn't be there when we raised questions. Not anger, but just silence. Isn't this very Japanese, avoiding confrontation?'

It may be safe to state, in concluding our discussion, that conscious efforts were made by many Nisei not to talk about the past, particularly about the internment, not to congregate together, and to assimilate as completely as possible. Such efforts were not natural, however, and this action was a hard-fought battle for Japanese Canadians that did not come easily, argued Terry Watada (1989, 142), a Sansei writer-musician based in Toronto. 'The second generation had to consciously concoct a design for the children; never speak of prewar days ... and never but never speak of the War. Never. Conspiracy of Silence was thus devised.'

For the Canadian Sansei the internment seemed to have had little bearing on their upbringing, as far as the individuals involved in our study are concerned. Generally, they seemed unaware of the enduring effects of the internment or its significance on the individual as well as the group. 'Nothing I can think of' or 'I've not given it much thought' are the typical responses to the inquiry. Instead, the internment was viewed as a distant and past tragedy, a tragedy in which the victims – their own parents and grandparents – were not necessarily viewed as actual victims. In the Sansei's own assessment, the victimization experienced by their elders during the internment has shaped their lives very little.

Nagata, however, argued that the cross-generational effects of the internment are manifested in a general sense by the Sansei's feeling of vulnerability. One of the significant findings from her study indicated that not only did American Sansei with an interned parent feel less secure about their status in the United States than the Sansei without an interned parent, but they also expressed a significantly stronger preference for Japanese Americans over Caucasian Americans. One possible way to explain this is, as the researcher interprets, 'the limited family communication about camp served to highlight rather than diminish the Sansei's sense of their parents' trauma. This, in turn, may have created the increased feelings of vulnerability and in-group preference' (Nagata 1990, 65).

There were a few respondents in the present study, three out of the sixty-four, to be precise, who mentioned the indirect yet long-lasting effects of the internment. One of them was Brenda, a Vancouver Sansei, who was introduced at the outset of this chapter. Her father had battled a drinking problem for many years. Life had been hard ever since her father left the internment camp. After the war ended, he had to curtail his plans to go back to his home in British Columbia to be a fisherman once again. Instead, he took any jobs available to him and after taking over a corner store from his relatives, he eventually ended up as its owner. Because of her father's problems, the family was 'dysfunctional and chaotic at times' and isolated from both Vancouver's Japanese-Canadian community and the community at large. Brenda became extremely withdrawn as a child, and, as an adult, she is still struggling with the tendency to be shy. 'I'd never figured out the reason why my father became such a heavy drinker when I was young,' said Brenda, but she wondered whether his alcoholism could be attributed to the internment, as her father tried so hard to suppress the anger and the frustration he had experienced during and after the war.

During the course of my interviews, two Sansei men also talked about the direct effects of the internment on their fathers and, indirectly, on them. The first was a forty-year-old man from Winnipeg whose father is 'emotionally extremely uptight.' The father worked as an auto mechanic to support the family of five children. He still has hard feelings about being interned because he lost his chance to finish his schooling. 'Coming home quietly from work, my father got mad at everybody about something because he was not allowed to blow up at work. He was never comfortable with his employer and co-workers at his place of work.' The son left home early, dropped out of high school (but went back in his twenties to complete it), and admits that he has difficulty in controlling his emotions when he becomes tense and uptight about something. 'I express my anger and anxiety in the same way that my father did. My wife could not handle it. It cost me my [two] marriages.' His parents' ethnic background, his father's feelings about being a minority and a victim of racism, an inferiority complex – the combination of all these, according to the son, affected him and his upbringing a great deal.

A thirty-five-year-old Toronto man was the second respondent who was also straightforward as he recalled the life of his father, who died in 1984 at age sixty-five. According to the respondent, his father suffered psychologically more from the internment than from anything else.

Being Japanese, my father was evacuated from his home and interned [to work on a sugar-beet farm in Alberta; the name of the place the respondent does not know]. As a result of that, he became bitter about his experiences during the war until the last moment of his life. He really lost his aspirations for life after that, I think. He said he was finished with his education when he came out here. He didn't think he would get very far even if he had education. He was very cynical. His first marriage came to an end after some years. The result of the war and his experiences made him not want to be part of the Japanese community. He really wanted to distance himself from it.

The son got the impression that his father would rather forget that he was Japanese. The father was one of the very few Nisei who had no Japanese friends at all. Instead, he became involved with Anglo Canadians as well as with Native Indians, becoming more 'Canadian' than the average Japanese Canadian. In the meantime his marriage with a Nisei woman broke up. The son was influenced by the choice made by the father 'not to be ambitious' and not to be part of the Japanese-Canadian community. The son had to live with that choice. After he tried to make a living by doing a variety of jobs, the Nisei father worked as a taxi owner–driver until he died.

This respondent was not taken to the Japanese Canadian Cultural Centre even once when he was a child, and while the father was alive, the son had nothing to do with the community. As the father rarely spoke about the past, about his parents and where they came from in Japan, the son now realizes that he knows nothing about half of his background: 'I don't know how I got here without knowing the detailed history of father's family.' It can be argued that the camp experience has robbed this Toronto Sansei man of his culture and his identity. A sense of self, a sense of history, connection to one's primary group and its community, which is basic to all Canadians, has been missed by at least some Sansei. Is this the price to be paid for 'the conspiracy of silence'?

How about the price paid for complete assimilation by abandoning the inherent values and the language of one's primary group in order to be accepted, safe, and secure? The relationships between the generations, particularly between the Sansei and their grandparents, the Issei, have suffered largely because of the loss of language. 'The Sansei have lost the opportunity to understand the world from the perspective of the grandparents, who have a different history, culture and language,' writes a Toronto woman (Omura 1993).

Many of our respondents admitted that they did not get to know their grandparents intimately 'as persons,' and that they did not have 'the right questions' to ask them, while they were still alive, in order to grasp 'the whole lot of their life experience.' Thus, the Sansei as a whole know relatively little of their respective family's past, their historical heritage, and, in particular, the Japanese-

Canadian internment, the very experience that distinguishes them from other ethnic groups in Canada. The gradual loss of generational continuity and the damage caused by this loss, whether psychological or otherwise, seems to have gone largely unnoticed by the Sansei themselves. What is the outcome of this loss of ethnic culture and generational continuity on the ethnic identity of the Sansei? This will be one of the topics discussed in the following chapters.

## Chapter Four

# Sansei Identity: Subjectively Defined

*Like most of my generation, I am the product of suburbia, a predominantly white school system and workplace ... As I grew older my 'ethnic difference' was a point of embarrassment, not pride. You know: 'Where do you come from?,' racist remarks, strange stares and, consequently, a lot of confusion and anger. It's taken me a long time to muster the courage to face what it really means to be a sansei.*

Norm Ibuki (1992)

This chapter examines what it means to be a Canadian of Japanese descent and analyses these questions. What does being a Japanese Canadian mean to each individual Sansei? How does the Sansei express his or her ethnic identity? What constitutes the basis for identification or consciousness for a person of Japanese descent born and raised in Canada? How important is one's ethnicity in one's everyday life?

Individuals can share a similar perspective and identify with each other for a number of different reasons. First, this chapter will explore the content and nature of ethnic identity among the Sansei or, more specifically, the reasons why they think that they are/are not members of an ethnic group. Depending on circumstances and the context, a different aspect of being Sansei appears and operates within the same individual. The content of identity varies among members of each generation as well as between the generations. To use Elkin and Handel's terms (1989, 101–2), ethnic identity 'expands and contracts,' and 'it changes over time, it looms large or small depending on the particular context and possibly on the advantage to be gained from manipulating the ethnic label.' To put it further in the constructionist approach (Nagel 1994, 1995), ethnic identity is also something of a product constructed both by external social, economic, and political processes and by ethnic groups and individuals themselves as they shape and reshape their self-definition and culture.

In the previous chapters we saw that Japanese Canadians, wherever they lived, have incorporated themselves into Canadian middle-class life very well. The Sansei were brought up to be '100% Canadian' and they themselves see their upbringing as totally Canadian. They grew up in their respective neighbourhoods as 'native locals.' The impact of socialization on their ethnic identity as it was discussed and previously analysed is probed here within the context of their highly integrated social and cultural environment, in which the process took place.

### Canadian or Japanese Canadian?

Numerous attempts to operationalize and to measure the concept of ethnic identity have been made by researchers in the field. Isajiw (1990, 37–49), for instance, proposed to dichotomize the concept: the external (objective) versus internal (subjective). External aspects of ethnic identity refer to observable behaviour, both cultural and social, that is, language, religious beliefs, foods, dress, dance, and so forth. Internal aspects refer to images, ideas, attitudes, and feelings. To measure the intensity of ethnic identity among various groups surveyed in Toronto (Breton et al. 1990), Isajiw utilized the gathered data to construct an Ethnic Identity Index with the three variables combined: (1) the respondent's self-definition in terms of the hyphenated or unhyphenated ethnic or Canadian label, (2) the importance the respondent placed on his or her ethnicity, and (3) the respondent's perception of the closeness of his or her ethnic ties. In this study that measures the self-identity of the Sansei subjectively, each respondent was asked about the relative salience of two different bases of identifiable categories: ethnic origin and being 'Canadian.' The question was phrased as follows: 'Do you usually think of yourself as a Japanese Canadian or simply Canadian?' Whichever label was chosen, the respondent was asked to elaborate the reason(s) for choosing that label against the other.

In their overall perceptions about their ethnicity the Sansei were more inclined to be ethnic Canadian than I had anticipated they would be. In fact, quite a few respondents mentioned that they became realistic and quite solid about their ethnic self-identity after they had become adults. Also, ethnicity does matter somewhat for many of them, although not so much in their daily lives, perhaps, and many respondents maintained that if possible they would like to preserve their ethnic identity individually, if not collectively. Thus, more than the Sansei perhaps realize, their actions and behaviour are 'somewhat different,' and could be considered 'Japanese.' In addition, these individuals would not necessarily reject these Japanese characteristics or traits.

In the usual manner of the Sansei, the response to the question of calling themselves either Japanese Canadian or simply Canadian was generally prompt and straightforward. The results from the sixty-four respondents were as follows:

Canadian                                             20
Canadian first, but Japanese Canadian        7
Japanese Canadian                                 37

A number of studies and surveys have previously been done in Canada to assess the ethnic identification of individuals in the country as a whole or in one region or city (see Driedger, Thacker, and Currie 1982 for a summary of the survey results). Differences in the population sample, the wording of questions, and the timing and location of the surveys make a meaningful comparison of the results almost impossible. One example is the 1973 study by O'Bryan and others (1976) involving ten ethnic groups in five Canadian cities, in which data on ethnic identification by the generational groups were provided. The analysis indicated that only 17 per cent of their third-generation respondents used an ethnic identification (simple or hyphenated) in responding to the question, What do you usually think of yourself? The remaining 83 per cent identified themselves as Canadian or something else.

The figures from the Canadian Sansei were also significantly different from those obtained from my in-depth interview study of Toronto Nisei conducted in the mid-1970s (Makabe 1976). Only five of a hundred Nisei indicated that they saw themselves without reservation as Canadian; the majority of them (66 per cent) had a dual identity. The remainder, close to one-third of the total Nisei sampled, saw themselves as 'Japanese.'

None of the Sansei in the present sample identified themselves as only Japanese, although I heard on and off during the course of the interviews remarks from the respondents such as 'As I grew older, strangely I feel basically I'm Japanese'; 'I realize there is a good comforting feeling in saying to others that I'm Japanese with no attached adjectives at all'; and 'You know, it's more fun to be a Japanese.' Indeed they all agreed that their ethnic identity has become more apparent as they grew older and left school, began to compete with other members of society, and firmly established themselves occupationally and socially.

Overall, the Sansei sampled for the study call themselves ethnic Canadian of Japanese descent rather than simply Canadian. A large majority of the respondents (69 per cent) had a dual identity, designating themselves either as 'Canadian first, but Japanese Canadian' or as 'Japanese Canadian.' The strength of this dual identity was implicitly expressed, and a slight difference in nuance implies a different context or basis of ethnic identity from individual to individual. The respondents somehow had to compare the idea or image of what it means to be ethnically Japanese with the characteristics of their family, the ways that they were brought up, and what they believe to be ethnic; in other words, a cultural grab bag of Japanese-Canadian traits and particulars. The differences in the choice between the 'Japanese Canadian' versus the 'Canadian-first' identity are subtly reflected in the statements cited below. These statements indicate considerable variations in the emphasis placed by these individuals on the Canadian component of their identity that was somewhat strongly and saliently expressed by some respondents compared with the ethnic component expressed by others. This means that these individuals carry a portfolio of ethnic identities that can change as they move through daily life, in accordance with variations in the situation and audiences encountered.

Michael Novak earlier described ethnic consciousness among white ethnics of the second and third generations as an ethnic memory that is 'a set of instincts, feelings, intimacies, expectations, patterns of emotion and behaviour: a sense of reality, a set of stories for individuals' (1972, 47–8). As I still recall vividly with the Toronto Nisei, there was a definite feeling that they think and feel in a way that others cannot think and feel, that their feelings involve a unique set of memories, instincts, tastes, and values. Over the years, therefore, the Canadian Nisei have maintained what Bellah et al. (1985, 153) call a 'genuine community of memory' – a community that people do not choose but are born into, where people inherit a commitment to historical ties through the community and commonly shared experiences. Perhaps because of these various elements and the complex feelings and emotions involved, some Nisei had difficulty in explaining and articulating the meaning of their ethnicity.

The Sansei, in contrast, seemed to find the query emotion-free or to consider it 'a fact of life issue,' unlike the Nisei, which may be an indication of ethnicity becoming less and less relevant to their life, and more and more peripheral or fragmentary. But neither is ethnicity something that they give no thought or notice to. It is a consciousness that is hardly ever expressed in their everyday life; it is a hidden social process of which they are often little aware.

The reasons the Sansei gave for defining themselves as ethnic Canadian, instead of simply 'Canadian' can be classified into two broad categories. The first category includes individuals with the dual identification of 'Japanese Canadian' or 'Canadian first, but Japanese Canadian,' who mainly see the advantages to be gained from identifying themselves as ethnic-group members. This group may be called the 'ethnic advantage/pride' type. For another group of Sansei the emphasis of their 'Japanese Canadian' identity is primarily placed on their socialization experience; that is to say, they think that their 'Japanese-Canadian upbringing' is somewhat unique, meaningful, and important. This group is thus referred to as the 'ethnic socialization/upbringing' type.

In the 'ethnic advantage/pride' category, the individuals are fully aware of their Japanese-Canadian heritage, in terms of their upbringing or the achievement made by the group, and they prefer to consider themselves, and to be considered by others, as Japanese Canadian. They see certain advantages to be gained from doing so and from belonging to a 'respectable minority group.' Therefore, being a Japanese Canadian invokes a positive feeling for those individuals in this dual-identity group; they evidence a feeling of pride, comfort, and pleasure in having a distinctive cultural background and an important historical heritage.

A young Sansei artist expressed this essence: 'I'm Japanese Canadian. I'm quite proud of being Japanese Canadian, certain history I'm proud of. People came to Canada, decided to make new life in a different place, which is a hard thing to do. We were messed around by the political system and the population at large, but we're still here. We're fine, well adjusted and integrated. This is a great part of ethnic-group stories in this country. I feel pride in who we are, our experience. I feel good about our heritage.' A thirty-two-year-old schoolteacher echoes the artist: 'I'm proud of what Japanese people have done in Canada since the war, particularly, and what they have accomplished. We've overcome lots of boundaries. I  feel proud of being connected with the history of the Japanese-Canadian group and its heritage.'

A thirty-five-year-old Toronto-born engineer said that his sense of being a Japanese Canadian is fairly strong and positive. He figured that that feeling comes alternately from his grandparents, parents, and their friends, and from associates that he has known. In his view, they are fairly strong, identifiable characters with good qualities such as being hard working, industrious, and smart. Wherever they are in this country they have earned this reputation on their own merits. 'Given a choice I wouldn't want to be anything else. I would rather be a Japanese Canadian and not be regarded as an Asian Canadian.'

A thirty-one-year-old female respondent, a 'professional traveller'/casual worker for the past few years, stated: 'The Japanese-Canadian identity is part of me. It means my family's heritage. You're the product of your family and the community. I feel I'm lucky that I come from such a strong family. They're all hard-working, committed to their community, and above all very decent. That gives me a good feeling and a sense of security.'

A fair number of the respondents expressed their feelings about being Japanese Canadian by using the word 'pride' and indicated a desire to feel at one with other Japanese in the community. They noted the advantages to being Japanese Canadian and seemed confident in their belief that the Japanese Canadians are generally well accepted, highly regarded, and respected.

A thirty-six-year-old company executive stated: 'I'm not simply a Canadian. I'm a Japanese Canadian. I've something extra which is important enough so that I'd never drop saying it. I think it is probably from the reaction to the way in which people that I associate with view the Japanese community and the Japanese experience in Canada. Their view is very positive, and that makes me want to be attached more to the community. That is why I always say that I'm Japanese Canadian.' This Sansei executive who is employed with a national retail establishment does not like to be viewed as part of the Chinese community in Metro Toronto where he was born and raised, or 'to be lumped in the Oriental group' as one of 'them.' He would like to separate himself from other members in this metropolitan area's fairly large Asian community, so he does not deal lightly with the occasional query by strangers about his ethnic background. He invests his time and energy to educate and enlighten 'those people who don't know the difference' by insisting on his ethnicity as Japanese Canadian.

Those seven respondents who stressed the importance of being Canadian by saying 'Canadian first, but Japanese Canadian,' seem to do so because their feelings, instincts, tastes, values, and the like are very Canadian and firmly ingrained. There is no way for them to get away from it. Some claim that they can maintain their self-identity as a unique individual without denying the significance of their ethnic-family origin, which 'happens to be Japanese Canadian.'

A thirty-five-year-old Toronto Sansei coffee-shop owner and operator, insisted that, in his perception, ethnicity has no effect on him at all. He does not consciously identify with fellow Japanese Canadians in casual or non-casual encounters, because he just does not feel there is a common ethnic heritage meaningful enough for him to share with them. He is 'Canadian first'; nonetheless, the Sansei man maintained that he cannot afford to deny his ethnic background. 'Doubtlessly I'm a Canadian by upbringing, but I would say being a Japanese Canadian doesn't hurt me at all. If people make any business decision based on names, and if they want to do business with me because I have a Japanese name, that's O.K. with me. People don't treat Japanese Canadians in a negative way. People think Japanese are somewhat smarter, a little bit hard-working. I think that's how they see us. It doesn't hurt me at all.'

A forty-two-year-old researcher-technician, who has been working in a university laboratory for fifteen years, maintained that Japanese scientists are highly respected for their conscientious attitude towards work. In the research field, ethnic identity is an asset that, in her perception, her fellow Japanese Canadians earned long before she entered the field: 'There's a good stigma attached to the Japanese in the field. All the Japanese work better in laboratories. The stigma is right, not a stereotype. I've never met Japanese scientists who are lazy, unproductive, regardless whether they are from Japan or Canada. That must have to do with our upbringing. I feel good and secure belonging to that group.'

To these individuals with this type of ethnic identity, ethnicity is perceived as an asset for them. It is advantageous to the Sansei in business to be able to draw people's attention merely by having Japanese names. They positively benefit from both the cultural heritage of their ancestral country and from the historical legacy of the Japanese Canadians to this country, said all the individuals in this group. They thus choose to be ethnic-group members who are capable of appreciating their unique background on their own rather than in response to the images and definitions of who the Japanese are that are formed by other non-Japanese in the community at large.

In discussing and elaborating on the meaning of ethnicity, the second broad category, a group of the respondents mentioned their 'upbringing' and focused on it when they defined themselves as ethnic Canadian rather than simply Canadian. Often the Sansei differentiated themselves from others by noting that they were somewhat differently brought up, and thus their outlook or codes of behaviour are a bit different from those of their fellow Canadians.

This sense of awareness is very similar to what was revealed by the Nisei respondents in my earlier study. In fact, in the Toronto Nisei this factor – broadly termed as the 'ethnic upbringing' type – was the most strongly endorsed basis for their being Japanese Canadian. Quite often the Nisei differentiated themselves from others on the basis of their strong awareness of their ethnic background, which was transmitted to them from their immigrant parents, the Issei (who were 'very Japanese'), and which had a significant bearing on developing their character and setting their attitudes, most appropriately towards work. Those Nisei further believed that their ethnic background, a very big part of their lives, had a significant influence on their day-to-day lives. Because of their 'reasonable upbringing,' it had become possible for them to achieve mobility and to approximate middle-class status in Canadian society.

For a forty-year-old Sansei mother of four, in contrast, ethnic identity as such is not important in her day-to-day life; therefore, she does not have any 'hang-ups' about being ethnic. She is a Canadian in everything she does, yet she feels she is a Japanese Canadian. An accomplished athlete, intensively involved in international competitions until she retired to a teaching career, this now 'full-time wife and mother' firmly believed that her goal-oriented attitudes were the core of values instilled in her by parents who were 'basically very Japanese.' They moulded her and accounted for her athletic spirit in competitive sports and for who she is today: 'I'd say I'm Japanese Canadian, perhaps more Canadian than Japanese. I've a lot of positive qualities from Japanese culture which mould you for what you are. I was raised by Japanese [Nisei] parents: my attitudes and values are from them. My

Japanese-ness is part of what I am, my way of thinking, my way of behaving.' Likewise a thirty-seven-year-old school teacher noted: 'I'm aware of difference existing between me and others. Even between my husband [non-Japanese] and myself. I still probably act the way that I was taught when I was younger; I still have to be better than others just to be at the same level and try harder in everything I do.'

A forty-five-year-old senior manager for a municipality: 'Through osmosis, through direct lessons and watching the behaviour of the elders in my family and their values and the way they react to certain things, the way they take care of each other, I attribute that being somewhat as an ethnic quality. I'm carrying some of those attributes as well. They're important.'

A thirty-five-year-old Sansei, general manager of a small manufacturing firm owned by his relatives: 'Inside me there's pride when I say I'm Japanese Canadian. Good comfortable feelings are there. I feel that I'm better than the next guy, just because I'm Japanese. That is the way I was brought up. Am I a racist? My sense of pride comes from [the fact] that I try to do things harder and better than others.'

A thirty-year-old general contractor: 'I'm a Japanese Canadian. My basic upbringing is Japanese Canadian. Japanese food and other ulture in me. I still want to be known and noted as Japanese Canadian by people in my business and by my customers. That Japanese distinction I like.'

The Sansei in the dual identification group consider their upbringing to be reasonable, meaningful, and positive. In this context, therefore, this type of ethnic identification is overwhelmingly positive, just as the 'ethnic advantage/pride' type of identification is. This is largely because the upbringing experienced by these Sansei involved none of the so-called minority experience and feeling in its content and tone, in the way their Nisei parents' connotation of upbringing inevitably did. Taught to 'behave well because you are Japanese,' every Nisei was also trained 'not to make themselves too obvious.' Thus, some of the Japanese-Canadian values to which their minority values are inherently attached, as well as their personality traits derived from the value system, are critically and negatively evaluated by certain Japanese Canadians. The Nisei personality traits – such as being docile, passive, timid, reserved, less aggressive – which have prevented Nisei from becoming widely involved in social activities and developing broader informal association with non-Japanese, are considered a definite drawback – the legacy of discrimination.

This is where a major difference in ethnic consciousness between the Nisei and the Sansei presents itself most clearly and distinctively. The Sansei are almost completely free of the psychological burden of being minority-group members and of people's negative definitions of their ethnicity. Negative identity takes shape, said Epstein (1978, 102) quite nicely, 'where the image of self rests chiefly on the internalized evaluations of others, and where accordingly much of one's behaviour is prompted by the desire to avoid their anticipated slights or censure.'

Not a single respondent in the present sample group thought that others ever treated him or her negatively as a Japanese or an Oriental, or in any way differently from other Canadians. None said that he or she is not fully accepted as Canadian, or made the comment that one cannot be Canadian unless one is white, as some of the Nisei did. Although the Sansei are aware of their identity as Japanese, or as Orientals within the larger society, this awareness does not extend to negative feelings about that identity.

For more than two-thirds of the Sansei I interviewed, accordingly, having an ethnic identity was for the most part something that brings them pleasure. Rather than being a handicap or a liability to full participation in Canadian society, ethnic identity is seen as giving them a sense of the worthiness of their group's ways and values, and conferring special status on them as unique individuals. Identity was largely a matter of 'feelings,' feeling good about being Japanese Canadian. This type of ethnic identity seems similar to the symbolic ethnicity initially termed by Herbert Gans, in his influential article published in 1979, the concept having been empirically elaborated more recently by Waters (1990) and Alba (1990). Based on his observation of white ethnic-group members in America, Gans argued that ethnicity has become increasingly peripheral to many people in their lives, but that does not mean they relinquish ethnic identity entirely. Rather, they adapt it to their current circumstances, selecting from an ethnic heritage a few symbolic elements that do not interfere with the need to inter-mix socially. Thus, Gans characterized contemporary ethnicity for white Americans as a matter of 'feeling ethnic,' as opposed to being so.

How is 'feeling ethnic' manifested by the Canadian Sansei who chose to refer to themselves as 'Canadian'? Twenty out of the sixty-four respondents (31 per cent of the total, or close to one out of three), responded to the question by saying that they would call themselves Canadian. Several responses given by the individuals that affirm their 'Canadian' identification are quoted in full because in both content and tone they present a good picture of these 'Canadian' respondents. Here again, it was not that easy for respondents to be sure what constitutes their self-identity as 'Canadian,' as opposed to being ethnic Canadian. Some were in a dilemma about being '100% Canadian' in their hearts and minds, yet at the same time '100% visible.' Even though each respondent tried to give a reason or reasons for his or her self-identification, it does not mean that the reason or reasons are fully inclusive. It may be more accurate to say that these individuals share the same per-spectives and views, to a greater or lesser degree. It is the degree to which ethnicity matters that is the important factor here, and of course this applies as well to the respondents with other types of identification.

A forty-two-year-old real estate sales agent: 'As far as I'm con-cerned, I'm a Canadian. I'm a Canadian as the next person is, probably more so. My ancestors were here since the turn of the century. We've been here so long, we're almost "white."'

. A thirty-seven-year-old engineer: 'I see myself as Canadian because I grew up in the white community. All of my friends, clos-est ones are white. I don't have a single friend who is Japanese. I was always treated equally. I've never felt that I was not white. It's difficult to think of myself not being white with my upbringing.'

A thirty-seven-year-old youth counsellor: 'I consider myself a Canadian. A Canadian is someone who wants to be a Canadian. I

don't speak a word of Japanese. I don't have any of the traditional
religion. I don't like Japanese food that much. So the way that I
look is the only thing Japanese with me.'

A forty-five-year-old auto mechanic: 'I must say I'm Canadian. I
cannot function as Japanese in any sense. I don't socialize with
other Japanese Canadians except the family. Even the family is now
becoming very multi-racial and multi-ethnic [because of intermarriage among the members]. I grew up differently from a lot of
Sansei. The only ties I have is the family, as far as anything Japanese
is concerned.'

A twenty-five-year-old industrial designer: 'I'm Canadian. I
wouldn't consider myself to be a Japanese Canadian because I
never try to identify myself with the Japanese-Canadian group
here. I have no Japanese-Canadian friends to associate with. My
boyfriend doesn't notice that I'm Japanese.'

A thirty-five-year-old courier: 'I consider myself simply as Canadian. I've no tradition to follow; no language, no religion. I know
little of the background. The 'Japanese' part may mean something, but it cannot be substantiated in my mind. I don't live and
die on that.'

Ethnicity seems to have little meaning for these individuals. It
seems inevitable for them to be 'Canadian.' From the quoted
remarks, the basic argument of the 'Canadian' respondents is
founded on four grounds: (1) they were born and grew up in Canada and have lived all their lives in Canada; (2) their education,
upbringing, values, and outlook are totally Canadian; (3) the
majority of their friends are non-Japanese and their social contacts
are exclusively non-Japanese; and (4) their racial and cultural
backgrounds have no relevant meaning to them, and other than
the fact they are racially classified as Japanese Canadian, they consider themselves as 'Canadian.'

The individuals in the 'Canadian' identification group were
more likely to grow up in small centres such as Chatham, Guelph,
Geraldton, Thunder Bay, and Ottawa and in the interior of British
Columbia, and they very likely went through early socialization
outside the influence of the Japanese community. Of the twenty
'Canadians' six were 'Torontonians,' and without exception these

Toronto residents from childhood to the present have had little
contact with the Japanese community and with institutions such as
the Japanese Canadian Cultural Centre or the Toronto Buddhist
Church. These places have remained outside of their normal lives.

All of the 'Canadians' admitted that their knowledge and practice of Japanese culture were not strong enough for them to be
able to say that they are Canadians of Japanese origin. Although
'Japanese things' – most distinctively, perhaps, eating rice as a staple food practically every day, and other odd customs and traditions – surrounded them in their parents' homes and are still there
and tangible, they are not certain what these Japanese influences
really mean to them, nor can they define the meaning of having
that particular background. Therefore, they cannot recognize
themselves as Japanese Canadians: 'My Japanese background has
no substance to claim at all'; 'I've little but my name, pedigree, and
diet of an occasional Japanese-Canadian meal.'

The involvement of these individuals in the ethnic community
has been minimal to none at all. 'The Japanese community as such
never existed, and does not exist in my life,' said a few of them.
Social contact at the informal level outside the family has also been
almost exclusively with the non-Japanese community. Therefore,
there is some resignation from those 'Canadians' in insisting that
they really have nothing with which to identify their Japaneseness
except their physical characteristics.

A forty-eight-year-old associate professor of medical science: 'I'm
Canadian. The Japanese part in my background means very, very
little. The Japanese group is so small, and I grew up outside the
community. I don't like to be thought of Japanese from Japan or
even as Japanese Canadian. I just like to be thought of pure, simple
Canadian. That is it. I think there are too many hyphenated Canadians. We have so many social problems because of that.'

A forty-year-old insurance broker: 'I'm Canadian. If you're Canadian, you're Canadian. In Canada everybody must be something
else than being a Canadian. That is ridiculous. We should all forget
about our background – ethnic, racial, nationality, or whatever.'

A forty-year-old sales clerk: 'I'm always Canadian. There's no
doubt in my mind. I don't care what other people think of me.

People look at me and think I'm a little bit different. That is their problem.' Through his daily interaction with customers and co-workers, the Sansei sales clerk receives clues indicating that others define him in terms of his ethnicity. He is still regarded as 'that Japanese guy' at his place of work, even after fifteen years of service and despite the fact everybody knows he is a third-generation Canadian. He accepts it when someone makes a friendly joke with racial overtones, which 'happens all the time.' Japanese Canadians cannot resign from or escape from being identified and treated simply as one unit of the racial group, commented the Sansei clerk who, because of his physical characteristics (and, partly, his rather lengthy Japanese name), is singled out from others in society wherever he goes. Every so often he has to confirm his own identity as Canadian by disregarding others' definitions of his ethnicity. 'Other definitions' thus reinforce 'self-definitions.'

As it can be gathered from the professor's as well as the insurance broker's remarks quoted above, some Sansei with the 'Canadian' identification expressed certain ill feelings when they had to deal with their ethnic background. They insisted that people should not be conscious of their backgrounds and should not speak about 'ethnic groups' because this consciousness and talking emphasize differences rather than similarities among Canadians. They contended that ethnic identity should not necessarily be singled out, either individually or collectively. The feeling was, the more salient and solid people's identity as being Canadian becomes, the better and stronger Canada becomes with less social and political problems. The sense of being a Canadian, as expressed by some individuals here, has thus a political tone.

It is interesting to note, in the present sample group, that renunciation of ethnic identity has been most explicitly expressed by those members of the 'Canadian' identification group. In a sense, to identify oneself as simply Canadian seemed to be the attempt on the part of those Sansei to protect the group's recently attained Canadian-citizenship status in its full sense, as much as the desire to dissociate themselves from certain immigrant/foreign elements in their background, as expressed by a thirty-five-year-old Sansei consultant-manager with a manufacturing firm. He was convinced that Japanese Canadians, or any other ethnic group for that matter, should deliberately dissociate themselves from their 'unCanadian-ness' and from anything linked with their ancestors' homeland. Japanese Canadians should deliberately de-emphasize their distinctiveness because their visibility is an extra burden, according to the consultant-manager. In order to truly become a part of Canadian society, a conscious, deliberate effort must be made among Japanese Canadians themselves to eliminate other people's awareness and definitions of their ethnicity. This can be done 'by acting Canadian' in the first place. Some 'Canadian' respondents evidenced no pride, nor did they see any advantage to their being 'Canadian' that might provide them with a strong basis for cultural or political identification, in contrast to the 'Japanese Canadian' respondents, whose ethnic identity was largely based on self-esteem or 'a sense of worthiness of one's own group's ways and values' (Epstein 1978, 103), which is manifested in one's attachment to them. After my conversations with these Sansei, I found myself wondering whether some of the respondents, despite their self-proclaimed 'Canadian upbringing' in its fullest sense, did not feel completely assured of their full acceptance in the larger society, in which they 'have every right and better claims to be Canadian' than do many other of their associates, as declared by the real-estate agent quoted earlier.

## Other Definitions of Ethnicity

Frederik Barth (1969) first introduced the concept of ethnic boundaries in his discussion of ethnicity, and examined the processes of constructing and maintaining boundaries by ethnic-group members. Ethnic identity is thus the product of a labelling process engaged in by an ethnic person himself or herself as well as by others. Wsevolod Isajiw (1974, 118), following up Barth's concept, pointed out a double boundary of ethnicity. Ethnic persons, maintained Isajiw, 'are identified by others as belonging to one or another ethnic group even if they do not actively share any more any cultural patterns with that ethnic group as long as a link to their ancestors can be made.' Thus, others' identification is as significant or important in the formation of identity as self-identification is for group members.

Waters (1990) likewise noted that ethnic identification involves both choice and constraint. In the analysis and discussion of Sansei identity thus far, we have seen more of the element of choice than of constraint. In reality, however, it is questionable whether they can choose those aspects of their ethnicity that appeal to them and discard those that do not. Is ethnicity for the Sansei really something that is flexible and voluntary, in the same way it is claimed to be for white ethnics?

In focusing her research on the nature of the ethnicity of white ethnics among third, fourth, and later generations of Americans of European extraction, Waters argued that ethnicity cannot for the most part be a matter of choice for non-white members in America. Such visible minorities as blacks, native Indians, and Mexicans, as well as Japanese Americans, are highly socially constrained without other choices available to them as long as they remain racially definable. Waters maintained that ethnicity has increasingly become a personal choice for members as a result of lessened differences among the ethnic groups – as far as white Americans are concerned – of whether to be ethnic at all and which ethnic group to identify with. Indeed, white ethnics have a lot more choice and room to manoeuvre than they think they do.

The situation for members of racial minorities, on the other hand, is altogether different. For those who experience racism or other forms of discrimination, ethnicity can mean the imposition of inequality, with the sense of belonging providing a retreat from oppressive circumstances. Thus, in reality, the lives of minorities are 'strongly influenced by their race or national origin regardless of how much they may choose not to identify themselves in ethnic or racial terms' (Waters 1990, 157). Their identity is something that cannot be voluntary, nor can it be an 'affective' attribute all the time. It also cannot be merely symbolic; it is non-symbolic, insists Waters.

Nagel's (1995) view on this matter, however, is quite different from Waters'. Regarding the ethnic renewal emerging among Indians in the United States that she has been observing in the past decades, Nagel noted that for many Indians their ethnicity has increasingly become a personal choice as their consciousness has been raised in reacting to external political forces within the United States. This change has encouraged individual Indians to claim or reclaim their Native American ancestry. The Indian consciousness raising has resulted in an increase in the number of Americans reporting Indian as their race in the U.S. census; this number has tripled between 1960 and 1990. For those 'new' Indians, ethnicity is thus regarded largely as 'a matter of individual choice' by Nagel (1995, 950).

For Japanese Canadians, particularly for the Sansei, because of their widespread social mobility and intermarriage, ethnicity has become increasingly peripheral to their lives. It has become perhaps more a matter of individual choice than of constraint. Yet, because of his or her physical or cultural characteristics, the Japanese Canadian is singled out from others in society. Many respondents told me that the experience of being singled out in childhood was really something hard to bear. They did not like it a bit because they did not want to be different from other children, or to be reminded they were different. They did not want to be classified as one of the typical Asian math/computer wizards, or regarded by their teachers as one of the kids who were 'born artistic,' either. They did not want to be thought of as Japanese Canadians. They were Canadians, as far as they were concerned.

The Sansei childhood consciousness of looking different and being singled out has largely disappeared now. As the group's status has moved up, racial distinctiveness has come to have far less impact in terms of the images of Japanese formed by non-Japanese. Yet through every daily encounter and interaction with members of the larger society, the Sansei almost automatically and instinctively notice that they cannot resign or escape from being regarded and treated simply as one of their racial group. Others never make a Sansei forget that he or she is an Oriental. In that way they do experience everyday racism. They cannot choose not to be a Japanese just as anyone visible enough cannot choose not to be Indian or Chinese.

A Sansei woman told me that she feels offended when she is

praised for her fluency in English. Surely the English accent must be just too perfect for an Oriental person. Furthermore, people are disappointed because a Sansei teacher does not speak Japanese and does not know enough about Japanese culture or its history. People think she is missing something. In certain places, people would ask, 'Why don't you speak in Japanese, dear?' or 'Why do you eat such strange food as raw fish?' For this young Sansei woman such comments are patronizing, very frustrating, and embarrassing. People do not understand how uncomfortable they make her feel. 'I feel upset and angry because certain expectations are there where there shouldn't be [any] in the first place.'

Outsiders form certain images of or beliefs about a minority group, and these images or beliefs affect their behaviour towards ethnic-group members. Depending on the pattern of relationships and the nature of interaction between the groups, the images become either positive or negative. The racial visibility of the Japanese made them a target for discrimination and rejection, which led to their eventual exclusion from the Canadian West Coast. In the pre-war period, the images were almost totally negative. One popular image formed by the members of the white majority was that Japanese were 'unassimilable,' that the Japanese diverged racially and culturally from others to the extent that they could hardly be assimilated. I still remember a comment made by a Nisei respondent when I was questioning him about what his 'Japanese Canadian' identity meant. There were no such people as 'Japanese Canadians' before the war, said the Nisei man; Japanese Canadians were all classified as Japanese and treated as 'Japs.' They were simply Japanese in the eyes of most *hakujin*.

No doubt some individuals are more sensitive than others to the stereotypes or the ethnic background imposed on them by others, but it has much less of an impact on the Sansei group as a whole than on the Nisei. None of the Sansei in the sample group would ever believe that their status as members of a racial minority is permanent and unchangeable, or that they are never free to forget their ancestry, in the same way the Nisei did. For them, ethnicity never becomes a burden, as it was for the Nisei, who expressed it as something that they had to live with throughout their lives.

When asked if it was a common experience for people to ask or comment about their ethnic backgrounds, the response from the Sansei respondents was fifty/fifty: half said they were almost always asked, and half said they were only occasionally asked; a fair number of the sample members replied that they rarely face such a query in their day-to-day lives. Some of them could not remember the last time someone had raised such a question, or that they encounter this query not more than a few times a year. People that the respondents know very seldom ask or comment, but complete strangers in ordinary interactions at, say, a grocery store or a PTA meeting do ask. A Sansei student working as a waitress reported that about twice a week a customer stops her and asks about her nationality (Takasaki 1991). In particular, people from Asian backgrounds appear to be more curious and inquisitive than others. Typically, the question is phrased as follows: 'Are you a Chinese or a Japanese?' or 'What nationality are you?'

The respondents are quite aware of the ways in which people use names to label them and, from the casual comments they hear, what physical features and names symbolize them to others. They are accustomed to answering the question either by saying, 'I'm a Japanese, not a Chinese,' or by giving a few additional phrases such as 'I'm a third-generation Japanese,' 'My grandparents were from Japan,' or 'I'm a Canadian of Japanese descent.'

Although there are considerable differences between the generations, outsiders treat all Japanese as if they are alike. Regardless of whether a person is a Canadian-born third- or fourth-generation Japanese or a recently arrived immigrant from Japan, to the outsider 'we all look Japanese.' Depending on how the question is raised and by whom, the query is perceived to be either a positive or negative experience. Depending on who asks the question, the response may change. The rules of thumb are, in one respondent's case, that if a Canadian-born person is asking, he says he is Japanese. If it is a person from another country, for example, an immigrant, he says he is Canadian.

Particularly disliked by the respondents is the question: 'Where do you come from?' 'You are a Canadian, I know, but where are you originally from?' A Sansei woman, currently a resident of St

Catharines, a small Ontario city, explains that she does not like the question because it insinuates that she is not from Canada. The question and accompanying comments people make not only often assume that she is not from Canada, but imply that she does not belong here. Depending on the way the question is phrased, her reply to the query can be, 'Oh, I'm from Mississauga.' Period. That puts people off, said the respondent, who would rather embarrass people who raise the question. 'My tolerance level goes down towards ignorance. I guess I expect more from people.' Another Sansei woman, a student waitress (Takasaki 1991), has written: 'I am not really offended by this [query by others], merely annoyed that people ask me what I would never ask of them. Still, I recognize that these questions come from the same voice I've heard all my life. A finger is pointed and a voice says: "You're different." No matter how the question is put, my answer is always the same. I tell them: "I'm a Canadian."'

Thus, questions about their ethnic background are felt by some individuals as constraints imposed upon them, something there is no getting away from. Some of them try to let the inquisitor appreciate the fact that anyone can be a Canadian, just like he or she is, despite the 'differences.' As a Sansei architect put it: 'If someone is very ignorant, I don't bother, but if someone is nice and knows that I'm Canadian, my answer is that my ancestor is Japanese. With unbearably ignorant ones? Then in that kind of situation I insist that I'm a Canadian, nothing but Canadian. I guess I try to educate people by insisting.' As audiences change, that is, depending on whether they are intelligent or ignorant, ethnic choices open to the Sansei architect seem to change. This is another aspect of ethnicity that is 'constructed' socially – as Nagel (1994, 152) put it, presenting the ways in which ethnic identities and boundaries are 'negotiated, defined, and produced through social interaction.'

For the majority of the respondents, the questioning by others about their background is regarded as 'something that Canadians always do' and 'a trait of being Canadian.' Newcomers to the country tend to be more curious to know other people's backgrounds, which is only natural. Some Sansei have learned to deal with the questioning with a bit of humour.

A Sansei man in a screen-print business in Montreal: 'Most people ask whether I'm a native Indian or not, not Japanese. Even
Indians would come up to ask me what tribe I'm from. It's only natural for people to wonder. It doesn't bother me, even being mistaken as an Indian or anything else.' A business manager in
Hamilton: 'It doesn't bother me, even when I'm mistaken for an
Italian, which happens occasionally. People don't think I'm Japanese.' A secretary in Calgary: 'When I'm cheeky, I say I'm a Canadian. Then I ask, "What do I look to you?"' A physiotherapist in
Toronto: 'At a Chinese restaurant, if a waiter doesn't speak to me
in English, assuming that I'm Chinese pretending not to know the
Chinese language, I just have to laugh at it. What else can I do?' An
auto mechanic in Guelph, Ontario: 'I don't get upset by people
asking. If they are just curious, there's no reason for an offence.
Sometimes I'm Chinese to them. It's just fine. I don't even correct
them.' A dentist in Toronto: 'My name can be mistaken for being
Irish. People sometimes comment on it. "Oh, I thought you maybe
are Irish or Italian." I tell them, "I'm indeed Irish, but I don't look
Irish."'

Some other respondents in the group said that they do not like to
be mistaken for someone from a broadly categorized Asian background. 'When I'm mistaken for being Chinese, that upsets me. I
just don't want to be perceived as Chinese,' a forty-six-year-old architect said. In the 1950s in Montreal's French district, where the architect grew up, every Oriental was Chinese. 'We Chinese were treated
roughly by the French Canadians,' he said, a memory he would
rather not recall. A thirty-one-year-old accountant in Toronto also
feels displeasure at being mistaken or regarded as non-Japanese – in
his case, as either a Chinese or a Vietnamese. If he encounters someone making a wrong reference at his workplace, for instance, he
makes a point of straightening them out once he has the opportunity, since he believes this is rather important for him. 'At my workplace I know sometimes I'm referred to as "that Chinese guy." For
some reason I always have to distinguish myself from Chinese. I
never want to be identified as being Chinese or anything else other
than Japanese. This is my prejudice. I guess my name, unlike Tanaka
or Suzuki, doesn't look very Japanese to *hakujin*.'

This accountant's 'prejudice' is based on his belief that the ethnic Chinese and Japanese in Metropolitan Toronto are not at all alike, and as a matter of fact are quite different, most notably in their orientation and attitudes towards assimilation and integration. Whereas Japanese work very hard to be part of the larger community by trying to disperse themselves and mingle with others in society, the Chinese are, to use the accountant's words, 'doing exactly the opposite.' The Chinese speak their own language, group together, and 'form pockets where they don't even speak English.' They are clannish and often keep to themselves. 'We just don't do that.' That is the big difference. More than a few respondents joined the accountant in expressing their unease when they are mistakenly regarded as Chinese or are lumped together with other Asian minorities. These racial attitudes can be characterized by a special type of what Gaertner and Dovidio (1986, 63) termed ambivalence or aversiveness. Aversive attitudes involve discomfort, uneasiness, disgust, and sometimes fear, as expressed here by some Sansei more outwardly than others. Gaertner and Dovidio argued that this type of racial attitude is very subtle, indirect, and less overtly negative, yet tends to motivate avoidance rather than intentionally destructive behaviour. In the minds of those aversive respondents, strangely, Japanese are somehow excluded from their classification of Orientals. They would be likely to attempt to avoid contact with 'those Oriental groups' to which they feel averse. It is not a very comfortable experience, they insisted, to be categorized by others indistinctly in such a racial group as 'Orientals.'

Furthermore, certain respondents expressed their concern and worry about the number of Asians moving into the cities where they lived, whether it was in Calgary, Kelowna, Vancouver, or Toronto. One of the respondents residing in the interior of British Columbia mentioned that a large number of Chinese (relative to the population size of the city) have recently been entering the region, even small cities such as Kelowna or nearby Vernon. This influx is quite rapid and noticeable. The public's image of Orientals is changing along with the movement of this population. A rumour that many houses had been sold to Asians in Calgary worried a young Sansei there because the public does not know that the Chinese, not the Japanese, are 'buying up.' He was worried that some Orientals might some day move into the suburban neighbourhood where he has just settled with his wife and a young child. These concerned Sansei tended to perceive other Asians, whether they are Chinese, Korean, or Vietnamese, as being different from the Japanese, in the same way that white people consider Asians (including Japanese) as being different from them. Often those Sansei seemed to share the anti-Oriental views and prejudices of the white majority – which is perhaps indicative of a reality perceived by some members in the community: 'The Sansei are just like *hakujin*. They think they are *hakujin*, and they act like *hakujin*.'

In this chapter we have observed that the Sansei as a whole, although they experience a high rate of social mobility, have not necessarily developed a weaker ethnic consciousness or a lessened awareness of their ethnic identity. Their ethnic awareness became apparent as they grew older, and the majority of them felt that they would 'hang on to it.' As grown adults, they noticed other people's definitions of their ethnicity and they also became more and more aware of the advantages of being members of a 'respectable' minority.

The Sansei are still categorized as Japanese Canadians even when they no longer actively share any cultural patterns with the Japanese, as long as links to their ancestors (most important, the racial link) can be made. There is a consensus that they are all resigned to being identified and racially defined as Japanese.

## Chapter Five

# Sansei Behaviour:
# With a Focus on Intermarriage

*On that fatal day when I first realized what happened to my parents, I remember thinking that I might have lived differently if I had known when I was younger. I might have married within my own race rather than outside. I might have learned to speak Japanese.*

Kathlyn Horibe (1991)

In chapter 4 we examined the subjective aspect of ethnic identity among the Canadian Sansei. The question central to that chapter was, What does it mean to be a third-generation Canadian of Japanese descent conceptually, emotionally, and ideologically, that is to say, what is the attitudinal dimension of ethnic identity? Now we are going to investigate the behavioural side of it. The questions to be considered here are, How is ethnic identity manifested by the Sansei in terms of everyday behaviour? Can we somehow determine the extent of identity maintained by examining the behaviour of the Sansei? And, keeping in mind the fact that there may be considerable variance as well as association between attitude and actual behaviour, how are the attitudinal variables related to the behavioural ones? In the process of probing the behavioural manifestation of ethnic identity, we will focus on the patterns of involvement and participation in social activities within the ethnic community and of interpersonal relationships among the respondents. As reported earlier, the Sansei are increasingly marrying non-Japanese. The sphere of interpersonal-marital relationships revealed among the respondents in this sample is scrutinized in depth in a search for the reasons for intermarriage and its consequences for ethnic-community participation.

We have learned that, because of the dispersal of the Japanese-Canadian population and the concomitant low rate of institutional completeness of the community, the extent of participation in ethnic institutions and organizations among Japanese Canadians, generally speaking, seems low everywhere, particularly in the regions and areas outside the two large population centres of Metropolitan Toronto and Greater Vancouver. Sansei involvement with and participation in existing ethnic institutions and organizations appears fairly limited and even meagre. Active and regular participants, as one may find any day in any one of the organized activities, for instance, at Toronto's Japanese Canadian Cultural Centre – perhaps the most well-established organization in Canada's Japanese community – are mostly the Nisei. One may find among the majority of the Nisei participators some Sansei here and there attending picnics, dances, bazaars, fund-raising dinner parties, wine-and-cheese parties, and sports tournaments sponsored by the community-wide organization. One can also see a fair number of Sansei volunteers working hard for Vancouver's Powell Street Festival every summer, with some new faces coming in sight each year; but, here again, the key players at the core seem to consist of a particularized segment of the entire group. Most events, such as the Powell Street Festival, staged for Japanese Canadians are attended by a relatively small segment of the community and attract more people from the larger community. The ties in the ethnic group are said to be expressed through membership in churches, the enrolment of children in language school or dance lessons, involvement in fund-raising campaigns, volunteering in the care of the elderly, or the maintenance of intimate relationships with particular Japanese-Canadian friends.

How many, then, of our respondents are actively involved in any of these activities? How meaningful and important is the involvement in those activities to the individual participants?

Early-childhood socialization experience was seen to be a critical factor in the explanation of the extent of one's exposure to and involvement in his or her own ethnic community and of the sense of one's ethnic identity (Isajiw and Makabe 1982; see also chapter 3). It was also pointed out that those respondents who grew up in the large centres most likely had at some time in the course of growing up the experience of being drawn into at least one ethnic organization or group activity, for example, the Buddhist church, the Christian church groups, the Japanese language school, the Japanese-Canadian hockey or baseball leagues, the Japanese martial-arts clubs, or the various social-recreational clubs within the Japanese community centre. Whether in Lethbridge, Montreal, or elsewhere, the respondents were exposed to the ethnic community through associational activities, albeit this exposure was fairly limited or fragmented. The personal contact with fellow Japanese Canadians, although less frequent and comprehensive, nonetheless occurred either through the involvement of the parents in ethnic institutions or through sporadic encounter.

### Organizational Affiliation and Memberships

In the following discussion our definition of voluntary organization includes churches, social or sports clubs, community or neighbourhood groups, civic or fraternal organizations, and labour unions, and includes both Japanese and non-Japanese organizations. The large majority of the respondents (close to 80 per cent) reported that they were members of at least one voluntary organization. Most often they were involved in recreational-sports clubs, local churches, PTAs, service-oriented community groups, and business-professional associations. A fair number of the reported memberships were 'fee-paying only,' but the majority of members could be considered relatively active in the sense that they at least attended meetings or participated in activities fairly regularly in the group, although they were not necessarily active enough to hold office or sit on committees.

About two out of five respondents (40%) reported that they currently belong to at least one Japanese organization. Those individuals were likely to be involved in non-ethnic associations as well; that is to say, their involvement in voluntary organizations was not restricted to ethnic associations. None of those members, however, tended to hold more than one membership with an ethnic association. Some men and women joined sports clubs and interacted with the members regularly; some others were involved in the Japanese Canadian Cultural Centre, the local chapters of the National Association of Japanese Canadians, Japanese-Canadian Christian churches, and the Buddhist church. A few Sansei parents took their children to language lessons, dance or music lessons, karate, or judo *dojyo* often offered within the community-cultural centre. Some claimed that they were more 'users' than participants of the programs or services offered by the community groups. Only a handful, a half-dozen of the sixty-four respondents to be precise, reported that their commitment to the ethnic organization had been consistent and important enough to allow them to spend a fair amount of time sitting in its board meetings or actively participating in group activities.

A forty-three-year-old Toronto Sansei dentist who has been active with a Japanese Christian church group since his childhood has his Caucasian wife and two children also fully involved in it. The social and spiritual life the family are deriving from the involvement in this church is fairly important to him, said the dentist: 'The membership with my church is the only contact that I have with the community. When I was at the age of ten, we started going to a camp operated by our church. That was where I started to encounter more Japanese people, and it turned out to have developed very good friendships. My best friends were from that church group when I was growing up, and are still largely so. My parents were involved in the church and we're raised in that church.'

A thirty-one-year-old Sansei engineer has also been a regular, active member of a Japanese-Canadian Christian church group in Hamilton. His parents and grandparents have been members of the church ever since the ethnic congregation was established in the city after the war. The small congregation from the beginning is one of the few Japanese associations that has been kept up by the Issei and Nisei residents in the area. The respondent is one of the few Sansei community members who has kept up his church membership, and he currently runs the youth group in the church. This

Sansei engineer regularly goes to the church and sits on the board, but these days, with the steady dwindling of church membership, the young man himself cannot be sure of the future of this small religious group. Even to the eyes of an insider like the respondent himself, whether the group is sustainable or not and for how long is a big question: 'Is the church going to be around? How long?'

A Toronto Sansei man, an assistant manager in a wholesale garment firm, was an exception among the respondents for his 'total commitment' to the Japanese Canadian Cultural Centre. The assistant manager strongly believes in voluntarism, which is his motivation for continuing to work with and for the institution, spending a fair amount of his spare time outside work. He finds great satisfaction in devoting his time and energy there because he feels that 'the Centre gives me more than I do to it,' as he put it:

> From my early childhood on, my father has been active with the Centre consistently. About ten years ago I started helping the Centre at the Metro Caravan, then volunteering in other events. I've sat on the board together with my wife who has also been very active. We socialize with our Sansei friends whom we got to know from the Centre. Ninety per cent of my JC friends are from the Centre. I don't spend all of my free time there, but it has been important because most of our close friends are from there. Recently we've joined a ballroom-dance group [within the Centre], and practise ballroom dancing once a week.

A Sansei mother and teacher, also in Toronto, was, in her words, a typical 'user only.' She uses programs offered by various community groups and participates in events taking place in the community mostly for the sake of her children. Since she works full time, the mother of two young children admitted that her social participation has been extremely limited; as a matter of fact she was not connected with any voluntary association outside the Japanese-Canadian community, with the exception of nominal membership in the teachers' union. She is fairly well informed about events in the ethnic community through her husband, who has wider contact with the community than herself. A group of the couple's

friends, who happen to be mostly Japanese, get together fairly frequently and participate in various child-centred activities. 'My husband is active in the Japanese community. He belongs to sports
groups, and participates in functions with the groups. I take my
daughter to the *odori* [dance] class and my son to karate class at the
Cultural Centre. We go to the Centre as volunteers, giving a hand
whenever they need.'

In Montreal, too, another full time mother and lab technician
said that her social association outside home was limited to once-a-
week attendance at the local church to which the family belongs.
The only contact she has kept with the Japanese group is through
the bowling league, which her parents started with the Japanese
residents in the city many years ago, and where the respondent
and her non-Japanese husband go to bowl once a week. Today less
than one-third of the members in the league are Japanese, and
most are strangers to the respondent. The Japanese-Canadian tag
attached to the league name is only nominal. A group like a bowling league, once established, tends to perpetuate, the Sansei
woman commented: 'There seems no reason for the members to
quit.'

Up in northern Ontario, in Thunder Bay, the Japanese-Canadian
Community Association, the only voluntary association for Japanese ever organized there, ceased to exist decades ago. The association was formed, immediately upon their arrival, by those who
came from internment camps to resettle in the northern community. Moving to a strange city and facing economic uncertainty and
anti-Japanese hostility from outside, the Japanese strongly felt the
need 'to be with our own kind.' The association initially started as a
mutual help/support group and became involved in the welfare of
the newcomers seeking resettlement. The group served to bring
the relocated families together to meet other Japanese so that they
could maintain ties of sociability. After achieving its goal, however,
the association lost much of its reason for existence. Interest was
waning in the mid-1950s, about the time the Nisei were busy building the foundation of their lives and their own families.

Decades passed before the community group was revitalized by
the redress movement in the 1980s, which involved a combined

force of the Nisei and Sansei members. A forty-year-old Sansei
man, an employee of a government-owned retail business and also
a home-town native from the area, became a member of the association just to give his moral support to the group's revitalization. He
was not convinced of how firm and lasting the group would be in
the future with only a few dozen active members widely scattered
throughout the area. In his observation, the continuity needed to
sustain such a small voluntary organization had been lost during
the inactive recent decades. But his teenaged son, together with
his retired parents, were active user-participants in various activities
currently organized at the community centre. His parents seemed
to need to be affiliated with the Japanese group for socializing, said
the son: 'I've been a member of the JC community association, not
very active myself. My son is taking a Japanese lesson now. My
mother teaches Japanese dance to a group of the Japanese. My
involvement with the association has much to do with my parents.
They are active, and I always help them in the folk festival or some
other events because my parents are doing them. I keep the membership partly because my son uses the centre too.'

As all the cases quoted above suggest, there seems to be a certain
degree of intergenerational transmission of involvement in ethnic
voluntary organizations. At most there seems to exist an intergenerational effect in the pattern of church memberships, although
the number of cases in the present sample is too limited to make a
systematic statement. As long as the parent/parents have been constantly involved with either the Buddhist or Christian groups, the
children have a better chance, at least at some point, of being
drawn into the religious institution. Those Sansei respondents
whose parents have long been detached from community activities
tend to have few affiliations with the ethnic community. However,
the correlative trend does not necessarily seem to hold; though the
parent/parents have been closely affiliated with the community,
both formally and informally, there are instances where the children have shown little interest of their own.

Also, for those who were well rooted, with lifetime residence in
the local community, their chances of holding or retrieving memberships with the ethnic association seemed much higher. One of

the female respondents, a thirty-two-year-old, born-and-raised Calgarian, was recently drawn back into the community, mostly through the influence of her father, who had been in the core of the community ever since he came to live in the city in the late 1940s. The daughter tries to give support to the community, more specifically to the Nisei community, which has persisted for decades against all odds, by participating in programs and events staged by the group. 'I've been involved in the JC community activities lately. I, with my father, edit the community newsletter. I'm learning a lot from reading what people have to say. It's quite rewarding. My husband [non-Japanese] and I go to a lot of community events; teas, barbecues, picnics, etc. We always do.'

On the other hand, for those respondents who migrated to the area from other regions of the country, chances to get involved in a community seemed few. A young Sansei artist came from Ontario to live in Calgary five years ago. During this period he met in total three Japanese Canadians. He has been involved in a group of local Artists of Colour – artists from African, Asian, and Native backgrounds. He has met a Japanese Canadian through that group, and through this person met another two Japanese Canadians who happened to be migrants to the city like himself, from somewhere else in the country. In this artist's vision the Japanese community as such does not exist in Calgary; at least it is not visible enough to his eyes. 'There may be a Japanese community here, but I really don't know. I don't know where it is. I don't know of any group either. I'm curious to know about the Japanese community, but too busy to go out of my way to find out. If there were a place like a community centre where I could go, it would be easier. There isn't such a place in the city; the closest is, I guess, in Vancouver.'

The large majority of the individuals interviewed in the present study (60 per cent) are neither joiners nor participants in any ethnic organization. Their lack of need to be with the Japanese community is the main reason given; or to express it differently, their interests do not lie within the realm of the community. Some do not feel a need for such organizational activities in the first place, and they would rather avoid joining any, no matter whether they be ethnic or non-ethnic. The voice of the individuals who do not belong to any ethnic association is well reflected in the remarks made by the following three Sansei men.

A thirty-seven-year-old engineer in Vancouver: 'I've not been involved in the Japanese community here in Vancouver as I don't identify as Japanese Canadian. I really don't feel drawn to the community. I've not felt any need to approach the community. My sister has actively been involved and she passes me information on what's going on there.'

A thirty-eight-year-old coffee-shop owner and manager in Toronto: 'I was not exposed to the Japanese community because of my father, who did not want to be part of it. I was not taken even once to the Cultural Centre when I was a child. I didn't have a Japanese friend to grow up [with] either. I haven't had anything to do with the community in the past and I don't think I'll have in the future.'

A forty-two-year-old self-employed wholesaler of fashion garments in Winnipeg: 'I haven't had a lot to do with Japanese people my whole life. I don't belong to any Japanese group and I never have been. Our social life evolves around our friends and people from business and from school. They're all Canadians [non-Japanese], except my cousin and his wife, with whom we've a close association.'

These remarks indicate the extent, much weakened, of linkages the average Sansei has to the ethnic voluntary association as well as to his or her fellow ethnics. They also provide another example of the change in behaviour between the generations, the Nisei and Sansei – in terms of involvement in ethnic organizations (Makabe 1976). This change seems to derive from various factors. Most noticeable to me in talking with my Sansei respondents was their lack of desire to join formal organizations for social relations with fellow ethnics. For most of the Nisei, keeping touch with friends would be the main reason for joining. They simply do not want to lose contact with Japanese. After joining a certain association group, small groups of friends are formed around common interests, hobbies, and sport activities – within the organization or not. The groups of friends then become the medium through which individuals find meaningful interactions with others.

The change in attitudes towards the community was also obvious. The Sansei respondents, quite unlike the Nisei, did not show a feeling of obligation or of allegiance owed to the community and its institutions at all. Very few expressed feelings that they should belong to Japanese organizations, nor did they believe that they should support the community financially by, for example, sending a membership fee to sustain the organization. While a large portion of the second generation still maintain a sense of obligation to participate in community activities simply to keep up the institutions, the Sansei children have indicated no notion of obligation or emotional attachment as such towards the community. Although the respondents accept the institutions of their predecessors (some giving emotional support to them at least), and claim that they would like to see them continue to exist, they are reluctant to accept the responsibility for sustaining them. They would not join a group for ethnic association unless they found it meaningful and sufficiently suited to their own needs or their children's.

**Friendship Patterns and Intermarriage**

Exactly half of the Sansei in the sample group reported not having a single person of Japanese origin currently among their friends or personal associates. The members of the group all have non-Japanese friends in the larger social circles within which they circulate. These people consist of their colleagues or former classmates from high school and university, and come from diverse ethnic backgrounds and all walks of life.

Owing to their upbringing in a highly integrated environment, the Sansei are open and secure about engaging in social relations with non-Japanese. The respondents generally claimed to have no preference for Japanese-Canadian friends, nor did they draw any distinction between Japanese and non-Japanese in informal group association. That they should feel bonds of intimacy with their non-Japanese friends is understandable in light of the fact that all of their close friends are people with whom they grew up or studied or worked together. Their playmates from childhood and friends from adolescence happen to be almost exclusively non-

Japanese. For those respondents who had friendships with Japanese, the relationship is rather peripheral in the totality of their personal association; the Japanese friends were made either in the neighbourhoods, at school, or through participating in activities with Japanese-Canadian groups. In other words, they experienced 'growing up together' at some point in their childhood or adolescence just as they have done with their non-Japanese associates. It is said that a large part of the non-kin friendship relationships of adulthood is rooted in the period of growing up. In determining one's intimate relationship with others, the importance of the peer group during the formative years cannot be underestimated.

As a result of free and open interaction with others in both formal and informal spheres of life, intermarriage has become a norm among Sansei, an 'everyday phenomenon.' The Canadian Sansei seem to be the group that has achieved full-scale structural assimilation, which according to Milton Gordon's description (1964, 71) means that the members have made 'large scale entrance into cliques, clubs, and institutions of host [mainstream] society on primary group level.' The case of the Sansei is indicative of the very high level of social integration attained, in the description of Blau et al. (1984, 591), 'because they [high rates of intermarriage] reveal that intimate and profound relations between members of different groups and strata are more or less socially acceptable.'

An unusual aspect to this accomplishment by a visible Canadian minority group is that the process has taken place very quickly – in just one generation, from the second to the third. It is completely unrealistic, as Gordon tells us, not to expect the children of different ethnic backgrounds to love and marry each other if their parents are similarly socially assimilated, belonging to the same country club and inviting each other to their homes for dinner and the like. It is rather unrealistic, however, to have such an expectation in the case of the Japanese-Canadian community, for assimilation for the Nisei has, up to the present, been much less than the level that Gordon implies.

The Canadian Nisei, too, have gone far beyond acculturation; nonetheless, the majority of them are still not found in the social cliques of Anglo-Canadian society, nor are they free from the psychological feeling of being a minority. I would instead argue that the majority of Nisei most likely stay within their own group for both formal and informal social interaction. Although they interact freely with non-Japanese colleagues and neighbours, they have not yet opted for extensive social participation outside the ethnicgroup boundary – certainly not by joining country clubs in mainstream society. Nor have they achieved intimate social contact with the white middle class they emulate; they do not get invited to their homes for dinner, not regularly at least, or do they feel at ease in inviting white folks to their homes for social evenings.

Thirty-nine out of the forty-nine respondents both currently married (including common-law relationships) and previously married had non-Japanese spouses or partners. The degree of intermarriage among our respondents is thus 80 per cent. This figure is about as high as the rates reported elsewhere in Canada and the United States. Japanese women are said to have outmarried at higher rates than men, but there was no gender difference observed among the members in the present sample. Regardless of education or occupation the Sansei are outmarrying at the highest level. Since marriage is the ultimate and most intimate form of social acceptance, the strikingly high rate of intermarriage among the Sansei confirms that there exists no barrier at all between them and other groups in personal interactions. And because all of them grew up in ethnically mixed or predominantly Anglo-Canadian neighbourhoods, without noting the influence of 'the Japanese community' as such, it is not surprising at all that they feel most in common with people they have known well within their communities, and thus meet marriage partners of 'mixed' backgrounds there.

Before the war intermarriage was taboo in the Japanese-Canadian community. A few Nisei who outmarried faced disapproval from the family and the community. Some of that disapproval may have remained among some Nisei. Now their 'reluctant approval' of Sansei intermarriage may indicate the acceptance of the majority (white Canadians) by the minority (Japanese Canadians) to the same extent it gives the converse indication – acceptance of the minority by the majority (Jiobu 1988, 152).

The respondents, both married and not yet married, agreed with the notion that ethnic origin is not important in their choice of partner, and they show no preference for ethnic endogamy. A Sansei woman who is married to someone of Jewish background said that she was aware of the ethnicity, race, and religion of potential marital partners when she was dating, but she never had the perception of 'crossing a boundary' in marrying her husband. 'It wasn't a decisive factor in my consideration,' she said. It might have been for her husband, indeed, but that is something that she has not yet been told. Often I heard some respondents who are married to non-Japanese, 'happily so far,' say that 'I would have married a Japanese if I had met one.' Likewise, one of the eligible bachelors in the sample revealed his honest feelings and interest by saying: 'I still want to meet Japanese girls and marry one: I'd like to say that my kids would be Japanese Canadian.' Another Sansei woman would have liked to have married a Japanese, but she just did not have the chance. Having grown up in the inner city of Toronto, she did not know where the Japanese were. She did not know where to go to meet them. Neither did her parents, who had no contact with the community at all. Her first marriage to a Caucasian partner ended in divorce after three years, a fact that was more gravely deplored by her parents than by the respondent herself.

One of the findings from Fujita and O'Brien's survey (1991, 137) involving three Japanese-American communities in California suggested that marriage to a non-Japanese spouse seems to have produced more problems than marriage to a fellow ethnic, resulting in a greater likelihood of the union ending in divorce. Among the current respondents there were five members whose first (and second) marriages had already broken up by the time of interviewing. All of the broken marriages in our sample happened to be cases of outmarriage. When asked whether or not they thought the act of marrying someone from a different ethnic-racial background might have led to problems in their marriage, the typical response I received from the divorcees was 'Maybe.' One of the Sansei divorcees insisted that for him the problems were personal, not ethnic-cultural. It is commonly accepted among Japanese

Canadians that the Sansei divorce rate is higher than the Nisei's partly because the former are increasingly intermarrying (and the divorce rate in the 1980s was up for all groups relative to the parents' generation). It is expected to rise as the majority of the Sansei pass through the marriageable years in the near future.

Most of the respondents reported that they had received from their parents no direct message about their marrying within the Japanese group or without. Most parents had made 'no comment' or put 'no pressure' on their children one way or the other. But many children acknowledged that their parents had occasionally showed a preference for them to find and marry someone of Japanese background. The parents did not push; nonetheless, the pressure was always felt. A forty-year-old Toronto pharmacist did not think that his parents had brainwashed him and his brother (who also married a Japanese), but he had always wanted to marry a Japanese, as far back as he could remember. So had his wife. They met at the Japanese-Canadian tennis club. They were one of the six inmarried couples in the sample drawn from the Toronto area whom I interviewed.

Outmarriage of the Sansei is not a matter of approval or disapproval, or even like or dislike, by the parents, but simply of the acceptance of the inevitable. Intermarriage has to be accepted; it is the 'fate' of the Japanese community. Simply stated, there is no critical mass in this tiny minority community for young people to meet and mate with each other. Intermarriage is largely a matter of 'social exposure,' or a consequence of 'pure demographics,' according to the respondents.

A thirty-year-old executive secretary in Calgary: 'My father always encouraged us to date somebody who was a Japanese. That was his feeling all right, but where am I going to see a Japanese person in this city? I remember questioning my father. Both my brother and myself ended up marrying non-Japanese. Half of my cousins are now married, most of them to Caucasians, with the exception of only one cousin.'

A thirty-eight-year-old Toronto architect: 'There was no big discussion about my not dating Japanese girls. It never became an issue at our home. My mother occasionally would make noises about how we should maybe find a nice Japanese person, but she knew as well as I did that there was little opportunity to find this person. My mother was not serious about suggesting. When I brought my first girlfriend home, my parents were fine; they liked her. I ended up marrying a non-Japanese. So did two of my sisters, but two of us ended up being divorced.'

A forty-three-year-old dentist in Toronto: 'My parents didn't indicate their preference over my dating mates or a marriage partner. For my generation in the family none has married another Japanese. It's a matter of social exposure. You just don't get exposed to many Japanese. My parents accept intermarriage as something inevitable for us. They may have preferred some of us to marry Japanese, but at the same time they knew that it was very unlikely.' This dentist has been steadily and actively involved in a congregation of the Japanese Christian church since his childhood. According to his observation, some fellow Sansei members have married each other within the community, but they were rather exceptional. Within his extended family, the rate of intermarriage among his generation is almost 100 per cent. Likewise, in northern Ontario, the number of intermarriages among marriageable members is increasing without exception; a long-term resident-respondent in the region reported that it is 'close to 95 per cent' among those currently getting married. The Canadian Sansei group has thus reached the point where the distinction between marriage and intermarriage vanishes, which can be seen as an indication of the absence of the distinction between minority and majority (Petersen 1975, 129).

There was little variation in the present sample among communities with respect to the rate of intermarriage. Among the residents in Metro Toronto, the area with the largest number of Japanese-Canadian population, the ratio of intermarriage was 75 per cent (18 couples out of 24), only very slightly lower than the overall figure. The respondents who were living away from Toronto or Vancouver seemed to assume that the Sansei residing in those areas could meet as many Japanese Canadians as they wished, from whom they could choose their partner freely and even randomly. That is a mere speculation or a false expectation.

The Japanese-Canadian population is widely dispersed everywhere. The proportion of Japanese in Metro Toronto, 17,000 plus Japanese among 3.8 million persons, is about same as it is in Calgary or Victoria: only about 0.4 per cent of the general population of a million in Calgary, of 280,000 or so persons in Victoria, and of 3.8 million in Toronto. So every region and area of the country, including Metro Toronto and Greater Vancouver, lacks a sufficient critical mass of Japanese population. Simply stated, there were not enough fellow ethnics to 'hang around' with and date where and when most of the Sansei were growing up. This factor of 'pure demographics' has no doubt had the strongest impact on the maintenance of ties to fellow ethnics. Among Sansei who do not have as compelling a set of shared experiences as the Nisei, the size of the local ethnic population seems to exert its greatest influence on friendships and interpersonal relationships.

I do not mean to insist that population size alone, or the distribution pattern of the population for that matter, is the determining factor as to whether community and inmarriage persist or not. Demographics work in combination with other factors. Thus, the Jewish group in Metropolitan Toronto, making up about 4 per cent of the total population in 1981, was the least intermarried group of all examined in Breton and others' survey (1990) – 19 per cent of the members among the third generation. In the meantime the Italians constituted more than twice as large a group (10 per cent of the total), but were among the most intermarrying group next to the Germans and Ukrainians – 71 per cent of the third generation. The Jewish third-generation members, noted Isajiw in his report (1990, 82), also retained the feeling of an obligation to marry within the group to the highest extent (66 per cent of the respondents surveyed), substantially higher than for the other groups. Endogamy seemed an important focus of ethnic-identity retention for Toronto's Jewish group.

How effective is the availability of fellow ethnics in the local area, nonetheless, on the maintenance of ties to fellow ethnics? How do demographic-ecological constraints affect the rate of ingroup interaction and the rate of ethnic endogamy? We have said that the size of the group is one factor. A Canadian study done earlier by

Ziegler (1979) in four neighbourhoods in Toronto involving adolescents from various ethnic backgrounds found that the relative
size of the group was positively and significantly related to individual friendship formation. When the student's own group was small
in proportion to the student body, he or she was more likely to
make friends of other ethnicities than when his or her own group
dominated the student body. The same thing applies to marriage.
Smaller groups generally outmarry more than larger groups. Findings from research previously done in the field, mostly in the
United States, confirm this tendency.

Blau et al. (1982), from their research on intermarriage in the
125 largest American metropolitan areas (using data from the
1970 U.S. census), presented evidence, first, of the inverse relationship between group size and outmarriage; the smaller the relative size of a specific group, the higher the rate of outmarriage for
the group. They also found statistically significant relations
between intermarriage and heterogeneity of the population in
terms of such measured variables as national origin, language spoken in the home, region of birth, diversity of industry, and occupation. Where heterogeneity is high, intermarriage is high, because
heterogeneity leads to intergroup contact, which leads to intermarriage. These findings suggest that the rate of endogamy will to a
certain extent be a function of the availability of mates from within
the group as well as of some residual social-cultural factors.

Results from another American study (Tomaskovic-Devey and
Tomaskovic-Devey 1988) were also indicative of endogamy being
highly influenced by demography – the density of a specific group
within a given population. This American study, using data from
the 1980 census, nationally compared single-ancestry rates as an
indicator of inmarriage rates for four white American ethnic
groups – Italian, Polish, Slovak, and Hungarian – and concluded
that outmarriage and single-ancestry rates were determined more
by the size and spatial distribution of the specific ethnic population or other structural opportunity than by cultural heritage as
such.

The recent study on American Indians by Nagel (1995) cites various data sources indicating that not only do American Indians

have very high intermarriage rates compared with other racial groups, but in the regions of the United States with historically small Indian populations the members are more likely to be inter-married – nearly twice more likely – than in the regions with larger Indian populations. Besides the size and density within a given population, racial intermarriage among Indian populations is also associated with such sociodemographic factors as the growth rate of population, urban-rural residency, and the language spoken in the home (Eschbach 1995).

The inference one can draw from these research findings is that when the relative size of the same group – that is, the Japanese Cana-dians – in different communities is examined, the population size should be inversely related to the extent of intermarriage. How valid can the inference be? In the following an attempt is made to examine the relationship within the Japanese-Canadian com-munity, using one existing measure of ethnicity – single-ancestry rates – which are available from the 1991 Canadian census.

Table 5.1 presents (1) the total Japanese population in 1991 for Canada's fourteen Census Metropolitan Areas, (2) the number of census respondents within that population who claimed only sin-gle Japanese ancestry, and (3) the single-ancestry rates. These rates were obtained from the proportion of respondents from the total ethnic population identifying ethnic ancestry who had claimed a single ethnic ancestry as Japanese. Thus, it is an approximate mea-sure of ingroup marriage in the last generation and of the intensity of current ethnic identification. Interestingly enough, the propor-tion of census respondents who reported a single origin for the Japanese group (74.0 per cent) was only slightly higher than the one for Canada as a whole (71.1 per cent);[1] this indicates blending in the Japanese-Canadian community had begun to occur by the late 1980s, and perhaps is occurring more rapidly than among many other groups in Canada.

We can see from table 5.1 that the highest single-ancestry rates were for Toronto and Vancouver, with about 80 per cent of all peo-ple claiming single Japanese descent. The rate was about 10 per cent lower for Hamilton, London, Montreal, and Winnipeg than it was for Toronto and Vancouver. The lowest single-ancestry rates

TABLE 5.1
Japanese Canadians: Total population, single-ancestry, single-ancestry rate, and
percentage of area population for Census Metropolitan Area, 1991

| CMA* | Total population | Single ancestry | Single-ancestry rate** | Percentage of area population |
|---|---|---|---|---|
| Calgary | 2,855 | 1,880 | 65.8 | 0.37 |
| Edmonton | 1,820 | 1,090 | 59.9 | 0.22 |
| Hamilton | 1,485 | 1,135 | 76.8 | 0.25 |
| Kitchener | 580 | 400 | 68.7 | 0.16 |
| London | 620 | 445 | 71.8 | 0.16 |
| Montreal | 2,365 | 1,690 | 71.4 | 0.08 |
| Oshawa | 305 | 100 | 32.8 | 0.13 |
| Ottawa-Hull | 1,275 | 825 | 64.8 | 0.14 |
| St Catharines–Niagara | 375 | 240 | 64.0 | 0.10 |
| Thunder Bay | 400 | 225 | 56.8 | 0.32 |
| Toronto | 17,065 | 13,710 | 80.3 | 0.44 |
| Vancouver | 19,845 | 16,090 | 81.1 | 1.25 |
| Victoria | 1,235 | 700 | 56.9 | 0.42 |
| Winnipeg | 1,380 | 980 | 71.0 | 0.21 |

Source: Statistics Canada, 1991 Census, Ethnic Origin (catalogue 93-315), table 2B
* Census Metropolitan Areas with fewer than 300 Japanese Canadians in 1991 are
excluded.
** Proportion of respondents identifying ethnic ancestry who claim a single ethnic
ancestry as Japanese.

for Census Metropolitan Areas in Canada were observed in such
areas as Oshawa (32.8%), Thunder Bay (56.8%), and Victoria
(56.9%), which all have very small Japanese populations. In these
areas, close to half of the Japanese-Canadian population
responded with more than one ethnic origin besides Japanese,
indicating that a great number of mixed marriages had already
occurred by the time of the 1991 census. These figures can be a
clue, although extremely simple and primitive, suggesting that
areas with larger ethnic populations have relatively greater opportunity for, and so higher rates of, ingroup marriage than smaller
areas with smaller ethnic populations.

The last column of table 5.1 illustrates the percentage of Japanese within the total population in the metropolitan areas – a measure of density. Here again we find the highest density is in

Vancouver (1.25 per cent), far outranking Toronto, the second
highest with 0.44 per cent. Density can also have some impact on
the rate of ingroup interaction. Glancing at the existing single-
ancestry rates, together with the density figures of Japanese population in Canada's major metropolitan areas, provides us with an
indication of a tendency consistent with the major finding from
the Tomaskovic-Devey analysis of American single-ancestry data –
the rates are highly influenced by structural opportunity, that is,
the density of a specific group within a given population.

Thus, ethnic-group endogamy can be a function of both the size
of the group and of the salience of group membership, and if so,
other ethnic-group behaviour, such as voluntary group association
and primary group affiliation, as we have examined earlier in this
chapter, can also be conditioned by the size of population, just as
marital patterns are. Fujita and O'Brien (1991) suggest that intermarriage reduces, to a moderate degree, most types of involvement in the Japanese-American ethnic community's life, as was
found among their respondents. Our sample is too small to make
such a generalization, except to suggest that the inmarried respondents – only a minority of 20 per cent of the total who were married – tended to have more Japanese-Canadian associates for
personal, informal interaction and sociability than did the majority
of the outmarried members.

The argument that ethnic-group behaviour is the result of structural opportunity rather than a reflection of cultural factors further suggests that differences in behaviour between the generations, that is, between the Nisei and Sansei – the comparison we
often use as the frame of analysis and discussion – should not necessarily be interpreted as a reflection of Nisei values or Sansei culture as such. Rather, it may be more accurate to say that the
members of each generation have had different opportunities, and
thus experiences, for interacting with other members of their generation group as a function of settlement patterns and dominant-
group reaction (Tomaskovic-Devey and Tomaskovic-Devey 1988).
Suffice it to remember the vast differences in growing-up experience between the Nisei and the Sansei. The Nisei lived in so-called
Japanese districts or communities on the West Coast for all those

years before the evacuation, and spent several years of incarceration together in the internment camps; they attended language school practically every day, and 'hung around' with other Japanese kids for most of their socializing. That was their growing up. Among the Nisei there was ample opportunity for developing close ingroup relations under the constrained segregation – physical and social – so that many ties to the group have been preserved from childhood up to the present. Generational differences in behaviour are the result of the fact that the Nisei once lived and played together, and eventually married within a segregated ethnic community. None of the above conditions has ever existed for the Sansei, and thus none applies. Indeed, this generation is genuinely a product of the Canadian community.

Before concluding our discussion on the ethnic-group identity of the Sansei, the relationship between an individual's self-definition of ethnicity (chapter 4) and his or her behavioural affiliation in a group needs to be explored. In order to investigate the relationship in our sample, types of ethnic-group ties as elaborated by Reitz (1980, 93–100) are used as an analytical framework.

Reitz, in his study on ethnic-group cohesion, begins by defining group membership. He includes in membership formation both an objective component – social interaction – and a subjective component – self-definition for the individual as a group member. Social interaction refers to ethnic-group 'networks' and communal life, including interaction in both formal and informal contexts; self-definition is one's identification subjectively defined as an ethnic, the feeling of belonging to a group based on one's ethnic origin. The three types of ethnic-group ties combining the two components of group memberships are conceptualized as full members, peripheral members, and non-members. The sixty-four individuals in our sample are now classified into the three types as shown in table 5.2 (p. 132).

Cell I is a category of twenty-six of the respondents (40 per cent of the total) who were classified as 'full members' of the ethnic community according to the typology; the individuals in this type group define themselves as 'Japanese Canadian' and they also have

TABLE 5.2
Types of ethnic ties: The case of the Sansei (N = 64)

| Social interaction* | Group identification | | | |
|---|---|---|---|---|
| | | 'Japanese-Canadian' | | 'Canadian' |
| Interact with Japanese | I | 59.1% | II-A | 20.0% |
| Do not interact with Japanese | II-B | 41.0 | III | 80.0 |
| | | 100.0 | | 100.0 |
| | | (44) | | (20) |

Notes: I = Full members; II-A = Peripheral members, latent; II-B = Peripheral members, nominal; III = Non-members
* The two categories of social interaction are constructed by the respondent's association with the Japanese group both formally and informally: 'Interact with Japanese' includes all those who reported that they associated with other ethnic Japanese informally and have a membership with any ethnic organization; 'Do not Interact with Japanese' are those not included in the first category.

social interaction with other Japanese Canadians on a regular basis, either through associating with ethnic organizations or through personal networking.

In contrast to the full members were sixteen non-members (25 per cent of the total) placed in Cell III. These members neither identified with the ethnic community nor interacted with other fellow ethnics at all. It should be noted here that one out of four Sansei have become non-members (the reason why they are sometimes called ex-members). These individuals are the ones who have very little to do with their ethnicity; their membership in the community has pretty well been abandoned. Yet, it should be remembered here that they are in the same boat as other Sansei in the sense that they are perceived by others as ethnically distinct. (Yinger [1994, 4] takes into account the presence of the perception of others in his typology of ethnicity and terms the category of non-members as stereotyped.)

About one-third of the sample held some discrepant or intermediate position. They are peripheral members and there are two types in this membership. The first type is what Reitz terms nominal members (Cell II-B), and it includes persons who feel that they belong to the ethnic group (calling themselves 'Japanese Canadians' in our case) without actually interacting with members of the community very much. There were eighteen 'Japanese Canadians' who had not a single Japanese person to interact with socially, nor were they involved in any ethnic voluntary association at that time. These individuals may very well live outside the ethnic community, in areas where the location of the nearest community centre is a '500-mile distance away.' Some may opt to stay away from the local community for various reasons, personal or otherwise.

The second type of peripheral membership includes 'latent members' or 'de facto members' (Cell II-A). Only four respondents were counted in this type from our sample. They were the ones who identified themselves as 'Canadian,' yet had formal or informal Japanese affiliations.

A certain tendency exists between the two measures of ethnic identity: the objective and subjective component (table 5.2). Thus, if an individual keeps an association with his or her fellow ethnics, either by joining voluntary organizations and participating in activities or by maintaining informal-personal relationships, this person tends to define himself or herself as an ethnic, say, as 'Japanese Canadian.' On the other hand, an individual who has few ethnic associates to interact with or is not involved in ethnic organizational life, is more likely to define himself or herself as 'Canadian.' The existing correlation, however, does not mean that the two dimensions of identity are always dependent on each other. One of the key findings from data in Alba's (1990) empirical study on the ethnic identities of white Americans of European ancestry was the absence of a relationship between ethnic social structures and identities (as measured by one's self-identification in terms of ethnic categories). Ethnic identity and its salience, Alba reported, had little to do with whether individuals belonged to organizations, whether they were intermarried, and whether they lived in ethnic neighbourhoods. With respect only to ethnic friendships the relationship between the two dimensions was strong enough. Thus, these variables are somehow interconnected with each other, though they may vary independently as well (Isajiw 1990, 36). It is probable that an individual may retain a higher degree of subjective (internal) than of objective (external) aspects, and vice versa.

Reitz argues that the number of non-members or ex-members, in relation to the number of full members, determines ethnic-group cohesion. In the Sansei sample the number of full members is the largest of the three memberships so far, larger than the non-membership or nominal membership. There were 15 per cent more full members than non-members. Is the combined rate of non-membership (25%) and of peripheral membership (35%) – 60% of the total – however, high enough to threaten the positive *raison d'être* of the Japanese group in Canada for sustaining its very existence as a distinctive ethnic group? Has the community as a whole already lost a large enough constituency of 'eligible non-members'? The implications one may draw in interpreting the evidence we see here are important in foreseeing the future of this small ethnic community. It depends on whether some day the ex-members, as well as peripheral-nominal members, come into first-hand contact with the ethnic community and become fully involved in it. In light of the prevalent intermarriage among the young generation, David Suzuki, a Sansei scientist-activist, predicts that the distinctive ethnic identity of Japanese Canadians will die out, perhaps before too long.

The nominal membership type, the 'symbolic' type in Yinger's typology, seems to have some common elements with the symbolic ethnic-identity type referred to in the previous chapter. The members of this type maintain an ambivalent attachment to a few ethnic symbols with no interactional contact or commitment. The members also do not interact with one another in a social-organizational context. Symbolic ethnicity thus imposes little cost on everyday life for the members, and the content of such identity often is 'superficial and intermittent' besides being symbolic. In Waters's (1990, 92) description, 'This symbolic ethnicity makes no claims or demands on individuals whatsoever. In fact these ethnic groups never have to meet in any meaningful sense, unless you call a Saint Patrick's Day parade a meeting, and yet there is a collectivity which one can identify and feel a part of in an individualistic and often atomistic society.' The nominal members were described by Reitz (1980, 92) as follows: 'They identify with the ethnic group but live outside it. Some nominal members may be cut off from the group by distance or other practical circumstance. Others may disdain the local ethnic community as being unimportant to ethnic belonging or to ethnic identity. Perhaps these nominal members believe ethnicity consists of abstract ideals or feelings about "the homeland."'

The Sansei members in the nominal-membership category were isolated and cut off from the local community. Their social contacts were exclusively outside the community, involving persons of diverse ethnic backgrounds. Yet they identified themselves with the ethnic collectivity; they would like to think of themselves as Japanese Canadians and would like to be considered likewise by others as well. The respondents in this category tended to reveal rather ambivalent feelings about being Sansei, or being an ethnic-group member, their ethnicity largely consisting of 'abstract ideals or feelings' about their background while having little to substantiate them culturally or behaviourly.

Indeed, the desire to maintain their Japanese-Canadian identity more or less symbolically as individuals was expressed by a fair number of the respondents. 'The personal identity as a Japanese Canadian' can be maintained, according to a young Sansei man in western Canada, 'as I've become more and more interested in my heritage and the group's history in this country.' His quest for ethnic identity thus requires some work to gain knowledge of the Japanese group's heritage and its historical past. This knowledge may not necessarily be extensive or objective, but the respondent said that he is 'willing to work on it before the historical legacy gets completely lost.' Also, such a quest necessarily takes the shape of, in Michael Novak's terms (1971, 73), 'the personal conscious self-appropriation of one's own cultural history.' The young Sansei man's views were repeated by many others in the group, including a young woman in southern Alberta: 'I'll do my part privately to keep the culture as I know it alive for me. I'll make sure my child knows the history of Japanese in Canada. I can pass the stories of my family on to the next generation. I've a strong sense of who I am without reaching out to the community. I don't seek out the ethnic community.'

A personal ethnic identification of 'my own and my family alone' can continue according to a Sansei father of two children in Toronto. For him the family's name (a rather lengthy one) is the only symbol of ethnic identity left for his mixed children and himself, and thus is important. So he gave his children Japanese middle names and taught them to say their full names in Japanese properly, 'without the Anglified accent.' A mother of a child in Montreal, retaining her maiden name, is similar. One day she decided to eat with chopsticks for the rest of her life, and she does it religiously, at least in her home. She hopes that her young child would do this too. This may be only a 'symbolic gesture,' but eating with chopsticks and 'some little things that I can do personally and privately' can become, if not substantially, then metaphorically a symbol of ethnicity, perhaps for many other like-minded people. Contemporary ethnicity is increasingly voluntary and optional among white ethnics, as has been pointed out in recent empirical studies done by Alba (1990) and Waters (1990) in the United States. It can nonetheless continue to play an important social role to the extent that people choose to act in ethnic ways.

Those white ethnics referred to by the American sociologists are typically suburban, middle class, and mobile. So are our Canadian Sansei. It may be true that an ethnic identity really does not affect everyday life much for most of Sansei. We have proved that it does not limit choice of marriage partner for them. It does not determine where they will live, who their friends will be, what job they will have, or whether they will be subject to discrimination – at least they do not perceive that to be so.

Being a visible minority, however, the Sansei ethnicity cannot be symbolic in the same sense that it is for white-invisible ethnic minorities. A Sansei woman's ethnicity, symbolic or non-symbolic, depicted in her own words is quoted in full before we conclude the chapter. She is forty-nine years old and a veteran teacher specializing in the teaching of handicapped children. Born and raised in Montreal, she has lived in a city in south-western Ontario for the past fifteen years with a Caucasian partner in a common-law relationship, having previously lived and worked in a few other cities in Canada, as well as abroad. In the living room of her suburban home there are a few ornaments and framed pictures with a 'Japanese flavour' that she has been collecting for some years, and she treasures them greatly.

It's nice to have Japanese things here and there. I've collected them piece by piece. Some of them are souvenirs that I brought back from Japan.

I know there are some Japanese families who have been here in the city for years after the war. I don't know any of them personally. I've not become friends with any of the Japanese here. I've never belonged to any Japanese-Canadian association or group since I left home. I just met and got acquainted with a few Japanese people from Japan when I was taking courses at university here.

I had some friends who were Japanese Canadian in my childhood in Montreal. There were a few families in the neighbourhood, inner city of Montreal, and we knew each other very well. I remember going to picnics in summer and concerts with them. I was involved in the Japanese United Church to the point that I taught the Sunday school until I left the city in 1968.

I'm more Canadian than Japanese, but I'm a Japanese Canadian. I went to Japan in 1970 for about three weeks. I could not relate to Japan or Japanese people at all. It was a very foreign country to me. I felt lost.

The Japanese-Canadian heritage has more meaning to my being a Japanese Canadian than anything else. The group's history of which I'm part is important to me. Therefore, redress was important to me. Although I was not involved in the movement in any organized way, I was fully supportive of it. At least financially I helped the movement. It is a very important part of our history.

I usually don't look at myself differently until someone makes it apparent to me. I don't think of myself as being different from everybody else. I've never experienced discrimination in my adulthood. Being a visible minority has no influence on my life, I would say.

I have certain manners or personality style that would be different from the average person. Japanese Canadians tend to be more reserved. We tend to talk more about emotions or feelings; we tend to think of others' feelings more. I notice myself that I'm more indirect when I speak to others, a part of my Japanese way of interacting. I cannot be direct like my partner. He's so direct and blunt.

The Japanese-Canadian institutions, the Cultural Centre in Toronto, for instance, are nice to have. I go to see some of the shows and events at the Centre, but I don't go out of my way to be part of the institution. If I'm the indication, I must say that the Japanese-Canadian community won't be around too long. It's not relevant to me and my life. But there're people like my sister in Toronto too. For her it is very important. She's the youngest in the family (I'm the oldest of the four), and got a lot less exposed to things Japanese when she was growing up. But she is very interested in maintaining the identity and trying to pass some of the things she learns to her children. She goes to the language school with her children.

I'm afraid that she's rather exceptional. Most of the Sansei I know are like me. The large majority of them, perhaps, wouldn't you say?

## Chapter Six

# Political Avoidance and Sansei Reaction to the Redress Movement

*... when you realize that the number of votes was 33,000 and the margin of 200 votes is a very small ... I'm sure that there were a thousand people out there who didn't vote for me because I'm Japanese. When you're part of a minority group those things happen.*

Art Miki (1994)

We have seen in the preceding chapter that the extent of involvement and participation in ethnic institutions and voluntary organizations among the Canadian Sansei remains rather low. No doubt there is a higher rate of participation in organizations in the community at large. Involvement in the organizational life of society is said to be associated with increased participation in political activities. What has the extent of participation of the assimilated Sansei been in contemporary Canadian political life?

We have also seen earlier that a number of our respondents shared the anti-Oriental views and prejudice of the majority – Oriental meaning every member of Asiatic origins excluding the Japanese in their classification – and expressed their discomfort with and dislike of being categorized as members of a broadly termed group, 'Orientals' (chapter 4). Overall, the expressed views and attitudes of the Sansei on political and social issues did not seem unlike the ones expressed by the so-called majority of Canadians or average Canadians. In fact, they were found to be quite alike. In this chapter we will report on the political attitudes and participation patterns of Canadian Sansei.

First, the opinions and views on multiculturalism revealed from a recent opinion survey undertaken by Decima Research in a nationwide scale can be cited as a case in point (Canadian Council of Christians and Jews 1993). Multiculturalism means different things to different individuals, but 72 per cent of Canadians polled in the survey said that the federal policy of multiculturalism is not working. Close to 70 per cent of the Sansei in the present study indicated likewise; they were critical either of the policy itself or of its implementation, insisting that the current government policy is not 'doing any good' for Canada. The criticisms of the policy were varied, but in the end the majority of those who voiced their opinion endorsed the discarding of the policy or its replacement by an alternative that would emphasize 'conformity' rather than differences in Canadian society. This view, central to the criticism, coincides with that of the majority of Canadians: they too were frustrated by the 'lack of conformity' in society, which has been viewed as a result of the government's policy. Canadians believed that different ethnic and racial groups should try to adapt to Canadian society, conforming to its values.

About half of the Canadians polled nationally, 50 per cent of them in 1974 (Berry et al. 1977) and 46 per cent in 1991 (Angus Reid poll), according to Reitz and Breton's (1994) citation, agreed with the statement, 'People who come to Canada should change their behaviour to be more like us.' The following statement, made by one of our respondents, a thirty-eight–year-old Sansei insurance broker in a small Ontario town, reflects the voice of Sansei, joining that half of the Canadians who responded to the surveys: 'I think some ethnic groups are pushing too far. We are too multicultural. We are no more Canadian. Why can't we be Canadians – of some background? Why do people always come here and enforce their customs on us? We'd better define what Canada is first, think of values and principles we believe in. So the newcomers can appreciate and accept our values and systems before they push theirs. I think the policy [of multiculturalism] is not doing any good for

Canada.' This statement can be interpreted as a manifestation of backlash, as Reitz and Breton suggested (1994, 37), against the concept of Canada as a cultural mosaic, the increased ethnic and racial heterogeneity of immigration, or the notion of a multicultural society. If there is a backlash, the above statement by the Sansei insurance broker implies that it is directed against all of those notions combined.

The responses to the questions on racism are another example. The vast majority of the respondents surveyed in the 1993 national poll cited earlier – 86 per cent of Canadians – agreed that there is at least 'some racism' in Canada, although they noted that the problem is not personally theirs, as they do not get direct personal exposure to experiences that can give rise to racism. An almost identical view was revealed by a great many of the Sansei respondents, as discussed earlier (chapter 2). Yet when the same people, both those polled and the Sansei respondents, were asked to name the most important problems facing the nation, racial issues were not high on the agenda at all. In fact, not a single Canadian responding to the poll mentioned racism as the most important problem in Canada.

Exactly the same response was obtained from the Sansei group. Responding to a request to name and discuss the issues – political, social, international, or otherwise – that the respondent feels most strongly about or is concerned about (the question is phrased differently here than the one used in the poll), not a single Sansei respondent brought up the issue of racism or issues related to racial-minority groups and human rights – not even as one of their concerns, let alone *the* concern. Very few mentioned the issues of racism / human rights as they related to the Japanese-Canadian experience as real victims of racism in this country. It is not surprising, then, that such issues as unemployment and the federal deficit emerged from the both surveys as the 'top problems' facing Canada in a time of economic hardship, restraint, and recession. Women's issues, the decline of the traditional family, and the destruction of environment were the concerns of many Sansei men and women in times of change, seen as 'too much, too fast' in every sphere of life. What was somewhat surprising was the lack of perception among our respondents of an identification with the plight of others who have been subjected to racism as their predecessors were, if not they themselves, which coincided with the lack of recognition of racism as an issue of importance. An experience that the Japanese group had endured for many years in this country has developed a certain kind of rage buried quietly and deeply among the members of the community. Oddly enough, however, the responses of the Sansei sample group were almost totally devoid of this feeling of rage. It may be safe to state, therefore, that the Sansei form no exception to the majority's view in every sense on almost every matter of concern, including racism and discrimination.

When asked whether they have done work in a political campaign or been involved in any political-social movement, our respondents were consistently and overwhelmingly negative in their replies: close to 90 per cent of them said, categorically, 'No' or 'None.' Nine out of ten Sansei declared that they have never helped out a party or a candidate at election time, nor have they even joined a political party. 'Politically, I've never been active, and won't be.' 'I'm one of the silent majority.' They kept saying, 'Politics is not my area of interest,' 'I don't go out of my way to do anything political except vote and pay taxes,' 'I'm definitely not an activist,' and so on.

Speaking of political participation, the most salient fact bearing on the Japanese in North America was their complete exclusion from political life in the pre-war era and, being disenfranchised, in the case of Canada (including those individuals born in Canada), until 1949. Disenfranchisement meant exclusion from a whole series of activities in the political and economic life of the country and the province. Consequently, Japanese are 'extremely naive politically,' Japanese-American sociologist Harry Kitano (1976, 191) once commented, and they lack political will and expertise. This condition is a historical legacy, according to an American historian (Sowell 1981, 274), of deliberately avoiding politics in times of adversity ever since the Japanese immigrated to North America. One of the findings of Fujita and O'Brien's California survey

(1991, 152) bearing on the contemporary political life of Nisei and Sansei indicated that their respondents are relatively active in the political arena, but more likely to be involved in what they called 'low-visibility activities' such as voting and contributing money, but less involved in more 'activist' pursuits. No significant difference was found between the American Nisei and Sansei in the measure of political participation. The researchers argued that the historical experience of Japanese in the United States, as well as their cultural and petit-bourgeois traditions, incline them to avoid more confrontational kinds of political activities.

Japanese Canadians have been almost completely 'out of place' in the political sphere. For example, only 4 per cent of Nisei respondents in the 1990 Toronto survey reported belonging to 'political' associations, but for virtually all of the joiners, the association they had joined was the National Association of Japanese Canadians, which was interpreted as a civil-rights group and thus a political association (Makabe 1990; see report in appendix 1). On the question regarding recreational-leisure activities of daily life asked in the same survey, 6 per cent of the respondents replied affirmatively by saying that they did engage in 'helping out at election time,' the lowest proportion of the twenty-two activities listed. The proportion of the Nisei participants in non-political-voluntary associations was higher than those for the general population in the community as a whole (Makabe 1976), so there are 'participatory norms' fostered sufficiently among them. Political activities seem, however, to be the exception to the norm for the majority of Nisei.

It is thus not surprising that, despite his or her 'middle classness' in other measures, as Ken Adachi (1976, 356) earlier noted, the Japanese Canadian has had negligible impact even on local, let alone national, political life. No Nisei has ever run for a major elective office up to the present.[1] Surprisingly, however, there is a similarly low, or even lower, rate of political involvement and participation among the Sansei, in spite of their very high level of education and relatively high level of income.

There was almost zero involvement in 'activist activities' found in all sixty-four respondents in the present sample group. Overall they were not interested in getting involved in political or social causes. The large majority were not active in any of the organizations involved in community concerns, compared with one-third of Japanese Americans who reported that they were (Fujita and O'Brien 1991, 151). Except for a handful, the Canadian Sansei have never actively worked for a party or a candidate during an election; neither have they contacted a local or federal government official about some issue or problem. Not a single respondent has formed a group or organization to solve some local community problems, compared with 14 per cent of Japanese-American respondents who have done so. Like many others in the community at large, Canadian Sansei do nothing beyond voting, and practise political avoidance (Gans 1988). Overall, they are not eager to participate actively because they dislike formal organizations in the first place, feel they cannot take time from work, or are reluctant to cut into the time reserved for family and leisure activities. Some respondents said that they are politically alert, but admitted that they too only play largely a spectator role. They watch, they vote, but they do not battle. Gans noted that about 5 per cent of the American adult population are categorized as activist. No reason seems to suggest the Canadian population is any different; however, the Canadian Sansei group does not meet even the North American participation level of 5 per cent.

The respondents, like most people, try to stay away from any formal organization that they can avoid. They said that they do not feel a need for organizational activities. They are basically anti–formal organization, and among the organizations they avoid most are the political ones. They are doubtful that they could change society even if they wanted to do so. They believe they get more satisfaction from working individually – whatever the cause may be, however personal the issue may be – without involving themselves in organized political action, which is often morally and psychologically unsatisfying. Many non-activists stated that they would rather deal with their concerns in small and personal ways with which they feel at ease. When asked which issues he feels most strongly about or cares about, the response of a Sansei father of two in northern Ontario was the destruction of environment and its impact on future generations. The father has taken action in the only way he feels he can be effective – as a leader of a local Boy Scout group: 'I'm concerned with the environment. Through the Scouts, I'm trying to do things I can do – planting trees. That's my project now. That is my way of helping our children.'

Similar concerns and approaches – always personal and individual – were repeatedly expressed by other respondents. Individuals are doing what they can both at home and at work to save energy, recycle, control waste, and so on. A Toronto mother of four volunteers to help the neighbourhood and school in promoting the idea of composting. She goes to school to teach children how to do composting. 'That's the only meaningful way that I can act on my concerns – pollution and environment,' said the mother.

The welfare of children and the future of the coming generation are the concerns of many respondents both as parents and as educators and professionals. A Calgary teacher believes in dealing with the problems at the grass-roots level – in her own classroom by her own efforts. 'I don't go out of my way to activate my concern, but I do a great deal in my classroom for the children by providing for them a secure environment. I'm doing it in a way I know well. It's making a difference in their lives. I'm right there at the grass roots, making a difference.' Another male professional's approach to act on his concern is similar to the above teacher's: he insists on working on tangible issues using his own resources and efforts instead of relying on organizational efforts. 'I'm concerned about people. I like to see people being able to function as a whole as much as possible. I spend a lot of time working with young people in our church, because that is one way I can help them carry on their lives in productive ways. I feel I can make more of a contribution in a personal way. If you can make a direct impact on a person's life, help the person to fulfil his or her life, that's better to me, rather than dealing with issues so distant, like world peace or pollution control.'

Thus, Sansei, like other people, continue to structure their lives around family, friends, and a variety of informal groups, where they can deal with concerns they feel are important and relevant to them. People participate actively in that way, in a small part of society, and stay away from larger formal organizations.

Given the general attitude of political avoidance among the respondents, it was not a surprise that this unresponsive attitude was repeated with the issue of redress for Japanese Canadians, and avoidance of actual involvement in the campaigning was practised by the same individuals. There was not a single individual in the sample who was fully and actively involved in the redress movement. None directly participated in any campaign activities.

*Justice in Our Time* (Miki and Kobayashi 1991) provides background information on the redress movement and on its process. The beginning of the movement in Canada goes back almost twenty years. During the 1970s, among some younger members of the community, 'a reawakening and a rethinking' had emerged around the time when the government's own documents and files were made fully accessible to the community. Now Japanese Canadians were 'officially' told that what was being done to them during and after the war was unnecessary and an abrogation of citizenship rights – that it was done as a political measure.

The year 1977 marked the centennial of the beginning of immigration from Japan to Canada. At about this time, the Japanese Canadian community began to hear a few individuals declare that they would like to take some action about the 'disgraceful wartime events' that remained unresolved. In Toronto, in the province where Japanese Canadians resettled in the greatest numbers after the war, a group of a few dozen volunteers came into being, and discussions began. In the same year the National Japanese Canadian Citizens' Association (renamed the National Association of Japanese Canadians [NAJC] in 1980) first established a Reparations Committee based in Toronto to investigate the question of redress.

Little was done, however, to publicize the issue in the Japanese-Canadian community across Canada. In 1980, media interest in Japanese-Canadian redress was sparked when the U.S. Congress established the Commission on Wartime Relocation and Internment of Civilians to assess the wartime uprooting and incarceration of Japanese Americans. In February 1982 the Commission's report, *Personal Justice Denied*, was released, and it recommended a public 'apology' and compensation of $20,000 for each uprooted

Japanese American. The news of substantial redress for Japanese-American individuals generated an outburst of public curiosity in Canada in the wartime history of Japanese Canadians.

Soon after the U.S. report was released, the National Council within the NAJC, with a newly elected president, decided to seek a negotiated settlement with the government, arguing the case for redress on the basis of the historical and documentary evidence. NAJC's (1984) brief to the government, *Democracy Betrayed: The Case for Redress*, called on the government to acknowledge the injustices suffered by Japanese Canadians during and after the Second World War, to enter into negotiations to compensate them, and to entrench equality rights in the Canadian Charter of Rights and Freedoms.

The NAJC (1985) also commissioned Price Waterhouse to conduct an economic-loss study in order to have an estimate of economic losses resulting from the uprooting and disposition of Japanese Canadians to justify the demand for meaningful financial compensation. The consulting firm's report provided the first documented calculation of losses suffered by Japanese Canadians from 1941 to 1949. The Japanese-Canadian community, according to the report, suffered a total economic loss of not less than $400 million, calculated in 1986 dollars.

During those years of ongoing negotiations with the government, in the mid-1980s, support for redress by the Canadian public had grown steadily. In March 1986 an Environics poll revealed that 63 per cent of Canadians favoured redress, and of those, 71 per cent supported individual compensation (Miki and Kobayashi 1991, 94). In September 1987 the U.S. House of Representatives passed the Civil Liberties Bill, which offered $20,000 to individual Japanese Americans who had been incarcerated in the United States during the Second World War, and a year later U.S. President Ronald Reagan announced his acceptance of Redress Bill HR 442.

Following the president's announcement, Prime Minister Mulroney of Canada soon announced his government's decision to endorse the Redress Agreement, which was signed between the NAJC and the government on 22 September 1988. The substantial settlement negotiated by the NAJC offered individual compensation of $21,000 to each Japanese Canadian directly affected by the injustices; a community fund ($12 million) to assist in rebuilding the community that was destroyed; pardons for those wrongfully convicted under the War Measures Act; the offer of citizenship to those exiled and to their descendants; and the establishment of a Canadian Race Relations Foundation to combat racism.

Those who were qualified for compensation under the 1988 agreement are defined as persons who were alive in Canada on 22 September 1988 and affected by the provisions of the wartime measures of the government during the period between 7 December 1941 and 31 March 1949, the last day on which the measures were in effect. Eventually there were over 15,000 who applied for and received the financial compensation. Expenditures by the government amounted to over $400 million in the end. It cost the government unexpectedly dear, in the opinions expressed in newspaper editorials and elsewhere by a segment of the public, to make their apology for the wrongdoings committed by a previous government. In the view of many Japanese Canadians, however, the compensation was just a token, 'too little, too late.'

Although the settlement marked a successful ending, those who joined the redress movement constituted a very small group in the Japanese community, wherever it was located. Japanese Canadians were people doing their upmost to work hard and achieve economic mobility to the greatest extent possible after the war, rising above their former second-class-citizen status to be recognized as full members of society at large. They were devoting all their energies to these aims. Thus, they had little left, either materially or psychologically, for political activity. Most of the Nisei raised in British Columbia before the war still bore traces of the discrimination against them like deep scars. They had an ingrained belief that the best way to act was to avoid attracting attention to themselves or to cause a stir in society.

From the beginning to the end, involvement of Japanese Canadians as a whole in the redress movement was limited to a very small segment of the population. The ending came rather unexpectedly and incidentally, and it was a big surprise for members both within and outside the movement. The Canadian government, following largely the U.S. settlement announced only days before, formally acknowledged the errors of its series of policies and actions during and after the war, treating Canadians of Japanese ancestry as enemy aliens regardless of their citizenship.

Throughout the years of the redress movement, the majority of Japanese Canadians remained silent and their attitudes were typically non-committal. These 'victims' found it difficult to talk about the wartime experience and some had never fully recovered from the camp experiences, as discussed earlier (see chapter 3). Thus, more than forty years later, it was still difficult for many of them to support a call for redress. Did this reticence partly arise from the fear that taking a stand on an 'unpopular issue' would elicit a response similar to what they had already experienced on the pre-war West Coast? Probably so, for a fair number of victims. Remarks made by many Sansei children verify the existence of the fear and reveal some insights into the Nisei as being hesitant in dealing with the issue.

In Toronto: 'My parents were not active during the campaign, typically like most Nisei. They were very cautious and at first were not in approval. They didn't like the idea of asking for compensation. They were very worried about the possibility of backlash, and were more afraid of that than seeking [to have] their rights upheld.'

In Thunder Bay: 'I know my parents went to public meetings, but they didn't take an active role in the movement. My father kept saying that he wished that people would just forget about it. "Why do they want to bring it up again?" he questioned. My parents preferred to have a simple apology from the government. They probably felt, by asking for money, non-Japanese people would be less likely to accept the concept of redress.'

In Hamilton: 'My mother was a bit embarrassed because she thought it was all water under the bridge. During the period of the movement, things were against the way she'd have liked to see. She was not interested in interfacing with other people, communicating with anyone including her own children. She was still not ready to deal with the internment. Father'd not shown any response to the question.'

In Ancaster, Ontario: 'My parents were both pleased and appre-

hensive, because redress brought welcome and unwelcome spot-
light on the community. They weren't sure of the public's reaction
and were overall low key about it. Carefully watched it, but didn't
battle it. Didn't get excited. They kept their emotion inside as
usual.'

Roy Miki, a Vancouver Sansei, acting as a chairperson of the
Redress Committee of the local NAJC chapter, summed up the
silence of the past (Miki and Kobayashi 1991, 132): 'I think it was
the community's own burden that led to a silence throughout the
1950s and the 1960s. There was the desire to put a painful experience behind, but also the fact that the homes, the properties, the
community facilities, the place in BC that had been "Japanese
Canadian" was gone. There was no point in dwelling on the past,
but only the important question of survival in the present.'

By and large, redress was a difficult process. At the time when 'a
reawakening and a rethinking' were just rising in the late 1970s,
there was no sign of an organizing movement emerging. The
actual organizing was an altogether different matter. It was a bold
step for a community small in numbers and lacking the necessary
political experience and influence. Before this, the Japanese-
Canadian community rarely, if ever, engaged in formal organized
activities dealing with any particular issue, including their internment experience. This was a wake-up call to a dozing community
comfortable in its post-war prosperity and anonymity, and it roused
them to an issue that not only caught the attention of the rest of
the country but that created very real dissension and division
between different communities, generations, families, and friends.
Because of the Canadian government's policy after the war, the
Japanese-Canadian community was completely scattered, not only
geographically but also psychologically. The consequent rupture
between the generations could not be avoided, and communication from one region to another ceased for a long time. If any consensus existed during the redress-movement period within the
community, we can say that it was limited to concerns of the Issei.
They were the victims who had taken the full force of the blows,
and they wanted to get things over with by any means possible with
the government.

Differences in views and attitudes towards the issue were indeed quite profound depending on the generation. Of the Issei born in the Meiji era (1868–1913), only several hundred across Canada were still alive to witness the whole redress process. Their true feelings may be summarized in such comments I heard as 'I don't care any more. It's a bother just to collect my thoughts.' 'There is no place for us to say anything any more.' 'It's too late. We are just too old to deal with it.' They had seen so many of their generation pass away for so long, and felt somehow uneasy about accepting anything as redress, even if it came about, just because they happened to have survived. There was some opposition among others to being compensated financially. They felt it made no sense to calculate the losses suffered at this late date, and at any rate the individual differences among those who owned or did not own property were so vast that the cases could not be treated equally. As a result, most of the Issei appeared to think that any amount they received would do or that no financial compensation at all would even be better: perhaps something small and symbolic for the sake of form, for the group called 'Japanese Canadians.'

The Issei attitudes were hard to understand and to accept for the Sansei, perhaps foremost conceptually. It would have been pointless to expect this post-war generation to understand the complex conceptions and expectations of their grandparents, who had no basis for communication when it came to basic concepts such as human rights, citizenship, freedom, or financial redress. The two generations were thinking in different languages after all, were separate from each other, and had utterly different value systems and standards for judging the world.

Nonetheless, the Sansei were the ones who took the major lead in the National Association of Japanese Canadians, which was at the centre of redress activity, although the number involved was very small, from a limited segment of the group. Not only was this young generation superior in its energy, it was steeped in the techniques of participation in the political process. They defined the issue clearly as a purely Canadian, domestic one of civil rights for Japanese Canadians. Its roots lay in nothing but the hateful notion of racism. The focal point of the movement was to convey this message and to clarify the situation to Canadians in general, and to win their support. For those activists who were leading the movement, individual compensation was the most important principle upon which the settlement was based; the individual Canadian – not because he or she was Japanese Canadian, but because his or her rights as an individual had been abrogated – had to be compensated. Thus, monetary compensation for an individual victim had to be a component of the 'redress package' in negotiation with the government because it was the only feasible and practical means of getting redress carried out.

The Nisei found themselves being placed between the two positions contended by the Issei and Sansei, and the majority took a position of no position. They either refused to give their support to the group leading the movement, or ignored the whole issue. They stayed away from the debate, as witnessed and reported by their children, the respondents in this study. Nisei involvement in the movement was indeed minimal; very few were personally vocal about seeking redress. Some participated only marginally by contributing money towards organizational efforts, attending public meetings and fund-raising functions sponsored by the NAJC, and/or signing petitions to support the demand for redress to the government. Not a few Nisei parents were involved only to the extent, to use some children's terms, of filling in the application form for monetary compensation after the settlement.

The following Sansei observations depict further the Nisei attitudes: 'This whole culture to the Nisei generation is strange. They never felt a sense of power. They were still powerless and polite. That was just their manner, and accepting. They're not the ones to rock the boat. I think of confrontational, ostentatious behaviour as not part of their style. They couldn't be part of the fight for their own cause' (Toronto). 'None of the Nisei I know were actively involved in it [the campaign]. For them the ending was like winning a lottery, I guess. They liked to take the compensation for sure. That's all they did, some of them' (Montreal). 'My parents said "forget about it"; "let it go." They paid no attention at all. I thought their wishes should be respected, so I did nothing' (Winnipeg).

The quotations cited so far in the discussion suggest that in the

Japanese-Canadian community there were a fair number of individuals who opposed redress – the concept of individual and financial compensation, especially – for a variety of reasons, some of which are reflected in the views expressed by the Issei, as mentioned earlier. Some saw seeking financial compensation as a kind of welfare, while still others thought that it was best not to reopen the wounds of the past. How many were there – the parents of the respondents who believed wholeheartedly in redress and tackled the issue as their own cause personally or collectively? Only a very few, judging from the information provided by the children.

In Steveston: 'My father was not interested in seeking redress. His only concern [after the settlement] was to divide the money among his children. He said that he really didn't want it. There was that sentiment, "too little, too late" within him, I suspected.' In Toronto: 'My parents were against redress. They were very uncomfortable during the years when the campaign was on. They were embarrassed with the result. My father donated a lot of the money to the church, giving us the rest. He didn't touch the money for himself. So my brother and I benefited from it.' In Montreal: 'My parents were not jumping up and down with it. I don't think they would have cared one way or the other, whether it happened or not. It happened. It wasn't a life-and-death issue. They weren't concerned about it. Not involved in the campaign at all either.'

Not only were there few activists and only a few supporters among Japanese Canadians, the community had no unified perspective on how to right the wrongs of the past, and no coordination of purposes. Since the events of some fifty years past were being brought up again, a range of ideas, expectations, and emotions emerged, so that problems inevitably became complicated. It is no exaggeration to say that agreement and consensus were unimaginable. The movement continued for five or so years without cease, and the very fact that it did continue meant a series of difficulties. Thus, driving forward with the movement was extraordinarily strenuous for those who were involved. The redress movement in the United States probably urged them to keep the flame of redress alive. Maryka Omatsu, a Toronto Sansei lawyer-activist, in her book *Bittersweet Passage* (1992), surveyed many of the dimensions of the movement and depicted the process with her own personal account of being involved.

What about the other Sansei? What did redress mean to them? How did they deal with it? What did our respondents have to say about it? All of them said that they were aware of the redress issue largely owing to the extra media coverage of it over the years. Little was discussed in the Japanese-Canadian home during the campaign; thus, the 'historical' reticence and non-communication were still intact. Many respondents followed the process with 'some interest.' Others observed what went on in the community with caution, feeling 'a bit uneasy' like their parents about the controversy on the issue of monetary compensation.

Approximately 9 per cent of the Sansei respondents in Nagata's survey (1990), conducted during the campaign in the United States, indicated that they had opposed the idea of monetary redress. There were also a few in our sample who revealed their opposition, being critical of the idea of monetary redress and of the way it was sought by 'the redress activists.' One Toronto Sansei man felt that 'the air was vengeful, negative, unforgiving, and greedy.' Seeking monetary compensation, he said, did not look good on the Japanese community, and actually was rather embarrassing. After all, getting money, which turned out to be a fairly significant expense for the government, 'did not change anything.'

For a Toronto Sansei woman, redress was something that she felt somewhat torn about because she had respected her father's wishes. The woman's father died during the campaign, and had told the family that he did not want monetary redress; an official acknowledgment and apology from the government were sufficient for the father. The surviving elders were, by and large, opposed to seeking financial redress, in this woman's observation, and their wishes should, first and foremost, be respected.

In a small city in the interior of British Columbia, where 'real victims' of the evacuation and internment were not many, there were also reasons, though slightly different, for a male respondent to be embarrassed with the movement: 'I think many of the members in the community were not ready for seeking redress. It was brought in here from outside – from Vancouver and Toronto. It wasn't our community's issue. There was some resentment and embarrassment, which I shared, among many members here. They just didn't talk about it. They didn't want to be publicized much here. Schoolteachers and people working in the public services felt that it would cause a lot of problems, being pointed out. Things are different in a small town.' Those who opposed redress were in the same boat with all the other 'no-positioners' in the sense that they did not demonstrate their opposition. Instead, they opted to stay away from the issue, following the ways of their parents, and avoided confrontation. They ended in not playing any role themselves in the process.

Some others, although only half a dozen of all the respondents interviewed to be precise, reported that they were indirectly and only marginally involved in the movement. They either wrote a letter to an MP on behalf of their aging parents, contributed money towards organizational efforts, or attended public meetings out of curiosity. The respondents all expressed repeatedly during the interviewing that redress was important, not as a sum of money, but rather as a symbolic gesture to acknowledge the injustice experienced by their parents and grandparents.

The movement helped a great deal to educate the public, including many Japanese Canadians like the Sansei themselves, about the facts of the 1940s. It did break down the barrier of silence for a good many of them. It reinforced their sense of ethnic identity and increased their awareness of racism. It gave one Sansei woman (Fukawa 1987) the determination to continue to urge her parents to talk about their experience; in doing so redress has finally become 'part of my legacy.' In favour of redress, an effort to seek justice for past victimization that would heal the wounds of the past, the majority of Sansei failed, nonetheless, to respond to the call for active support of the campaign.[2]

Was there not anything, besides giving one's moral and financial support, that the individual could do? What stopped them from getting involved? Reasons given to me for their lack of involvement were twofold. First, redress did not seem to be their issue or cause. For instance, in Toronto: 'Redress was not relevant to me. I was not born when it [incarceration] happened. It had nothing to do with me. I didn't have anything to say about it.' In Hamilton: 'It wasn't my cause. My parents never made me think otherwise.' In Guelph: 'I was not involved. I knew my father didn't want to talk about it. I didn't know anything about the campaign until the issue was settled. It wasn't my cause. Later I was told that I was eligible for the compensation, and I got it.' In Geraldton: 'I didn't pay any attention [to redress]. Why would I bother? It wasn't my cause. The money came to me, to my biggest surprise, but there was no reason for me to get it. I haven't [had] anything to do with the money. I don't know what to do with it.' In Montreal: 'Redress didn't interest me personally to the point that I would fight for whatever the goal might be. I didn't feel strongly about it.' In Lethbridge: 'Redress was a cause for my parents. It wasn't important to me at all. I didn't think it was really my place to get involved.'

The prime reason to be drawn from the sample statements above seems to be that redress was not an issue to many individual respondents. The 'events' occurred nearly fifty years ago, long before many of them were born. The individuals were convinced that the incident did not affect them directly or indirectly, and thus redress was not considered to be their cause; rather it was the cause of the people who had actually suffered from the uprooting and incarceration.

The younger segment of the respondents in the sample tended to maintain more than the older ones that the cause was not theirs. But even those who were born before 1949, who happened to be eligible for the individual compensation, admitted (as shown in the above quotations) that they could not relate to the issue; 'the concept of redress was beyond my concern, outside the context of my experience.' Those who were born in the 1960s were 'too young' to be involved, being wrapped up more in themselves than in political causes. Had the redress movement begun now instead, a few mentioned, they would be involved in it very much.

Many were thus observing the process with some interest as an outsider or 'casual onlooker,' avoiding participating in battling the cause. The stance of the NAJC in defining redress as a 'Canadian' issue, not merely relevant to Japanese Canadians alone, seemed not to be persuasive enough to the 'public,' including many Sansei. The struggle for redress was important as a test of how the country dealt with its 'mistakes,' a Vancouver Sansei activist (Kobayashi 1987) argued, in an attempt to draw the attention of Sansei in the community. Japanese Canadians were seeking to right the wrong not just for those members who suffered, but for all the victims of both past and, theoretically, future mistakes. That is why, the argument went on, redress was an issue for post-war Sansei, new immigrants, and all Canadians who care about clearing their national conscience.

It was pointed out earlier (chapter 3) that most Sansei were sheltered from knowing much about the internment, especially the traumatic aspects of it, by their elders, and had not been taught about the event in their previous schooling. Little was told by their own parents personally about their victimization. Thus, internment was viewed by and large as a distant and past incident that would probably never happen again and that, more important, had no enduring impact on or significance for post-war Japanese Canadians, especially the Sansei themselves. There was no notion perceived at all of the negative impact of the historical event on their life chances and experiences. The idea of Sansei or later generations being 'heirs' of the internment was thus completely absent in Sansei minds, and they saw little relevance in redress to the contemporary Japanese-Canadian community, and thus no reason to be involved.

Unlike in the United States, there were no public hearings held in Canada as part of the redress process. The U.S. Presidential Commission on Wartime Relocation and Internment of Civilians, a nine-member body formed within Congress, held public meetings in 1981. The nationwide hearings received ample media attention and captured the attention of Japanese Americans and the general public. In total, more than 750 witnesses – evacuees, former government officials, public figures, interested citizens, and historians and other professionals – testified before the commission throughout the nation (Commission on Wartime Relocation and Internment of Civilians 1982). An American historian, Roger Daniels (1991, 189), argued that the creation of the commission and the hearings held by that body helped dispel much of the scepticism prevalent among Japanese Americans and 'created a communal climate of opinion highly favorable to redress.' Victims' testimonies were powerful, not just in terms of the psychological task of 'working through' their personal internment experiences, but in letting the public as well as other victims know that they should no longer suffer from the pain and agony of false guilt. Japanese Americans accepted their experience 'as part of our heritage ... part of our history,' to quote activist Uno's remark made earlier (1974, 109–11).

Even just a dozen witnesses, instead of 750, would have been sufficient to draw some Canadian Sansei's attention to the issue and lead them to be part of the redress movement. But, in contrast to the American scene, even with the campaign in full swing, silence about the past was broken very little in Canada. Only after the issue was eventually settled did Japanese Canadians either reveal or discuss both the immediate and the enduring consequences of the wartime victimization openly and publicly.

The second reason for non-involvement on the part of our respondents was their lack of connectedness with their community. One group of respondents felt that they were out of place in the campaign organization because they had few connections to their ethnic community. They did not know how to be effective in the campaign, even if they were to be involved, without finding 'the right contact' within the community. 'If someone approached me, I could have been involved, or could have done something.' 'You have to be asked to get involved. Nobody asked me.' One Sansei woman said she did not resolve the issue in her mind in terms of how to right those wrongs for her parents, and she needed to discuss this with someone. She was not invited to meet with a group by anyone, and the opportunity for discussion was missed. 'I'm not a type of political activist. How could I suddenly become an activist even with redress for Japanese Canadians?' questioned the woman. Not only did these people feel they could not do anything individually; nobody approached them to be part of a group either. These remarks reflect, more than anything else, the extent of contact loss

for many members in the ethnic community. A busy Sansei executive from Toronto said he was sufficiently interested in the issue
and wanted to do something at one point, mostly on behalf of his
parents who 'would be absolutely incapable of participating in any
political process even if they wanted to.' But he had no time to
make a contact to get involved. Had he been approached by someone personally and persuaded to be part of a committee or a
group, he might have made time, said the executive. Indeed, he
was confident of being able to help in organizing an effective campaign and lobbying activity, using the skills that he had acquired
from his experience in business – how to move politicians as well as
the general public and how to use media effectively. What was missing for the executive were opportunities to get involved. And for
many, many others.

One is reminded here that, as the redress movement progressed,
Japanese Canadians were living apart and the 'activists' were struggling across thousands of miles to reach out to the members who
lived well outside the ethnic community. Ethnicity has become
largely peripheral to them. More than half of the Sansei are not
'full members' of the community any more (see chapter 5). Half of
them are either 'non-members' or 'nominal members.' They have
very little interaction with the community both formally and informally. It is unlikely they will interact with Japanese persons in their
daily life; neither are they likely to be associated with any ethnic
voluntary group. Their membership within the community has
pretty well been abandoned.

For a Toronto activist, Maryka Omatsu, working in the redress
movement was a great discovery of a whole new world of what she
called 'aliens' – most people she encountered in the process were
people she had never met before. She found herself sharing with
the 'aliens' bewildering similarity and pleasure and joy, as she
became friends with them while working together. And whomever
she met for the first time, as Japanese Canadians often experience,
she found someone who was distantly related by blood, marriage,
or some sort of tie in this small community. The conversation
always began with the question, Where is your family from?
Redress was thus a coming together of the personal and political

for Omatsu. Through personal connectedness, one finds a place to belong and feels a sense of togetherness.

I would gather that, among those members of the community who remained silent throughout the process of redress, there must have been a fair number who 'had to be asked to get involved.' Many members of the community had been passed over in the process so significant in the history of the group. 'No other event in our history had so much vitality, so much heart, so much purpose, so much fullness of meaning' (Miki, 1992). The movement was so crucial, according to activist Roy Miki, one of the principal organizers in Vancouver, that the course of the history of the Japanese-Canadian community could be changed forever after. It is rather ironic to see that redress activists such as Miki and the core of the NAJC leadership, who were largely Sansei, contributed so much effort and energy in an attempt to demonstrate the relevancy of the redress issue to the post-war generation of the community, while the majority of the same generation's members remained silent and passive throughout the whole process, missing opportunities to get involved. The story of the redress movement, will, nonetheless, remain a prime example of one small ethnic community's struggle to overcome the devastating effects of racism, and to affirm the rights of all individuals in a democracy for future generations of Canadians, including Japanese Canadians.

The following story of a Sansei man, one of the non-members (or ex-members) of the community in our sample, tells what redress meant to him. His growing-up experience provides the background for, and the reasons, why he has become a non-member. The respondent was born and raised in Toronto, and currently resides in a city located two hundred miles away from his home town. He is forty-five years of age, and married.

> I was not involved in the redress movement. I didn't know whether there was a group organized here or not. We are not activists in formal ways with organizations. Personally I was not interested in the issue particularly and I was not paying attention at all, until the ending [the settlement] came.

I was born in 1948. I was told that I was eligible for applying for the compensation. Up to this day I have not done that, and I don't think I will.

I was born in Toronto. We lived in the inner city and when I was sixteen moved to a suburb, the west end of Metro. I remember being brought up to think of myself as an Anglo-Canadian. I tried to think of myself as Canadian. I didn't like to think of myself as Japanese Canadian and didn't like to be treated as Japanese either. It was a conscious effort. I went to the local Anglican church and was confirmed at age nine. I got more encouragement in trying to be an ordinary Canadian from my mother than my father.

My parents seemed to make it clear to me that they were glad that they were Japanese and that they were not Chinese or anything else. They also gave me mixed signals that they didn't want to tell the whole world that they were Japanese. They only wanted to be Japanese in their home with the door shut. Outside they behaved as very integrated Canadians. My mother, particularly, behaved as being a completely assimilated Canadian, not mentioning that she was glad to be Japanese.

The food at home was always Japanese, but I developed a great dislike for steamed short-grained rice. For the period between age eight and ten, I was not eating properly, so my mother made two dinners, one for me and one for the rest of my family. I probably didn't like that staple food of our people.

I refused to learn the Japanese language, although my parents encouraged me to attend the Japanese language school more than a few times. My grandmother lived with us for some years, but there was little communication between her and me because of the language barrier. I didn't get to know her as a person.

I didn't like associating with Japanese people at all. I actively avoided Japanese, both Sansei boys and girls. I made an effort not to become special friends with Japanese boys. I joined the Boy Scouts from age seven to sixteen where other Japanese boys were involved. I made an effort not to become special friends with any of them. I made sure that my closes friends were *hakujin*. It seemed to me others were doing the same things I was.

I used to think I'm Canadian, Anglo-Canadian. Now I must say

I'm Canadian. But it's not simple any more to me. I cannot deny my background. I'm very strongly Canadian. I'm a member of the Anglican church community where I feel I belong. The Japanese part has become more meaningful in the past ten years in my life after I rejected my ethnic background for so long. I realize now that I will never be able to run away from it, so I'd better become friends with it.

My internal struggle is not over yet. I need more time. That's why I could not relate to the redress issue as my issue. I cannot do so overtly and fill out the application form. I have still not faced standing up and saying, 'I'm a Japanese and give me money.' I'm not a victim, because I was only an infant during the period. The thing that stops me is that I'm not comfortable enough being Japanese to fill out the form required and go to the lawyer for verification. This feeling is very difficult to explain. My mother, not so much my father, has strongly urged me to apply for it. But I don't think I will. It is still too painful for me to identify myself as Japanese.

## Chapter Seven

# Conclusion

*What does it matter if a small group of Japanese Canadians assimilates and disappears? There are millions of Japanese back in the land of the rising sun. And certainly race mixing is a better alternative to racial segregation. If North America's visible minorities follow in our footsteps, wouldn't Martin Luther King's dream become a reality?*

Maryka Omatsu (1992, 172)

The third generation of those of Japanese descent in Canada, as represented by the sixty-four individuals who have appeared in this study, can best be described as the generation of security. The group has shown no urgency to escape the world of the second generation, which is epitomized by the tensions of success and marginality, nor any eagerness to reject the middle-class status attained by their parents. Its members have achieved mobility within the dominant economic institutions successfully enough. They seek security and greater integration just as much as their parents have done, yet they value autonomy and freedom beyond mere economic security. The supreme goal in their career pursuits, as many of them claimed, is to be independent and self-sufficient, whatever the occupational spheres they happen to occupy. Their work is mostly, if not only, a means of achieving a good life – although the good life to which the Sansei aspire does not conform with the traditional North American emphasis on materialistic success. Also, their definitions of work and a good life are quite unlike those of their parents.

The Sansei are the generation that has become 'native Canadian' in the fullest sense, being born and raised in the Canadian community. They have gone through socialization in mainstream institutions of society outside the Japanese minority culture and the boundaries of the ethnic community. Because of the geographical dispersion of the Japanese population after the Second World War, the Sansei, regardless of the region where particular individuals reside, are no longer insulated by the ethnic community. They have won a measure of acceptance that their predecessors never knew, and they have been well incorporated into the Canadian middle-class world. Their upward mobility also has led them into an almost exclusive level of social interaction with non-Japanese groups in society at large; the tendency among the Sansei to marry non-Japanese has become a routine phenomenon to such an extent that the distinction between marriage and intermarriage has vanished. Thus, the 'Japanese community' does not have meaningful relevance in most of the Sansei's minds: 'The Japanese community is something I never grew up with and I've very little to do with,' summed up one respondent.

Consequently, the Sansei are nearly identical to the majority group not only in achievement, but in interests, social values, and belief systems. The concept of Japanese Canadians as a disadvantaged group vis-à-vis the majority does not perhaps define 'minority group' any longer as far as the Sansei are concerned. One element in the definition of a minority group is the group's awareness of itself as possessing a depressed status relative to other groups in society (Elliott 1971). This very awareness seems almost completely absent from the minds and souls of the Sansei I encountered in the course of interviewing, the term 'minority' itself having seldom or very rarely been mentioned by the individuals in describing Japanese Canadians in general or themselves specifically.

The hypothesis that the evacuation-internment experience may be a central component of the distinctive Japanese-Canadian identity had to be rejected by the present Sansei group just as it was by the Nisei (Makabe 1976). Only a few respondents stated that they perceive the incident as having been so unique as to distinguish Japanese Canadians from other ethnic groups in Canada. For many of them the internment is not a reminder of 'differences in background' that they might occasionally come to be aware of.

The testimonies of the respondents have, however, provided sufficient evidence of the attempts on the part of their Nisei parents to obliterate the bitter years of the event. Indeed, almost all of the Sansei children interviewed in this study have revealed that, growing up in a Japanese-Canadian family, they encountered was an unwillingness among the Nisei to discuss the issue with others, including their own children, unless specifically questioned about it. Also, there was an insistence on minimizing the uniqueness and historical (or other) significance of the event, and a reticence in recognizing any of the effects of this experience on Nisei themselves as well as on forthcoming generations. Furthermore, the silence and non-communication were not broken for decades, even with the redress movement in the 1980s.

These Nisei attitudes affected the ethnic experiences of the Sansei. Practically all the respondents indicated that they have not had a serious discussion with their parents on the internment and on the victimization of racism – the legacy of Japanese Canadians. Consequently, the Sansei have little awareness of family history, the unique historical background of the group, racism and discrimination in general, and the internment and forced resettlement in particular. The negative impact of the event on Sansei's life chances and experiences is perceived to be almost non-existent, as it is on their ethnic identity.

Yet the Sansei are not unaware of their ethnicity. At least 60 per cent of them call themselves 'Japanese Canadian' instead of simply 'Canadian.' However, they do not feel that their upbringing was significantly different from that of other Canadians. With their lack of self-awareness as a minority, they are, unlike their parents, completely free from negative 'minority feelings.' What is crucial in explaining the changing content and extent of ethnic identity between the Nisei and Sansei are the external conditions that affected the process of socialization. The Sansei went through the basic process of socialization among the majority members of

Canadian society, and were unaware of the fact that they were 'different' from the rest of the society in their 'upbringing' or by virtue of racism and discrimination – with which they were, in their perceptions, seldom faced (chapter 3).

More important in affecting the process of socialization that the Sansei have undergone are the attitudes of the group towards assimilation and integration, and the strategies adopted by its members to achieve such an end. The Nisei's basic orientation to and emphasis on greater integration and total assimilation into the Anglo-Canadian way of life, their de-emphasis on Issei heritage, and the self-imposed physical dispersion have had a combined impact on Sansei socialization to a great extent. This pattern – adopted by the Nisei throughout the post-war period – has continued to provide the baseline along which the ethnic-historical heritage is being transmitted from Issei and Nisei to Sansei. As a consequence, we have seen, the Sansei have had very few formal or informal ethnic affiliations.

In primary-group associations of friendship, dating, and marriage, it was found that there is indeed no boundary separating the Sansei from the majority group. The very high rate of intermarriage observed elsewhere among the Canadian Sansei was confirmed with the present sample group as well. Symmetrical relations with the majority group and the absence of other-imposed economic and social barriers have made it possible for the Sansei to achieve marital-structural assimilation, and thus the incorporation of this generational group into Canadian society has proved to be full and almost complete.

In assessing the Sansei identity – by focusing on the maintenance and continuation of ethnic identity – this study noted as critical the impact of 'other definitions' of ethnicity. Practically every respondent acknowledged that they are perceived in terms of certain stereotypes; the definitions of their ethnicity by others are as significant as their own definitions. 'Other definitions' reinforce 'self-definitions.' Also, almost every respondent indicated that their ethnic awareness became more apparent as they grew older, 'got into the real world,' and began to compete with other mem-

bers of society. It was then that they noticed other people's definitions of their ethnicity and became aware of the advantage of
being a member of a 'respectable' minority. Therefore, the most
commonly expressed type of identity among the present Sansei
was, overall, a positive, self-imposed one of so-called ethnic pride.
Those 'Japanese Canadians' feel good and comfortable with being
ethnics. They identified themselves as Japanese Canadians by
choice rather than in response to the majority's definitions of
them. Or, to put it in other words, those individuals who 'feel good
being ethnics' were inclined to evaluate positively others' definitions of their ethnicity.

Nonetheless, the Sansei are still categorized as Japanese Canadians or Orientals, even if they no longer actively share any cultural
patterns with such an ethnic group and have little to do with others who are categorized as Orientals – so long as a link to their
ancestors (most important, the racial link) can be made. No Sansei
can escape this fact. This reality thus leads one to conclude that
ethnic identification is not merely a reflection upon genuine ethnic culture as such. It is also a response to a question posed by society at large in terms of its categories. It involves a broader process
on the part of the individual of coming to terms with one's own
definitions of the self as well as the perceptions created and
imposed by others and by society at large. Whether the majority
group's definitions are positive or negative, they promote the continuation and development of ethnic identification. And they may
also condition new forms of social organization.

In the absence of 'other definitions' of ethnicity – which is possible
a few generations down the road in light of the prevalence of intermarriage – the distinctive ethnic identity among Japanese Canadians may die out indeed – a view shared by many of our respondents. Among the Toronto residents, as well as all others elsewhere, there seems to exist the commonly accepted notion that
the Japanese-Canadian community is bound to disappear in the
long run. Its demise is inevitable in due course, although it may
take a very long time. 'It's sad, but it's a sinking ship,' as one put it.
According to another, 'it is an evolution. The community is chang-

ing for the better, sooner or later completely blending. You cannot be sad about it.' Maryka Omatsu, quoted at the beginning of this chapter, was in agreement with these sentiments.

Simply put, the Japanese population is not replacing itself with a minimal rate of growth. This is a result of both immigration and intermarriage. The predominance of intermarriage among the members (including the post-war immigrants), discussed previously (chapter 5), is likely to produce, in everyone's eyes, more and more persons of mixed ancestries. This leads to significant declines in community involvement, and with already weakened linkages between not only individuals but also generational subgroups, further decreases the possibility of continuing contact among the members.

Japanese immigration in the post-war decades has been extremely modest. Since the Second World War some 17,000 altogether have immigrated to Canada from Japan – about 380 a year according to immigration statistics (see chapter 1). Placed in the full context of Canadian immigration in the post-war period, the flow from Japan has been so slight as to be almost negligible. From the 1960s, the number of immigrants from Asian origins such as Hong Kong, India, and Pakistan increased sharply, in such numbers as to make the number of Japanese utterly insignificant. These immigrants unfailingly settle down just after entering Canada, and thus their numbers increase steadily, while many of the Japanese immigrants have opted to return to Japan after some years in Canada, the timing coinciding with a period of great economic growth in Japan.

The immigrant group, with both pre-war and post-war members combined, makes up about 20 per cent of the total Japanese-Canadian population today. The large majority are newcomers who have come to live in either Vancouver or Toronto. Like their predecessors, they are quickly assimilating to society at large. So few in number wherever they have settled, the majority tend to be independent, intermarried, and isolated, and do not need to rely on the Japanese community, unlike the pre-war immigrants. In turn, their influence in community affairs has been rather insignificant and their presence in Canada, in relation to Nisei and Sansei, has remained uncongenial and inharmonious. New immigrants with energy and new ideas create conditions that reactivate the ethnic ties both of older immigrants and of those in younger generations. The complete cessation of immigration over the period of twenty years after the end of the war prevented the reactivation, and thus the reinforcement, of Japanese culture. Hence, the likelihood of new immigrants coming into first-hand contact with the 'native' generations in the Japanese community, as we see it today, has proved to be rather limited.

Unless there is a large influx of immigrants, with hundreds of them continuing to arrive yearly in Canada and settle in one area, the Japanese community, as seen by one Calgary woman, will be 'doomed to extinction.' The few people newly immigrating to Canada from Japan do not, she added, come to live in such small centres as Calgary, her home town. The city's religious groups and other community associations, which are currently barely surviving, are going to vanish, in the view of the respondent, by the time the Nisei are gone. By contrast, a few hundred immigrants are received by Toronto and Vancouver each year. Even when factoring in zero repatriation, however, there is no doubt the number itself has proved to not be substantial enough to reactivate the ethnic ties within the existing community.

Institutions and organizations need a population base for continued survival. The Japanese-Canadian institutions and organizations may have been surviving quite a while, but are bound to disappear in the long run and, as many respondents speculate, will merge with the larger society. Individuals in all ethnic groups tend to lose their group identities over time, and particularly after the third generation. Reitz (1980, 139), speaking of Toronto's major ethnic groups, noted that ethnic communities must constantly be replenished by new immigrant arrivals if they are to survive indefinitely, even though the decline of ethnic community attachment remains a gradual, long-term process.

The attitudes and views of the Sansei towards the ethnic community in general and its future specifically were inconsistent and unsure overall. To cite a few comments given by the respondents as examples: 'I'd like to see the group keep existing in Canada forever, but I don't see the ethnic-group identity fitting that much into my life.' 'I don't see any need to maintain the community in my life, yet I don't want to forget my cultural or historical background.' 'I'm not inclined to do anything collectively in order to maintain or strengthen ethnic identity. My community is my family and friends, not the ethnic collectivity.' 'I don't need to belong to the community. It doesn't mean that I don't care, but I'm not sufficiently interested in getting involved in the Japanese groups and clubs.'

The ambivalent feelings among Sansei seem to be derived from the awareness that their knowledge and practice of Japanese culture and their ethnic contact are not comprehensive enough, nor are they as firm and as significant as their parents'. There is every reason to expect that the progress of assimilation will continue into the forthcoming generations. It then becomes especially difficult to maintain the existing personal network, already reduced to such a feeble substance, which is an element most essential to the survival of any community, ethnic or otherwise.

A Sansei man who grew up with the Japanese Buddhist church in Montreal sees neither energy nor motivation among the few surviving members of the institution to maintain it for the future. His grandparents and his parents were once running the church and it meant a great deal to them. There was a strong connectedness between the Issei and Nisei in terms of keeping the institution intact. Even if the grandson wanted to take the responsibility over from his predecessors, it is simply unfeasible. The Sansei man knows that he does not have 'a base of people that I can rally around' to sustain the routine activities of the religious institution. 'I'll be too alone there with only one or two others'; the task is too enormous. 'It seems that we just don't have that drive to go in order to keep up the church,' says the father of two young children. Collective action requires a good deal of mutual trust and a commonality of interests and priorities. There is not enough Sansei membership to develop sufficient trust in Montreal's Japanese Buddhist church, a problem shared by almost all other religious groups within the Japanese community today, whether in Hamilton, Ontario, in Kelowna, British Columbia, or in Toronto.

A Toronto Sansei man who is acquainted with many Sansei individuals since childhood, observed: 'I know that the Sansei don't get together to form a group. They don't want to get organized even in an informal way. I don't see a common thread to pull the Sansei together. We don't have the tie into the community. We didn't grow up there to form informal social networks, as our parents did.'

Another Sansei man, who has for a long time been actively involved in Toronto's Japanese Canadian Cultural Centre, the major ethnic institution in the community, commented: 'Community is a place where people have feelings of sharing common experiences, a sense of history, cultural heritage, etc., so that people have 'I'm just like you' feelings, in the way the Nisei do. They have a sense of commonness or connectedness.' He wondered: 'Do the Sansei have that sense? I don't know. Maybe not.' After thirty years of operation, the Japanese Canadian Cultural Centre has become a well-established institution in the metropolitan community. It may decline in its strength after the Nisei have gone, but it will not disappear, 'at least in my lifetime,' says the aforementioned Sansei man, whose views were echoed by many respondents, both within and outside Toronto. These days, preservation of a sense of ethnic community seems to be the main task of the centre. Because of the symbolic presence of the centre, many people, both Japanese Canadians and non-Japanese, think the Japanese community thrives, although the Japanese-Canadian community represented by the cultural centre is, for a Toronto female Sansei, 'definitely not my community.' This is probably the case for many others as well.

In the end, a study must come up with some explanations for the phenomenon under investigation by touching upon theoretical questions. In the case of the present study, they are, How and why has such a small community managed to maintain its identity – at least up to the present? How has the Japanese-Canadian community developed, sustained, or transformed its distinctive group identity so that it can be maintained by future generations? What are the basic reasons for the changes in the Japanese-Canadian identity over the generations, the past and future? In short, the study ends up with the same old fundamental question dealt with in the field of ethnic studies: Why do ethnic groups persist? Most, if not all of them, do. Why do some of them then fail to exist?

For the five decades since the expulsion from the West Coast, the Japanese community in Canada has somehow persisted as a social and cultural community. Despite the large-scale dispersion of the population and the high degree of assimilation and integration, the community has lived on mostly as a subcultural group. The community has never ceased to exist, however small it has become. More or less a product of wartime events, being shaped by similar experiences in the hands of the former internees, the present community was formed anew largely by the Nisei for the Issei and Nisei themselves. The commitment to the group on the part of individual Nisei, which turned out to be lifelong, has been solid and persistent enough to sustain the community as we see it today.

The core of this strong identity among the Nisei resides in their interpersonal relationships with other Nisei, with individuals with whom they feel comfortable. It is thus an ethnic community, but strictly a personal community without much social structure, physically less visible yet very persistent. It is sustained by the perception that the Nisei still see significant social boundaries between their group and others in mainstream Canadian society. As most of them believe that they are somewhat 'different' from many of their fellow Canadians, they have retained a relatively high level of participation in the institutional life of their ethnic community. I am convinced that as long as, and to the extent, they are able to do so, the Nisei will continue to be motivated to support the social organizational mechanisms crucial to retaining their community life.

There are good reasons – factors both outside and inside the group itself – that explain this 'successful' retention of group cohesiveness among Japanese Canadians to the present. The most crucial, I would argue, is the Nisei socialization process, the fact that they once lived and grew up in a genuine ethnic community and went through the wartime experience together. The Nisei community is an example of what Bellah et al. (1985) called a 'community of memory.' These people have known each other and each other's families quite well, and often their relationships are life-long. There is a sense of history among the members in this ethnic community of memory. The history, particular to the Nisei, has meanings, full and real, as well as symbolic effects.

In Fujita and O'Brien's recent study (1991) on Japanese-American ethnicity, the central theme was also the issue of ethnic persistence. Based on the findings from their survey of the Japanese-American communities in California these researchers argued a very strong case for the persistence of the ethnic community. The evidence obtained showed overall very small variations in behaviour and attitudes between the two generations under investigation, the American Nisei and Sansei. According to Fujita and O'Brien, the absence of major significant differences indicates a great deal of continuity between the generations. Such a high degree of generational continuity, together with an equally high level of participation in ethnic voluntary associations and other behavioural involvement in ethnic community life among California's Japanese Americans, is considered to be a good indication of the level of retention of ethnicity. The researchers' attention was then focused on examining and explaining how and why the Japanese Americans have been successful in retaining their ethnicity, while at the same time moving to and incorporating so fully into mainstream society.

Fujita and O'Brien insisted upon the importance of cultural and social organizational forms in determining the ability of an ethnic group to support ethnic community life in the face of structural assimilation. The Japanese-American experience demonstrates, according to them, the compatibility of cultural and social organizational forms with structural assimilation where 'cultural principles' are in operation:

> [T]he persistence of Japanese American ethnicity stems from elements in traditional Japanese culture that structure social relationship among group members in such a way that they are able to adapt to changing exigencies without losing a group cohesiveness. These

cultural principles have generated for Japanese Americans, as they
have for the Japanese in Japan, a strong sense of peoplehood, allow-
ing them to adopt major elements from other cultural systems without totally sacrificing social relationships within the group. (Fujita
and O'Brien 1991, 5)

There is a notion, generally accepted in the field, that structural
assimilation eventually leads to destruction of the ethnic community. To the extent to which members of an ethnic group are incorporated into society at large, ethnic identity becomes less and less
salient for the members. Assimilation is seen, therefore, as having a
direct, negative effect on the capacity of ethnic groups to survive.
Fujita and O'Brien, in interpreting their research evidence, fundamentally contradict this assumed notion. Although they do not
explicitly argue against such notions of assimilation as a zero-sum
phenomenon, they do seem to believe that structural assimilation
and retention of some forms of ethnic identity can take place
concomitantly. The experience of the Japanese Americans can
be seen as a reflection of the complex interaction between these
two phenomena. Thus, as Isajiw contended (1990, 35), ethnic-
identity loss should not, by itself, be interpreted as an indication of
assimilation.

The experience of the Japanese Canadians in the post-war era is
not dissimilar to the American experience, in that Japanese Canadians have also become incorporated into mainstream society to
the extent that Americans have. Both groups have retained a relatively high level of involvement, at least to the present, in their ethnic communities despite a high level of mobility and integration.

The evidence presented in this study, however, confirms, at the
same time, that fundamental changes have been taking place
within the Japanese community in Canada. The aspect of change
has largely been overlooked in Fujita and O'Brien's study, with the
emphasis being placed on generational continuity and the high
level of participation in ethnic voluntary associations observed
among their sample groups. The changes in the Japanese-
Canadian community seem fundamental, in my observation – far
more considerable, and even commanding, than the American
counterparts, and are most notably and strongly evidenced in the

high incidence of intermarriage occurring among the third- and fourth-generation members. Overall, these individuals have long lost their connectedness to each other and to their community, since there is no common ground to pull them together nor is there the chance for them to mingle with other Japanese socially or otherwise. Intermarriage is inevitable for those unconnected individuals in such a small and widely scattered community.

At the end of intensively talking with some sixty Sansei, I have failed to see any sign of a community that is to be continuously maintained, as it has been done by the Nisei. With the communities I visited, there was not sufficient interchange or first-hand contact observed between the various subgroups in either formal or informal associations. If the persistence of ethnic-community involvement depends, in part at least, on the preservation of strong ethnic associational ties, as is commonly assumed in the field, I would suspect that, with the lessened associational membership as it is, the involvement of members in the community as a whole has pretty well come to an end. After all, less than half, two out of five, of the Sansei in our sample group (in contrast to 69 per cent of the Japanese Americans in Fujita and O'Brien's California sample) were holding such ties, many of them being marginal and nominal.

In fact one out of four Sansei have already become what is called 'non-' or 'ex-members' of the community (see chapter 5). These individuals neither identify with the ethnic community nor interact with other fellow ethnics at all. Combined with another segment of the sample group, the 'nominal members' who feel they belong to the ethnic group but do not have a single Japanese person with whom to interact socially and are not involved in any ethnic voluntary association, 60 per cent of Sansei have very little to do with their ethnicity. We must say, then, that ethnic identity is a relatively small part of most of the Sansei's identities. Whether or not this rate is high enough to threaten the positive *raison d'être* of the Japanese group in Canada, in its efforts to sustain, its very existence as a distinctive group, remains a matter for speculation. It seems undeniable nonetheless that the community has already lost a large constituency of 'eligible non-members.' But it does not mean that all of the kinds of ethnic ties have entirely disappeared –

at least not with the Sansei group under investigation. It is possible at the same time that the long-term outcome of change may be an eventual dissolution of the ethnic community. If such a dissolution is inevitable, as David Suzuki predicts it will be, it will take place 'five or six generations after the time of the last wave of immigration,' as suggested by Reitz (1980, 232). This translates into more than a century. Indeed, this small ethnic community may take a very long time to die.

Why, then, is the situation of Japanese Canadians today unique or different from that of many other ethnic groups that have achieved similar levels of structural assimilation in Canadian society, other than the fact that the group is a visible minority? Has the assimilation-oriented behaviour of Japanese Canadians in the postwar decades been significantly different from that of other groups? What are the basic reasons for the changes in Japanese-Canadian identity between Nisei and Sansei? What forces have led to structural assimilation to such an extent – never thought possible for a visible-minority group – over such a period of time as just one generation?

I would argue against the notion that structural assimilation, however willingly and voluntarily it may have been pursued, has been a major causal force leading to the dissolution of the Japanese community in Canada. Rather, external events in accumulation – the endless discrimination and racism experienced by Japanese Canadians from the time of their arrival in this country to their incarceration in concentration camps during the Second World War and their forced dispersal and resettlement – account for the circumstantial break-up of the community and the consequent lack of generational continuity. It is the result of both structure and agency – a dialectic played out by the ethnic Japanese group and the larger society.

Specifically, the federal government's policy of assimilation implemented through the means of geographical dispersal should be noted as a major force in breaking down this tiny ethnic community so fully, physically and otherwise. Policies and regulations to induce the resettlement set by the government over a period of seven years between 1942 and 1949, highlighted by the 1944 order of dispersal, were pre-eminent. The dispersal was forced upon each Japanese Canadian, and was fundamentally coercive in nature.

One can note similarities in the series of assimilation policies of the same national government in an earlier era towards other minority groups, most notably the native Indians. The Indian Act of 1876, which was designed to promote coercive assimilation, has completely taken power away from native people by eradicating their languages, religion, culture, traditions, and customs with the expectation that they would/should become self-sufficient members of Canadian society. 'The extinction of the Indians *as Indians*' (Harper 1945, 127) was the ultimate end pursued by the policies. The means adopted to enact the policies with natives were education, Christianization, and settlement on reserves (Ponting and Gibbins 1980), while with Japanese Canadians it was the physical dispersal and resettlement of the population.

The Canadian government policy of dispersal of the Japanese (although it was part of wartime policy, and thus relatively short-lived) was not only forcible but also turned out to be quite effective, fully achieving its purpose by spreading the population widely and sparsely and by destroying the ethnic community almost completely, aided as it was by a conscious and conscientious effort by Japanese Canadians. With their very survival at stake, the Japanese Canadians, with 'an innate respect for authority' (Adachi 1976, 355), recognized and accepted the necessity of dispersal in order to achieve mobility and to be welcomed by society at large. At first reluctant to 'cooperate with the government,' they later took to dispersing voluntarily or involuntarily as a way to achieve assimilation and integration. In contrast to the 'success' attained with the Japanese, the government policy of assimilation largely failed with Indians, argued Ponting and Gibbins (1980, 18), because of Indians' isolation, marginality to the labour force, and the cultural gulf between the Indians and the white community. Heterogeneity as a group would be a factor making them a more difficult group to assimilate than others. Canadian Indians have never accepted assimilation or 'cooperated' with the government in the way that the Japanese did.

The dispersal policy, on the one hand, turned out to have benefited the victims of coercion in the long run; the relocation process, on the other hand, destroyed the organized communities, broke up the closely integrated institutions, and disrupted various associational groups and friendship ties. The outcome was indeed overwhelming. Once the community had become so widely scattered, the distance caused real disconnection and discontinuity between individuals and their families, which further affected the socialization of future generations to a magnitude that no one had ever thought possible.

It should be repeated here that structural-voluntary assimilation per se was not a major force leading to the destruction (the weakening, more precisely) of the Japanese community in Canada. Physical factors surrounding the group externally, specifically the politically motivated and forced dispersal and resettlement, account largely for the present state of the Japanese-Canadian community and the lack of connectedness, as well as the resulting generational discontinuity. The Japanese-Canadian experience provides us with an instance demonstrating that ethnic group behaviour is, among various factors involved, more likely to be the result of external-structural constraints on the opportunities that confront both individuals and their groups. Externally enforced government policies and institutions can be a powerful source of ethnic identity and social experience. Japanese-Canadian ethnicity, as it is today, seems to have less to do with 'cultural principles' (Fujita and O'Brien 1991) or even economic-opportunity factors, which are usually given prominence in explaining differences in behaviour between groups as well as generations in the field of ethnic studies in North America.

It is now ten years since the settlement of redress for Japanese Canadians. One outcome of this settlement was the establishment of a $12 million fund to rebuild the community. The fund has helped in aiding the existing ethnic social structure, the cultural-community centres in both large and small centres, the National Association of Japanese Canadians both nationally and locally,  the seniors' housing projects, the Heritage Centre to be constructed in

Vancouver, and other capital projects across the country. The Japanese language schools in major centres and other types of organizations, which have also been rebuilt and reinforced, may contribute to the survival of Japanese-Canadian identity by responding to the interests of its members. Once established, organizations tend to create their own vested interests, and this contributes to group survival and continuation. They tend to perpetuate. Ethnic identity can be maintained in that way to a significant degree by 'organizational momentum' (Reitz 1980, 216) alone.

Books, films, ethnic newspapers, and festivals have also found support from the redress fund. Several national conferences and seminars have taken place in various places across Canada on leadership, seniors, intergenerational relations, intermarriage, and education, with the result that a fair number of Japanese Canadians, especially the young ones, have for the first time been given a chance to get acquainted with others from various regions and backgrounds. A question, however, still remains: Has a viable Japanese-Canadian community re-emerged? Is it emerging? It is seen to be emerging by some, but many others seem to remain unconvinced. Memberships in Japanese organizations have been steadily declining across the country since the redress, as noted by Terry Watada (1996), a Toronto Sansei writer and an adept observer of the community at first hand. He argues that there must be real change to see a real rediscovery of ethnicity within the ethnic institutions and organizations, change that recognizes and accommodates the needs of the younger generations and acts upon those needs.

The cost of assimilation is high. Japanese Canadians are trying to revitalize the community through the establishment of institutions and organizations. However, the lack of interest fostered by the vigorous pursuit of assimilation over the decades makes such efforts extremely strenuous, if not futile. It seems less than likely, I must say, that the community will see the development of a new and distinctive social-cultural structure.

It is possible, however, that we will see a sustained identity, perhaps in more symbolic ways, with support and interest from the wider community. It would even be more desirable for the ethnic-cultural heritage to be fostered and reshaped by fellow Canadians at large. With Japanese not separated from others, the group's identity can be openly displaced and shared with citizens in the wider community. An 'open-attitude policy' that can draw many young members of the community from mixed backgrounds is favoured by many respondents in the study. Openness is inevitable, and 'a matter of fact' according to one respondent, for the retention of Japanese culture as such is impossible for such a small group as the Japanese in Canada.

Thus, Toronto's Japanese Canadian Cultural Centre can become an 'all Canadian' institution and last perpetually, with the attached name of 'Japanese Canadian' retained as something symbolic for the sake of memory or history. While the minority group of Japanese Canadians merges with the mainstream, it is possible to see that selected aspects of the group's structures, institutions, and identities might become part of the mainstream (Isajiw, 1996). Gans, in his attempt at 'updating' the original concept of 'symbolic ethnicity' that he elaborated in the late 1970s, highlighted the future of symbolic ethnicity by saying that '[ethnic identity] is shaped as much or more by needs, wishes and opportunities that originate in the larger society as by those created from internal changes in the ethnic group' (1994, 588).

In such an open and tolerant society as Canada, ethnic lines may not disappear for quite a while – not in the foreseeable future. The issue is not, as Yinger sees it (1994, 343), assimilation versus ethnicity, but a matter of assimilation *and* ethnicity.

So the search for a sense of community seems to continue for Japanese Canadians. So does the attempt to define and redefine what the Japanese community is. At least for the time being.

# Appendix 1
# Myth of a 'Model Minority'?:
# Social Mobility and Integration
# Achieved by Canadian Nisei in a
# Metropolitan Community (1991)

This paper seeks to assess the degree of social mobility and integration achieved by the second generation of Japanese Canadians (Nisei) in Metropolitan Toronto,[1] by examining two sets of data – gathered in 1976 and 1990, respectively – dealing with the same generational group of Japanese Canadians residing in the same metropolitan community. The author was engaged in both the 1976 study, part of fieldwork she conducted for her doctoral thesis (Makabe 1976), and in the 1990 community-wide study of needs assessment among Japanese-Canadian seniors as well as the middle-aged (Makabe 1990).[2] The latter study, funded by the federal government and sponsored by a Japanese-Canadian organization, allows the author to closely examine and empirically double check Nisei experience in the longitudinal context.

Previous studies conducted on Japanese groups in Canada and the United States had consistently produced evidence of considerable socio-economic mobility achieved by the second and third generations, the Nisei and Sansei, after the Second World War. The 1976 study by the researcher empirically elaborated on the process of the Nisei group's progress after the internment and relocation in the Toronto community. In short, the Nisei were able to achieve 'success,' in approximating standards of the Canadian middle class. They worked hard, wherever they resettled, to become accepted by and integrated into the larger society. Integration and assimilation, because they had formerly been denied, were highly valued and vig-

orously pursued. The great majority spent the post-war years working to ensure basic economic security and to re-establish a life from
scratch. Their main concerns were to achieve the highest possible
social mobility in Canadian society.

In the mid-1970s, when the researcher's early study was conducted, the Nisei as a group were in the prime of life and at the
zenith of their occupational careers. At the same time they were
still striving to attain higher social status than they had already
earned. Fifteen years later, in 1990, for the majority that struggle
was over. After fulfilling work and family duties and attaining
senior-citizen status, many Nisei themselves seemed in a position to
ponder their own achievement relative to fellow citizens. This
paper, written as the battle of the Nisei was near its end, seeks to
assess the outcome of the struggle over a period of fifteen years;
how high a status after all has been achieved by the Toronto Nisei?
How valid is the 'success story' of the Nisei (Petersen 1971) in
Canadian terms? To what extent has the Nisei's socio-economic
mobility promoted assimilation and integration?

### Data

The group sampled for the 1990 study consisted of 208 Nisei,
Canadian-born residents of Toronto, including 103 men and 105
women. Most of these individuals came to Toronto after they had
been forced to leave the coastal area of British Columbia and were
incarcerated in internment camps during the Second World War.
The large majority came to live in the East between 1942 and 1946,
travelling directly from relocation camps established by the federal
government. The mean age of the sample was 66.4, ranging from
55 to 85 years of age. Nearly 60 per cent of them were retired from
gainful employment at the time the survey was conducted. Personal interviews with the respondents sampled were conducted in
January through May 1990.

The principal source of information for the 1976 study was a
series of intensive qualitative interviews with one hundred Nisei.
The respondents defined as 'the heads of the household,' consisted of ninety-eight men and two women. They were interviewed

TABLE 1
Years of schooling completed, Nisei respondents, 1990 (*N* = 205) and 1976
(*N* = 100)

| Years of schooling | Nisei 1990 | | Nisei 1976* |
|---|---|---|---|
| | Men | Women | |
| Elementary: 0–8 years | 13 | 12 | 5 |
| High school: 9–12 years | 57 | 65 | 63 |
| College: 1–3 years | 11 | 13 | 7 |
| 4 years or more | 19 | 10 | 25 |
| | 100 | 100 | 100 |
| Mean | 12.0 | | 12.8 |

* Includes 98 men and 2 women

in the period of September 1974 through May 1975. The mean age
of the sample then was 51.3, ranging from 38 to 64 years of age.
Aged exactly fifteen years apart – from 51.3 to 66.4 measured in
the mean ages – the two sample groups were thus nearly identical
age cohorts, although the earlier sample consisted almost entirely
of men.

## The Limit of Socio-Economic Mobility Achieved

In terms of almost all measures of socio-economic success, the
group has made considerable strides. Their progress is particularly
evident in the higher-than-average educational attainment of the
Nisei group, in particular the younger segment of the generation.

Table 1 indicates that 13 per cent of Nisei men and 12 per cent
of Nisei women in the 1990 sample had eight years or less of formal education; 57 per cent of men and 65 per cent of women had
nine to twelve years. Thirty per cent of Nisei men and 23 per cent
of women in the sample had thirteen years of schooling or more.
The mean years of education completed for this Nisei sample
group as a whole was 12.0 years.

Almost one out of four Nisei respondents seventy years of age and
over attained only an elementary-level education (table 2, p. 184).

TABLE 2
Years of schooling completed, Nisei respondents, by age and sex, 1990

| | Age | | | |
| | 55–69 | | 70+ | |
| Years of schooling | Men | Women | Men | Women |
| --- | --- | --- | --- | --- |
| Less than 8 years | 6.8 | 7.3 | 28.6 | 20.6 |
| 9–12 years | 60.8 | 71.1 | 50.0 | 55.9 |
| 13–15 years | 13.5 | 10.1 | 3.6 | 17.6 |
| 16 years or more | 18.9 | 11.6 | 17.8 | 5.9 |
| | 100.0 | 100.0 | 100.0 | 100.0 |
| | (N = 74) | (N = 69) | (N = 28) | (N = 34) |

Of those Nisei who were educated in Canada aged between fifty-five and sixty-nine, on the other hand, nearly seven out of ten managed to complete schooling of at least high school level: furthermore, 27 per cent were able to move beyond the high school level; half of these individuals completed college. These findings were consistent with the findings from the 1976 study: over half of the Nisei men surveyed, for example, had high school education, and 34 per cent had post-secondary education (table 1).

The aged seventy and older category (table 2) includes an older segment of the Nisei group. These older Nisei, often the oldest in large families, had held various family responsibilities. Because they often had to provide financial or other help to their younger siblings, they rarely had the chance to attend university. That was particularly the case with older Nisei men than women in the group aged seventy years and over. The figures in the table show that the proportion of those with only an elementary-level education was 8 per cent higher among men than women in the group aged seventy years and over. With their relatively low level of education, many older Nisei found it almost impossible to achieve higher mobility, even within economic institutions newly open to them after the war. They seem to have lived with the limitation of few opportunities to upgrade their education, as there was no change observed in the level of educational attainment by age over the duration of 1975 to 1990 under investigation.

By contrast, the war affected the younger segment of the Nisei group quite differently, for many enjoyed the privilege of attending university or college in the post-war period.

The Nisei educational attainment can be compared with that of the general population in the community through data available from a survey conducted in Metropolitan Toronto in 1982 by Richmond (1986). As Richmond notes, Canadian-born of foreign parentage who were of non-British ethnic origin in Toronto (such as the Nisei), have achieved substantial educational mobility as well, particularly the younger segments of the population. Thus, even for the group aged fifty years and over, nearly 30 per cent of second-generation men were reported to have obtained some university education, a figure close to that of the present Nisei group. For Toronto women of the same age group, however, the proportion with some university study was far lower – only about 5 per cent (4.5%) in Richmond's survey sample. Mean years of schooling was 12.8 for the Toronto men aged fifty years and over and 10.9 for women, respectively; 12.0 for both the Nisei men and women fifty-five years and over. The level of upward mobility in education experienced by Metro's non-British second generation as a whole was indeed remarkable. From this data Richmond argued that inequality of educational opportunity based on ethnicity no longer existed. This was certainly the case in Metropolitan Toronto, where opportunities for post-secondary education and training exceeded those in most other parts of Canada.

It seems fair to state that in their educational record, the Nisei have made strides equal to, or even greater than, their contemporaries in the metropolitan community. This proves that they were not handicapped by their ethnicity, at least in educational pursuits.

Education is an important determinant of one's initial position in the job market, affecting subsequent opportunities as well. The data obtained by the 1990 survey provided information on the occupational backgrounds of both those respondents retired from active employment for some time and those who were still working

TABLE 3
Occupation of Nisei respondents by employment status, 1990

| Occupation | Currently employed | | Retired | |
|---|---|---|---|---|
| | Total | Men | Total | Men |
| Managerial-proprietary | 15.0% | 18.0% | 10.3% | 26.2% |
| Professional | 18.7 | 25.1 | 14.7 | 14.3 |
| Clerical | 20.0 | 8.2 | 19.8 | 2.4 |
| Sales | 4.4 | 1.5 | 1.9 | 2.4 |
| Skilled work | 20.0 | 23.8 | 14.7 | 28.8 |
| Semi-skilled work | 13.3 | 15.6 | 18.1 | 14.2 |
| Unskilled work | 7.8 | 7.8 | 20.5 | 11.0 |
| | 100.0 | 100.0 | 100.0 | 100.0 |
| | (N = 90) | (N = 61) | (N = 116) | (N = 42) |

at the time they were interviewed. For retirees who had worked in more than one field, their major occupation was considered. The information from the two groups, currently employed and retired from employment, is shown together in table 3, so that the group's experiences can be compared.

Eighteen per cent of those Nisei men who were currently employed and 26 per cent of those who were already out of the work force were either managers or self-employed proprietors. Most were owners of small companies or stores, earning their living from self-employment, or held managerial positions in companies or government agencies.

As shown in the table, nearly one out of four men currently employed were in professions, the largest occupational category in the group. In contrast, skilled work was the largest occupational category for those who were retired; 29 per cent of the respondents in the sample population reported their major occupation as skilled work, another 14 per cent as semi-skilled, followed by another 11 per cent as unskilled, typically factory work. Over half of the retired respondents (56%) had thus ended up working in blue-collar jobs.

Here again, the potential for occupational attainment has not been uniform for every segment of the Nisei population, young and old. After relocation and resettlement in Ontario, older members of the Nisei group were most likely to continue in the blue-collar sphere of the economy. Men of this group typically began careers as such skilled or semi-skilled workers as electricians, auto mechanics, carpenters, or radio and television technicians. A large number of the women took jobs in the garment trades (Makabe 1976).

The analyses of large-scale survey data nationally collected in the mid-1960s in the United States provided similar evidence for the American Nisei as well (Bonacich and Modell 1980; Levine and Rhodes 1981). One-third of the Nisei men in their sample were in the professions and another third were engaged in blue-collar labour. At the same time, close to half the Nisei surveyed in the American study were owners or employees of ethnic small businesses. Bonacich and Modell maintained that this economic form of so-called middleman, uniquely strong among Japanese Americans from pre-war days, was retained most among the oldest and least educated Nisei males.

Many of the younger Nisei, both Canadian and American alike, attended university and college after the war and entered various professions or took white-collar employment. The figures in table 3 tell the occupational histories of Nisei men and women. Most noticeable is the upward mobility achieved by the younger group of men (currently under sixty-four years of age) in particular; nearly half of this group had either managerial or professional jobs.

With the lifting of all discriminatory practices after the end of the war, the group's economic picture brightened everywhere in this country. It is generally thought, nonetheless, that the group in eastern Canada, Toronto in particular, enjoyed more favourable social circumstances than those in other regions. There are a few Nisei who 'made it big' indeed in professions and businesses.

In his discussion of the post-war Japanese community in Canada, Nisei writer Ken Adachi (1976) maintained that being minority members seemed to have little relevance to the majority of Japanese Canadians. This notion has been supported by the respondents of the 1990 study. In responding to the question 'Have you

ever experienced difficulties, or felt handicapped in getting a job
or in other employment situations because you are of Japanese
descent?' more than seven out of ten Nisei interviewed responded
negatively by saying, 'No, not much.' Those who admitted having
experienced some difficulties constituted a minority of 19 per
cent. Men and women, young and old, were alike in maintaining
that being of Japanese descent did not limit their opportunities for
advancement or restrict them in their occupational pursuits. They
themselves had not encountered job discrimination personally.
Generally, discrimination in such areas as employment, education,
housing, and public accommodation was not perceived to be
affecting the Japanese Canadians in the metropolitan community.

However, how realistic would this perception be? There is
enough evidence indicating that only a few, a select group of Nisei,
have climbed to the top or executive level of major Canadian corporations or government bureaucracies. Whether or not an unoffi-
cial quota system is operating seems a factor Nisei generally tend to
be ignorant of or are underestimating the importance of. 'Opportunity for advancement? I'm not ambitious to advance myself or to
get higher up anyhow, so why do I bother?' was a typical remark
made by some respondents. Thus their response to the question
on discrimination referred to earlier was a definite 'No.' Many like-
minded Nisei reported that they have experienced few difficulties
in ascending the corporate ladder, because they seldom participate in such competition to begin with, assuming that top positions are reserved for Anglo-whites anyhow. This may be one way of
adapting to being a minority. Internalizing feelings of inferiority
and social-psychological perceptions of being a minority, as Kitano
(1976) suggests, may thus prove as effective in limiting upward
mobility as discriminatory laws and practices.

Regardless of their perception of discrimination and insistence
on its non-existence, it may be safe to state that social mobility
achieved by the Nisei – limited by their success in finding positions
commensurate with their training and experience – did not go
beyond the 'middle' position at the highest. In sum, as Adachi
(1976, 359) depicts: '[I]n their drive for middle class status, Nisei
have not bloomed as public or corporate figures and have not pen-

etrated the levels of power, prestige and privilege in terms of the hierarchical ranking or social stratification of Canada's "vertical mosaic.'"

## Integration and Social Participation

The Nisei had gone far beyond assimilation in much of their cultural practice, as reported in the 1976 study. The majority of them, however, were not found in the social clique of the Anglo-Canadian society. This was true in both formal and informal spheres. For instance, 'the per cent self-selection' – friends or intimates (excluding relatives) of the same ethnic group as the respondents, one of the indicators to measure the extent of social integration – was 80 per cent among the Nisei sample. If this figure is regarded as an index of the degree to which a group has maintained its distinctive social identity, the Nisei in Toronto, presumably the most integrated generational group of all in the country, have maintained a strong distinctive ethnic identity. The question then was what factors made them maintain that identity, or what factors had prevented them from going beyond the level of cultural assimilation.

In 1990, the friends with whom the Nisei closely associated were reported to be still largely Japanese Canadians. The respondents in the survey were asked to choose which of the following statements best described their friends and associates: (1) most of my friends are Japanese Canadians; (2) half of my friends are Japanese Canadians; or (3) most of my friends are non-Japanese. More than half of the Nisei respondents (57%) identified most of their friends as being Japanese Canadian. A further 26 per cent described half of their friends as being Japanese Canadian. Only 17 per cent said that their social associates were almost exclusively non-Japanese. These figures provide strong proof that a majority of the Nisei stay inside Japanese-Canadian confines for the closest of non-familial ties. This may have resulted from an urgent need among Japanese Canadians to maintain their social network for physical and emotional support in response to the community's physical dispersal and dissolution after the internment. Such informal networking has nonetheless persisted firmly for decades, and this may remain the strongest and most compelling integration indicator.

Examined in terms of patterns of social participation, the majority of Nisei were found to be actively involved in various voluntary organizations and groups. At the time of the interview, 24 per cent of the respondents in the 1990 sample belonged to no organization at all, whatever its make-up and purpose. Of those who belonged to an organization, seven out of ten were members of what was largely Japanese Canadian in composition. Of all the clubs and associations named by the respondents, 67 per cent were described as 'Japanese' – meaning that the members of the organization were almost exclusively Japanese; 14 per cent were described as 'mixed,' with a significant portion of the membership being non-Japanese; and another 19 per cent of the organizations were identified as 'non-Japanese,' that is to say, were outside the ethnic boundary in the community at large. Thus, not many Nisei were found in groups and mainstream organizations in the larger community. Only a minority of the Nisei sampled had developed contacts outside the ethnic boundary. The majority were much more likely to affiliate with Japanese-Canadian groups than with others.

In the mid-1970s, of all the participants in organizations and groups that the Nisei sample belonged to, more than half (57%) were members active only with Japanese-Canadian groups, while less than half of them (23%) were active only in non-Japanese groups. Twenty per cent of the 1976 respondents were categorized as participants in both Japanese and non-Japanese associations. The findings from the two survey on group affiliation of the Nisei (although the measures used were different) were thus fairly consistent with each other, and constituted proof that their major formal associations – clearly identifiable as ethnic – limited their social participation in mainstream society. Such findings also suggest the persistence of an ethnic community despite the absence of a physically defined one, as seen in Toronto's Nisei community. A tightly knit network of informal, personal relations, this is a community of people who are psychologically contiguous more than anything else.

TABLE 4
Ethnicity of friends and income of Nisei respondents (N = 178)

| | Monthly income* | | |
|---|---|---|---|
| Ethnicity of friends | Less than $2000 | $2000–$3000 | $3000+ |
| Japanese** | 63.3% | 62.9% | 47.5% |
| Non-Japanese | 36.7 | 37.1 | 52.5 |
| | 100.0 | 100.0 | 100.0 |

* The average of disposable net income monthly
** Friends closely associated with who were mostly Japanese Canadian
are categorized as 'Japanese,' and friends closely associated with who
were mostly non-Japanese (or half or more of whom were non-Japanese)
are grouped in the 'Non-Japanese' category.

A certain pattern characterizes the social integration of the
Nisei. Economically successful Nisei were far less likely to associate exclusively with other Nisei or belong to Japanese-Canadian
associations than were those who were less mobile. Measured by
income, education, or occupational status, the same relationship
holds.

Table 4 indicates, for example, that as the level of income of the
respondents advanced, their friends were more likely to be non-
Japanese: over half of the group with monthly disposable income
of $3000 or more said that people with whom they associated were
primarily non-Japanese or that half of them were non-Japanese.
For over 60 per cent of the group whose monthly income was less
than $3000, by contrast, the large majority of friends were identi-
fied as fellow Japanese Canadians.

Correspondingly, people in professions or managerial positions were far less likely to belong to Japanese-Canadian associations than were those in the blue-collar sector (table 5). For
members who held blue-collar jobs, ethnic-voluntary organizational membership was general and widespread. It was also noted
earlier that higher socio-economic status was frequently associated with the younger segment of the group. These upwardly
mobile members, younger and better educated, tended to be

TABLE 5
Ethnicity of voluntary associations that Nisei respondents belong to by
occupation, 1990 (N = 158)

| Ethnicity of associations | Occupation | | |
| --- | --- | --- | --- |
| | Professional-Managerial | White-collar | Blue-collar |
| Japanese-Canadian | 54.0% | 64.9% | 71.4% |
| Non-Japanese | 46.0 | 37.1 | 28.6 |
| | 100.0 | 100.0 | 100.0 |

active members in larger community-wide organizations in society rather than in ethnic organizations. Among older, less well-educated Nisei, however, there was a lingering affiliation with Japanese-Canadian groups.

The Nisei, while they were growing up on the West Coast, had for the most part been determinedly barred from the cliques, social clubs, and churches of white Canada. Consequently they have reconstructed, even in the post-internment community of Toronto, their own network of organizations and institutions, and their own 'social world.' Doubtless many Nisei feel comfortable in it, while in the larger community some of them may feel 'out of place.' They are the ones who have failed to develop free and open social relationships with the majority group.

The area in which the Nisei have been almost completely 'out of place' has been the political sphere. Only 4 per cent of the Nisei respondents in the 1990 survey reported participating in political associations, but these were virtually all Japanese Canadian, for instance, the National Association of Japanese Canadians (NAJC). On the question regarding recreational-leisure activities of daily life, 6 per cent of the respondents replied affirmatively to 'helping at election time,' which was the lowest proportion of all twenty-two activities asked about. Nisei have rarely become free of minority experience and feelings, which may have prevented them from playing a role in society's political processes. The Canadian Nisei's almost total lack of participation in political life clearly indicates the substance as well as the extent of integration attained by native-born members of a visible-minority group.

## Conclusion

The present report has reviewed, first, the social mobility attained by the Nisei group in the post-war decades in Metropolitan Toronto. According to the measures of socio-economic success the Canadian Nisei, like their counterparts in the United States, have made impressive gains. Whether such socio-economic mobility necessarily leads to structural assimilation and integration is the question this report has aimed to assess using the existing data.

It has been argued that while Nisei might attain structural integration, as defined by Gordon (1964), the considerable structural separation and the high degree of social distance characterizing the early years of their lives have limited assimilation and integration more than it would otherwise be possible.

In fact Rose (1985), in his discussion reviewing Asian Americans as a group in the United States, concluded by stating that they 'are not and will not be fully assimilated, at least not in the foreseeable future' because of racism in North American society. Lee (1989, 387) as well argued that they will remain 'yellow' in the eyes of the members of the majority and marginal, as long as cultural racism and nativism remain integral parts of American culture and society. The Canadian Nisei's experience to the present, as discussed here, supports these observations to a fairly large extent.

## Notes

1 The 1991 Canadian census returns reported 17,065 Canadians of Japanese origin living in the Census Metropolitan Area of Toronto, about one-third of the total Japanese population in Canada. The Toronto community has remained small, like every other Japanese community in the country. It is generally thought that the economic level of the group in Toronto is most favourable. Also, this group is more integrated than other Japanese communities in different regions of Canada.

2 *A Study on Needs Assessment of Japanese Canadians, 55 Years and Older*
(1990) is a report of research sponsored by Momiji Health Care Society,
an elderly care group established in Toronto in 1976. The study cov-
ered issues pertaining to the living situations of middle-aged and elderly Japanese Canadians residing outside of institutional settings in
Metropolitan Toronto. A total of 259 individuals (128 men and 131
women) aged 55 years and older made up the sample group, and of
them 208 were Nisei. These individuals were selected through a random process from the population sample of Japanese Canadians in the
area.

# Appendix 2
# Interview Questions

## Family Background and Upbringing

1. Family History. Grandparents, parents, and as far back as you can remember.
    Who in your family were the original immigrants?
    Where (in Japan) did they come from?
    How long ago did they come here?
    How old were they when they immigrated?
    Do you know why they left?
    Why did they choose Canada?
    Where did they settle?
    Occupation, education?
    Did their whole family come or just them?
    Discrimination they faced? – describe that as much as you know.
    How do you know this information?
    What kind of work did your father (and/or mother) do when you were growing up?

    _____

2. Where were you born?
3. Where did you grow up?
4. Where else did you live?
5. How long have you lived in the area you live now?
6. What is your religion? Were you raised in it? About how often would you estimate that you attend religious services?

7. Did you speak Japanese at home growing up? How much was spoken, where and by whom? Did your parents, grandparents speak?

8. Did you ever attend the Japanese language school growing up, or any other Japanese school either in Canada or Japan?

9. Do you speak Japanese (or any other language than English) at home now? How often? On what occasions?

10. Describe to me the neighbourhood where you grew up. What was the most common ethnicity in it? Were any friends, neighbours Japanese Canadian? How different were they?

11. How did your parents feel about their ethnic background? Did they talk about it often?

12. Did your parent/parents say much about internment and relocation? When did you first become aware of it? Do you feel you know enough about this part of the history of Japanese Canadians? What is your feeling about all the things that happened to your parents and grandparents during and after the war?

13. Do you think your parents' being of Japanese-Canadian origin has had an influence on your upbringing? Do you feel that you were brought up somewhat differently from your friends? If so, in what way?

14. Did your parents belong to any ethnic organizations or clubs? Are they still active with any of those organizations?

15. When you were growing up did you consider yourself a member of the Japanese-Canadian community?

16. Was it important to you or to your parents for you to date someone of the *Nikkei* background?

17. Did you ever go out with someone who was not Japanese-Canadian?

18. If yes, how did your parents react? How did your friends react?

19. Did (would) you marry someone from the same ethnic ancestry? (if married) How long have you been married?

20. [Re: marital partner] – What about outside of your religion? Do you think both of these things were equally important to your parents?

21. Did any of your brothers and sisters or aunts or uncles marry

outside the *Nikkei* group? How was this seen by the rest of the family? How did they treat them?

22. Can you think of any particular value/values that were emphasized by your parents when you were growing up? Are family values different for the Japanese Canadian? In what way?

## Ethnic Identity

23. Do you think of yourself primarily as a Canadian, a Japanese Canadian, or a Japanese? Why? – Ask to elaborate the response.

24. When people ask you what your ethnic background is, what is your answer?

25. Is it a common occurrence for people to ask or comment on your ethnic background? Can you recall the last time someone asked or commented on it? How do you answer the question?

26. Do you belong to any Japanese-Canadian organizations or clubs? What do the organizations do? How active are you there?

27. Do you belong to any other (non-Japanese) organizations or clubs? How active are you in the organizations?

28. Would you say that being a Japanese Canadian is important to you or not so important?

29. Can you think of times in your life when being a Japanese Canadian has been more or less important? Can you give me an example of when it has been important?

30. Have you ever felt any personal discrimination or hostility in getting a house or an apartment? Getting a job or a promotion? In any other way? Can you recall the last time?

31. Do remarks, comments, or jokes people make on Japan, Japanese, or Japanese Canadians bother you?

32. Do you think Canadians have a stereotypical notion of Japanese Canadians? What is it?

33. Is there any validity to it? Where do you think this stereotype comes from?

34. Do you ever find that people expect you to behave according to the stereotype(s)?

35. Have you ever visited the country any of your ancestors came from (i.e. Japan)? Do you want to visit there?

36. Do you feel more comfortable being around Japanese Canadians than non-Japanese? At what times? Any idea why?

37. Do you ever feel a special sense of relationship to Japanese Canadians? Any idea why?

38. Is your neighbourhood characterized by a particular ethnic group? If so, what is it? If not, do you think you are missing something?

39. Describe to me your friends, people outside home that you feel closest to.

40. Can you describe some of the Japanese-Canadian customs or practices that affect your everyday life, i.e. food, music, cultural events, or anything else?

41. Do you eat any ethnic foods regularly?

42. What are the holidays which you and your family celebrate that are the most important?

43. Are there any family traditions you follow on New Year's Day?

44. Have you ever done work in a political campaign? For whom, what did you do? Have you:
   - been active in an organization involved in community problems?
   - contacted a government official about some issue or problem?
   - formed a group to attempt to solve some local community problem?
   - done anything else?

45. Were you involved in the redress movement for Japanese Canadians? What did you do? If not, why not? What did redress mean to you?

### Career, Mobility

46. Would you tell me all the occupations (full-time job) that you have engaged in up until now since you started your occupational career? What is your feeling about your job/career? Do you think you have reached a social rank that is higher than your father's?

47. Would you describe yourself as working class, middle class, or upper class?

48. What does 'success' mean to you? Is success in your work important to you? What is a 'good life' to you?

49. Do you think your ethnic background was an obstacle at one time in the past? Do you think it may be an obstacle to your future somehow?

## Issues and Opinions

50. What do you think of the policy of multiculturalism?

51. What are the issues, political, social, international or otherwise, you feel most strongly about or care about? What actions have you taken or might have taken with respect to the issue(s) of your concern?

52. (If they have children) How important is being a person of Japanese descent to your children?

53. Would you prefer your children to marry within their ethnicity? religion? race? Why?

54. Do you think that Japanese in Canada should preserve their ethnic identity in the future? How do you think the identity should (or can) be maintained?

## Demographics

55. What year were you born?

56. What is the highest grade of school you completed?

57. Are you currently employed (self-employed) full-time?

# Notes

## Introduction

1 Among the Japanese in North America, individuals can identify with their ethnic group as a whole or with a generational segment. Those who were born in Japan and emigrated at an age when they could make their way in the world are called *Issei*, meaning 'the first generation.' The offspring of the immigrant group, who are Canadian-born and Canadian-reared, are called *Nisei*, or 'second generation'; the children of the latter are called *Sansei*, meaning 'third generation.'

2 *Hakujin*, literally means the white, or white people. Among Japanese Canadians the term, in meaning and use, refers to non-Japanese, to distinguish them from Japanese.

3 Throughout the manuscript I use the term 'assimilation' or 'structural assimilation' interchangeably with 'integration' or 'structural integration,' in the sense commonly understood or in the way used by the respondents in the study as daily language. Assimilation means, as one dictionary defines, to blend the culture and structure of one group, that is, Japanese Canadians (as a minority), with the culture and structure of another group, that is, Anglo Canadians (as a majority). It is generally assumed that in the process of assimilation the majority remains the same while the minority changes to become like the majority; in the process of integration, on the other hand, each group is changed by integrating with the other without completely losing its own identity, and thus the groups remain complementary but individual. In reality the two processes through which an ethnic community becomes an integral part of a larger community (i.e.,

Canada as a whole) stand alongside each other, and are empirically interwoven. When I say that the minority group of Japanese Canadians has structurally assimilated and integrated into the larger society, I mean, empirically, and largely following Gordon's (1964) definition, that the group has attained large-scale entrance into the primary as well as the secondary levels of the larger society.

4 See Isajiw (1974) for a comprehensive discussion defining ethnicity, and Nagel's (1994, 1995) recent articles for the constructionist's approach to ethnic identity, which stresses the socially constructed character of ethnicity.

### Chapter One: The Japanese-Canadian Community

1 Postwar Japanese immigration, 1949–92

| | | | |
|------|------|------|------|
| 1949 | 11 | 1971 | 615 |
| 1950 | 11 | 1972 | 684 |
| 1951 | 3 | 1973 | 1020 |
| 1952 | 6 | 1974 | 810 |
| 1953 | 46 | 1975 | 587 |
| 1954 | 71 | 1976 | 474 |
| 1955 | 97 | 1977 | 387 |
| 1956 | 120 | 1978 | 348 |
| 1957 | 178 | 1979 | 576 |
| 1958 | 188 | 1980 | 701 |
| 1959 | 191 | 1981 | 756 |
| 1960 | 159 | 1982 | 598 |
| 1961 | 116 | 1983 | 308 |
| 1962 | 134 | 1984 | 246 |
| 1963 | 174 | 1985 | 198 |
| 1964 | 137 | 1986 | 247 |
| 1965 | 203 | 1987 | 446 |
| 1966 | 500 | 1988 | 344 |
| 1967 | 858 | 1989 | 541 |
| 1968 | 628 | 1990 | 369 |
| 1969 | 698 | 1991 | 502 |
| 1970 | 785 | 1992 | 603 |

*Source:* Citizenship and Immigration Canada, *Immigration Statistics,* 1992

The immigrant group makes up over 20 per cent of the total Japanese-Canadian population today. The large majority of the post-war immigrants live in either Toronto or Vancouver. The influence of the immigrants from Japan in 'community affairs' has been insignificant, and their presence in Canada, in relation to the Nisei and Sansei, has remained uncongenial and inharmonious. Separate from these postwar immigrants, there also exists a sizable group of Japanese businessmen and their families, although the number does not appear in official statistics. Posted in Canada by their companies on a short-term basis of from three to five years, they tend form a 'community' of their own. Their numbers had been steadily increasing because of ever-increasing business and trade relations between Canada and Japan, especially in the two decades up to the economic recession of the early 1990s.

2 Since the 1970s previously classified federal documents have been opened for public scrutiny, and more information regarding the treatment of Japanese Canadians during the Second World War has become available. The best single collection of documents can be found at the Public Archives of Canada (see Sunahara and Wright 1979). Mona Oikawa's thesis (1986) investigates the measures taken by the Canadian government in the implementation of its forced resettlement of Japanese Canadians between 1944 and 1949, utilizing documents housed in three Canadian archives: the Public Archives of Canada, the Public Archives of Ontario, and the United Church of Canada Archives.

## Chapter Two: Social Mobility

1 The high level for Japanese Canadians may be partly explained by the smaller proportion of immigrants compared with other visible minorities under investigation.

2 For example, Tang's (1993) research dealt with the career histories of American engineers, both Caucasians and Asians, followed from 1982 through 1986. One of the findings was that native-born Asian engineers have achieved earnings parity with Caucasians, but they have not yet attained occupational equality. They are relatively less represented in management, and their prospects for promotions are also poorer. Asians and Caucasians with comparable training, skills, and experience do not have the same opportunities for promotion. Tang sug-

gested that it is necessary to modify or expand the major competing theories to explain the racial disparity in career achievements between Caucasian and Asian engineers.

## Chapter Five: Sansei Behaviour

1 Among the Asiatic groups, according to the 1991 census returns, the single-origin rate was 90% for the Chinese, 96% for the Koreans, and 90% for the Filipinos. These high rates are partly due to the higher-than-average proportion of immigrant populations in these groups. For the white ethnic groups, the Jewish group's single origin was the highest, with 67%, following by the Italians with 65%, and only 39% for the Ukrainians.

## Chapter Six: Sansei Reaction to the Redress Movement

1 Art Miki from Winnipeg, Manitoba, ran for the Liberals in the federal election in October 1993. He was the first Japanese-Canadian candidate to run for elective office at the national level. Miki lost by a margin of only 219 votes. A Vancouver-born Sansei, Miki had been the school principal in the riding for years, and was involved in the redress movement since 1984. As the president of the National Association of Japanese Canadians, he led negotiations to achieve the redress settlement from the government in 1988.
2 Among the American Sansei, too, the level of participation in the redress movement was reported to have been low (Nagata 1993, 198). Approximately 43 per cent of the Sansei with previously interned parents surveyed reported that they were not active at all; 55 per cent of the Sansei with parents of no camp experience were likewise inactive during the entire process of the movement.

# References

Adachi, Ken. 1976. *The Enemy That Never Was.* Toronto: McClelland & Stewart.

Alba, Richard D. 1990. *Ethnic Identity: The Transformation of White America.* New Haven: Yale University Press.

Barth, Frederik. 1969. *Ethnic Groups and Boundaries.* Boston: Little, Brown.

Berry, John W., W.R. Kalin, and D.M. Taylor. 1977. *Multiculturalism and Ethnic Attitudes in Canada.* Ottawa: Supply & Services Canada.

Bellah, Robert N., et al. 1985. *Habits of the Heart.* Berkeley: University of California Press.

Blau, Peter M., Carolyn Beeker, and Kevin M. Fitzpatrick. 1984. 'Intersecting Social Affiliation and Intermarriage.' *Social Forces* 62: 585–606.

Blau, Peter M., Terry C. Blum, and Joseph E. Schwartz. 1982. 'Heterogeneity and Intermarriage.' *American Sociological Review* 47: 45–62.

Bonacich, Edna, and John Modell. 1980. *The Economic Basis of Ethnic Solidarity.* Berkeley: University of California Press.

Breton, Raymond, Wsevolod W. Isajiw, Warren E. Kalback, and Jeffrey G. Reitz. 1990. *Ethnic Identity and Equality.* Toronto: University of Toronto Press.

Canada. Department of Labour. 1947. *Re-Establishment of the Japanese in Canada: 1944–1947.* Ottawa: King's Printer.

Canada. House of Commons. 1944. *Debates.* Ottawa: House of Commons.

Canadian Council of Christians and Jews. 1993. *Canadians' Attitudes Toward Race and Ethnic Relations in Canada.* Toronto: Canadian Council of Christians and Jews.

Citizenship and Immigration Canada. 1992. *Immigration Statistics.* Ottawa: Citizenship and Immigration Canada.

Commission on Wartime Relocation and Internment of Civilians. 1982. *Personal Justice Denied.* Washington: Government Publishing Office.

Daniels, Roger. 1991. Introduction to part 8, 'The Redress Movement,' in Daniels et al., eds, *Japanese Americans. From Relocation to Redress*, 188–90.

Daniels, Roger, Sandra C. Taylor, and Harry Kitano, eds. 1991. *Japanese Americans. From Relocation to Redress*. Revised edition. Seattle: University of Washington Press.

Davis, Morris, and Joseph F. Krauter. 1971. *The Other Canadians: Profiles of Six Minorities*. Toronto: Methuen.

Driedger, Leo, Charlene Thacker, and Raymond Currie. 1982. 'Ethnic Identification: Variations in Regional and National Preferences.' *Canadian Ethnic Studies* 14: 57–68.

Elkin, Frederick, and Gerald Handel. 1989. *The Child and Society*. 5th edition. New York: Random House.

Elliott, Jean Leonard, ed. 1971. *Immigrant Groups*. Scarborough, Ont.: Prentice-Hall Canada.

Epstein, A.L. 1978. *Ethos and Identity*. London: Tavistock Publications.

Eschbach, Karl. 1995. 'The Enduring and Vanishing American Indians: American Indian Population Growth and Intermarriage in 1990.' *Ethnic and Racial Studies* 18: 89–108.

Fujita, Stephen S., and David J. O'Brien. 1991. *Japanese American Ethnicity: The Persistence of the Community*. Seattle: University of Washington Press.

Fukawa, Masako. 1987. 'Conspiracy of Silence: Redress from a Sansei Perspective.' *The Bulletin*, no. 4 (April). Vancouver: Greater Vancouver Japanese Canadian Citizens' Association.

Gaertner, S.L., and L.F. Dovidio, eds. 1986. *Prejudice, Discrimination and Racism*. New York: Academic Press.

Gans, Herbert J. 1979. 'Symbolic Ethnicity: The Future of Ethnic Groups and Cultures in America.' *Ethnic and Racial Studies* 2: 1–20.

– 1988. *Middle American Individualism: The Future of Liberal Democracy*. New York: Free Press.

– 1994. 'Symbolic Ethnicity and Symbolic Religiosity: Toward a Comparison of Ethnic and Religious Acculturation.' *Ethnic and Racial Studies* 17: 577–92.

Gordon, Milton. 1964. *Assimilation in American Life*. New York: Oxford University Press.

Harper, Allan G. 1945. 'Canada's Indian Administration: Basic Concepts and Objectives.' *America Indigena* 4: 119–32.

Henry, Frances. 1994. *The Caribbean Diaspora in Toronto*. Toronto: University of Toronto Press.

Hirschman, Charles, and Morrison G. Wong. 1986. 'The Extraordinary Educational Attainment of Asian-Americans: A Search for Historical Evidence and Explanations.' *Social Forces* 65: 1–27.

Horibe, Kathlyn. 1991. 'What happened to my parents fifty years ago.' *Montreal Gazette*, 8 December.

Ibuki, Norm. 1992. 'Exhibit Chronicles: Life before and after Japanese American Internment.' *The Bulletin*, no. 8 (August). Vancouver: Greater Vancouver Japanese Canadian Citizens' Association.

Isajiw , Wsevolod W. 1974. 'Definition of Ethnicity.' *Ethnicity* 1: 111–24.

– 1990. 'Ethnic Identity Retention.' In Breton et al., *Ethnic Identity and Equality*, 34–91.

– 1996. 'On the Concept and Theory of Social Incorporation.' Unpublished paper.

Isajiw, Wsevolod W., and Tomoko Makabe. 1982. 'Socialization as a Factor in Ethnic Identity Retention.' Research paper no. 134, Centre for Urban and Community Studies, University of Toronto, Toronto.

Jiobu, Robert M. 1988. *Ethnicity and Assimilation*. Albany: State University of New York Press.

Kitagawa, Muriel. 1985. *This Is My Own*. Edited by Roy Miki. Vancouver, BC: Talonbooks.

Kitano, Harry. 1974. *Race Relations*. Englewood Cliffs, NJ: Prentice-Hall.

– 1976. *Japanese Americans: The Evolution of a Subculture*. 2nd edition. Englewood Cliffs, NJ: Prentice-Hall.

Kobayashi, Audrey. 1989. *A Demographic Profile of Japanese Canadians*. Ottawa: Department of Secretary of State.

Kobayashi, Cassandra. 1987. 'For JCs Who Say Redress Is Bad for Business.' *The Bulletin*, no. 9 (September). Vancouver, BC: Greater Vancouver Japanese Canadian Citizens' Association.

Kogawa, Joy. 1983. *Obasan*. Toronto: Penguin Books Canada.

Kuwabara, Bruce. 1994. 'Report of Ai.' A Symposium of Japanese Canadians in the Arts. 16–17 April 1994. Toronto.

La Violette, Forest E. 1948. *The Canadian Japanese and World War II*. Toronto: University of Toronto Press.

Lee, Sharon M. 1989. 'Asian Immigration and American Race Relations: From Exclusion to Acceptance.' *Ethnic and Racial Studies* 12: 368–90.

Levine, Gene, and Colbert Rhodes. 1981. *The Japanese American Community: A Three Generation Study*. New York: Praeger.

Lieberson, Stanley, and Mary Waters. 1988. *From Many Strands: Ethnic and Racial Groups in Contemporary America*. New York: Russell Sage Foundation.

Makabe, Tomoko. 1976. 'Ethnic Group Identity: Canadian-Born Japanese in Metropolitan Toronto.' PhD dissertation, Department of Sociology, University of Toronto.

– 1980. 'Canadian Evacuation and Nisei Identity.' *Phylon* 41: 116–25.

– 1982. *Shashinkon no tsuma-tachi* [*Picture Brides*]. Tokyo: Miraisha Publishing.

– 1990. *Needs Assessment: Japanese Canadians (55 Years and Older) in Metropolitan Toronto*. Toronto: Momiji Health Care Society.

– 1995. *Picture Brides: Japanese Women in Canada.* Translated by Kathleen Merken. Toronto: Multicultural History Society of Ontario.

Mass, Amy Iwasaki. 1991. 'Psychological Effects of the Camps on Japanese Americans.' In Daniels et al., eds, *Japanese Americans, From Relocation to Redress*, 159–62.

Miki, Art. 1994. 'Art Miki: Will I Run again?' *Nikkei Voice* (Toronto), no. 1 (February).

Miki, Roy. 1991. 'Redress: The Personal Inflected.' *The Bulletin*, no. 10 (October). Vancouver, BC: Greater Vancouver Japanese Canadian Citizens' Association.

– 1992. 'The Community Imagined.' *Nikkei Voice* (Toronto), December 1992–January 1993.

Miki, Roy, and Cassandra Kobayashi. 1991. *Justice in Our Time*. Vancouver, BC: Talonbooks.

Moritsugu, Frank. 1991. 'Musings on the Third Anniversary of Redress.' *Nikkei Voice* (Toronto), November.

Mura, David. 1991. *Turning Japanese*. New York: Atlantic Monthly Press.

Nagata, Donna K. 1990. 'The Japanese American Internment: Exploring the Transgenerational Consequences of Traumatic Stress.' *Journal of Traumatic Stress* 3: 47–69.

– 1993. *Legacy of Injustice*. New York: Plenum Press.

Nagel, Joane. 1994. 'Constructing Ethnicity: Creating and Recreating Ethnic Identity and Culture.' *Social Problems* 41: 152–76.

– 1995. 'American Indian Ethnic Renewal: Politics and the Resurgence of Identity.' *American Sociological Review* 60: 947–65.

National Association of Japanese Canadians. 1984. *Democracy Betrayed: The Case for Redress*. Winnipeg, Man.: NAJC.

– 1985. *Economic Losses of Japanese Canadians After 1941: A Study Conducted by Price Water House, Vancouver, BC.* Winnipeg, Man.: NAJC.

Novak, Michael. 1971. *The Rise of the Unmeltable Ethnics*. New York: Macmillan.

O'Bryan, G., J.G. Reitz, and O. Kuplowska. 1976. *Non-Official Languages: A Study in Canadian Multiculturalism*. Ottawa: Supply & Services.

Oikawa, Mona. 1986. 'Driven to Scatter Far and Wide: The Forced Resettlement of Japanese Canadians to Southern Ontario 1944–1949.' MA thesis, Department of Education, University of Toronto.

Oiwa, Keibo. 1986. 'The Structure of Dispersal: The Japanese-Canadian Community in Montreal 1942–1952.' *Canadian Ethnic Studies* 18: 20–37.

Omatsu, Maryka. 1992. *Bittersweet Passage: Redress and the Japanese Canadian Experience*. Toronto: Between the Lines.

Omura, Sharon. 1993. 'Burnt bridges and a generation gap.' *Globe and Mail* (Toronto), 10 April.

Petersen, William. 1971. *Japanese Americans*. New York: Random House.

– 1975. *Population*. 3rd edition. New York: Macmillan.

Ponting, J. Rick, and Roger Gibbins. 1980. *Out of Irrelevance: A Socio-Political Introduction to Indian Affairs in Canada*. Toronto: Butterworths.

Reitz, Jeffrey G. 1980. *The Survival of Ethnic Groups*. Toronto: McGraw-Hill Ryerson.

Reitz, Jeffrey G., and Raymond Breton. 1994. *The Illusion of Difference*. Toronto: C.D. Howe Institute.

Richmond, Anthony H. 1986. 'Ethno-Generational Variation in Educational Achievement.' *Canadian Ethnic Studies* 18: 75–89.

Rose, Peter. 1985. 'Asian Americans: From Pariahs to Paragons.' In Nathan Glazer, ed., *Clamor at the Gates: The New American Immigration*, 181–212. San Francisco: ICS Press.

Shamai, Shmuel. 1992. 'Ethnicity and Educational Attainment in Canada – 1941– 1981.' *Canadian Ethnic Studies* 24: 43–57.

Sowell, Thomas. 1981. *Ethnic America History*. New York: Basic Books.

Statistics Canada. 1993. Census of Canada, *Ethnic Origin*. Catalogue 93–315. Ottawa: Statistics Canada.

– 1995. 'Visible Minorities: A Diverse Group.' In *Canadian Social Trends*. Ottawa: Statistics Canada.

Sunahara, Ann Gomer. 1981. *The Politics of Racism*. Toronto: James Lorimer & Co.

Sunahara, Ann, and Glenn T. Wright. 1979. 'The Japanese Canadian Experience in World War II: An Essay on Archival Resources.' *Canadian Ethnic Studies* 11: 78–87.

Suzuki, Bob M. 1977. 'Education and the Socialization of Asian Americans: A Revisionist Analysis of the "Model Minority" Thesis.' *AMERASIA* 4: 23–51.

Takasaki, Elizabeth. 1991. 'When the voices say "You're different."' *Globe and Mail* (Toronto), 3 May.

Tang, Joyce. 1993. 'The Career Attainment of Caucasian and Asian Engineers.' *Sociological Quarterly* 34: 467–96.

Tomaskovic-Devey, Barbara, and Donald Tomaskovic-Devey. 1988. 'The Social Structural Determinants of Ethnic Group Behavior: Single Ancestry Rates among Four White American Ethnic Groups.' *American Sociological Review* 53: 650–59.

Uno, E. 1974. 'Therapeutic and Educational Benefits.' *Amerasia Journal* 2: 109–11.

Ward, William Peter. 1978. *White Canada Forever*. Montreal, Quebec: McGill-Queens University Press.

Watada, Terry. 1989. 'The Conspiracy of Silence.' In Cassandra Kobayashi and

Roy Miki, eds, *Sprit of Redress: Japanese Canadians in Conference*, 141–8. Vancouver, BC: JC Publications.

– 1996. 'Paradigms Lost.' *Nikkei Voice* (Toronto), September 1996.

Waters, Mary. 1990. *Ethnic Options: Later Generation Ethnicity in America*. Berkeley: University of California Press.

Wong, Morrison G. 1982. 'The Cost of Being Chinese, Japanese, and Filipino in the United States 1960, 1970, 1976.' *Pacific Sociological Review* 25: 59–78.

Yinger, J. Milton. 1994. *Ethnicity: Source of Strength? Source of Conflict?* Albany: University of New York Press.

Young, Charles (with Helen R.Y. Reid). 1936. *The Japanese Canadians*. Toronto: University of Toronto Press.

Ziegler, Suzanne. 1979. 'Demographic Influence on Adolescents' Cross Ethnic Friendship Patterns.' In *Child in the City*, Report no. 4, Centre for Urban and Community Studies, University of Toronto.

# Index

Acadians, 25
acculturation of Canadian Nisei, 121
activist activities, 143
Adachi, K., 5, 21, 30, 31, 149, 177,
187
age cohorts, 183
Alba, R., 97, 133, 136
ambivalence (or aversiveness) as a
form of discrimination, 109
Ancaster, Ontario, 10, 149
Angler, Ontario, 78
Anglo-Canadians, 35; society, 23, 122,
189
Anglo-conformity, 69
Angus Reid poll, 140
anti-Oriental views and prejudice, 110,
139
apology, 146, 148, 149; official
acknowledgment and, 154
Artists of Colour, 54, 118
Asian Americans, 193: career advanc-
ment of engineers, 203; education
and income of, 56, 57; upward
mobility of, 56
Asian Canadians, 92, 109–10; as
minorities, 109

Asian community of Metro Toronto, 93
assimilation, 6, 23, 68, 76, 85, 109, 121;
cost of, 179; cultural, 189; definition
of, 201; need for, 69–70; quest for, 8,
166; structural, 121, 174, 176, 178.
See also integration

backlash, 141, 149
Barth, F., 102
BC Security Commission, 28
Beeton, Ontario, 78
Bellah, R.N., 91, 172
Berry, J.W., 140
black Americans, 103
Blau, P., 121, 127
blue-collar jobs, 46, 47–8; of Nisei,
186, 187, 191
Bonacich, E., 42, 187
bon-odori, 66
Breton, R., 88, 140, 141
British Columbia, 11, 17, 20–1, 22, 31,
39, 43, 46
Buddhist church, 63, 72, 74, 100, 104;
in Montreal, 63, 170; in Raymond,
Alberta, 74; in Toronto, 73, 100
Buddhists, 63; practices of, 70

Calgary, 10, 34, 77, 79, 108, 109, 169
Canada, Department of Labour, 21
Canada, House of Commons, 22
Canadian Charter of Rights and Free-
    dom, 147
Canadian Council of Christians and
    Jews, 51, 140
Canadian Race Relations Foundation,
    148
Census of Canada, 1991, 17, 129, 193
Census Metropolitan Areas, 16, 128,
    129, 193
census tracts, 18
Chatham, Ontario, 10, 68, 79, 99
Chinese Canadians, 204; in Metro
    Toronto, 109–10
Chinese community in Metro Tor-
    onto, 93
Christian church groups of Japanese
    Canadians, 74; in Hamilton, 114; in
    Toronto, 114
Citizenship and Immigration Canada,
    202
Civil Liberties Bill, 147
civil rights, 151
Commission on Wartime Relocation
    and Internment of Civilians, 146,
    157
common-law arrangements, 11, 122,
    137
community of memory, 91, 172–3
community (redress) fund, 148, 178
compensation as a means of redress:
    individual, 35, 152, 153, 156; mone-
    tary-financial, 35, 152, 153, 154
concentration camps, 176
consciousness raising of American
    Indians, 104
conspiracy of silence, 82, 855
constructionist approach, 88, 202

cultural mosaic, 141
cultural principles, 173, 178
Currie, R., 88

Daniels, R., 157
Davis, M., 22
Decima Research, 51, 140
demographic-ecological constraints,
    effects on endogamy, 126
density of population, impact on inter-
    marriage, 129–30
desegregation, 26
discrimination (against Japanese
    Canadians), 4, 20, 21, 23, 41, 46, 58,
    62, 176; impact of, 5; laws and prac-
    tices of, 187, 188; legacy of, 70, 90;
    Nisei perception of, 51, 188–9; as a
    problem, 5; reverse, 54; Sansei per-
    ception of, 51–6; stigma of, 50
disenfranchisement, 2; measure of,
    20, 142
disloyal Japanese Canadians, 24, 25
dispersal of JC population, 18, 23, 25,
    27–8, 68; order of, 176–7
divorce rates among Sansei, 124
dojyo, 73, 114
double boundary of ethnicity, 102
Dovidio, L.F., 109
downward mobility, occupational, 48
Driedger, L., 89
dual identification, 91

education: of Asian Americans, 41–2;
    of Asian Canadians, 41; of Nisei, 40,
    183–4; of Sansei, 39–45; emphasis
    on by JCs, 40–5
Elkin, F., 41, 60, 87
Elliott, J.L., 164
employment-equity programs, 54, 55
enemy aliens, 21

Environics Research, 147
environment, 144–5
Epstein, A.L., 97, 102
Eschback, K., 128
ethnic advantage/pride type, 91–2, 96
ethnic association, 114, 132–3; involvement in, 117; Nisei participation in,
   119; Sansei participation in, 118–20
ethnic awareness of Sansei, 6
ethnic boundary, 102
ethnic churches, 9
ethnic consciousness, 91, 97
ethnic difference, 71, 87
ethnic endogamy, 123, 130; rate of,
   126, 127
ethnic-group cohesion, 15, 131
ethnic-group persistence, 8, 172;
   impact of mobility on, 8; of Japanese Americans, 173; of Japanese
   Canadians, 173
ethnic heritage, 7, 8, 14, 92–3, 94
ethnic identity; as a choice or constraint, 104–5; comparison of, 4;
   behavioural, 15; objective (external), 88, 133; portfolio of, 91;
   renunciation of, 101; subjective
   (internal), 88, 133, voluntary-
   optional, 136
Ethnic Identity Index, 88
ethnic labels, 8
ethnic memory, 91
ethnic renewal of American Indians,
   103
ethnic small businesses, 46, 187
ethnic socialization/upbringing type,
   92; of Nisei, 95, 96–7; of Sansei,
   95–6
ethnic traditions and customs: retention of, 42
ethnicity: as a burden, 105; census

definition of, 16; impact of mobility
   on, 8; indication of, 91; retention of,
   172, 173; of Sansei, 3, 6, 7, 15
Etobicoke, Ontario, 64
evacuation (and relocation) of
   Japanese Canadians, 14, 23, 30, 31

family history, 13
fieldwork, 6, 12
Filipino Canadians, 204
Fraser Valley, 22
French Canadians, 29, 109
Fujita, S.S., 123, 130, 142, 173, 174,
   175, 178
Fukawa, M., 155
full members, 131–2, 134, 159

Gaertner, S.L., 109
Gans, H.J., 97, 98, 144, 180
generational continuity, 86, 173, 174
Geraldton, Ontario, 10, 74, 99, 156
German Canadians, 126
ghost towns, 22
Gibbins, R., 177
go-han, 60
Gordon, M., 69, 121, 193, 202
government policy: of assimilation,
   18–19, 176–8; of dispersal, 177–8; of
   evacuation and resettlement, 31; of
   multiculturalism, 140–1; toward
   native Indians, 177; of wartime in
   the U.S., 24
'groupness' among Japanese Canadians, 34
Guelph, Ontario, 10, 99, 108, 156

hakujin, 5, 6, 58, 73, 105, 108, 110; definition of, 201
Hamilton, Ontario, 10, 61, 108, 149,
   156, 170

Handel, G., 41, 60, 87
Harper, A.G., 177
Henry, G., 50
heterogeneity of population, 127; of immigration, 141
Hirschman, C., 41
Horibe, K., 111
human rights, 54, 141. *See also* racism

Ibuki, N., 87
immigrant reception area, 27
immigrants: Asian, 168; British, 21; Japanese, 19, 20, 36, 203
incarceration of JCs, 15
income of Toronto Nisei, 191
Indians: American, 103–4, 128; native, 85, 108, 177
inferiority complex of Nisei, 84
informal networking among Toronto Nisei, 190
informants, 12
ingroup marriage, 128; rate of, 127, 129
ingroup preference among American Sansei, 83
institutional completeness, 112
integration 6, 26, 76, 109; definition of, 201; indicator of, 191; of Nisei, 15, 122, 181; of Toronto Nisei, 189–93. *See also* assimilation
intermarriage, 9, 15, 121, 169, 175; of American Indians, 128; of Canadian Sansei, 120–5; rate of, 9, 125
internment: cross-generational impact of, 75; effect on Sansei, 82–6; experience of, 8, 67, 71; 'heirs' of, 157; legacy of, 9, 75–82; victims of, 9, 82, 158
internment camps, 21–2, 36, 82, 182
interpersonal relationships: of Sansei, 9, 120–1

interviews: intensive, qualitative, 4, 11, 182
Isajiw, W.W., 8, 102, 113, 126, 134, 174, 180, 202
Issei, 5, 28–9, 95; attitude and views on redress, 151; definition of, 201
Italian Canadians, 126, 204

Japanese Americans: community of, 123; income of, 57
Japanese Canadian Citizens' Association, 32, 35, 146
Japanese Canadian Committee for Democracy, 32
Japanese Canadian community, 6, 16–18, 34, 44, 85, 172; future of, 10, 167–71, 179–80; of Hamilton, 61; of Metro Toronto, 31, 33; in northern Ontario, 70; as a social-cultural community, 31, 36; of Vancouver, 33
Japanese Canadian Community Association in Thunder Bay, 116
Japanese Canadian Cultural Centre (Toronto), 33, 36, 65, 69, 72, 73, 85, 100, 112, 114, 115, 171, 180; of Hamilton, 63
Japanese Canadian values, 37, 40
Japanese immigration, 18, 169–9
Japanese language schools, 65, 71, 72, 73, 179
Japanese population: in BC, 31; in Canada, 16–17; in Metro Toronto, 194
'Japanese Problem,' 23
Japan town, 19
Jewish group, 40, 204; in Metro Toronto, 126
Jiobu, R.M., 57, 122

Kelowna, BC, 10, 109, 170

Kingston, Ontario, 10, 40
Kitagawa, E., 26–7
Kitagawa, M., 27, 30
Kitano, H., 142, 188
Kobayashi, A., 18, 46
Kobayashi, C., 146, 150, 157
Kogawa, J., 16, 28
Korean Canadians, 110, 204
Krauter, J.F., 22
Kuwabara, B., 35, 51

La Violette, E.E., 22, 24, 26
latent (de facto) members, 133
Lee, S.M., 57, 193
Lethbridge, Alberta, 10, 156
Levine, G., 187
Lieberson, S., 57
London, Ontario, 10, 40, 77, 79
low-visibility activities, 143
loyal Japanese Canadians, 23, 25

Mackenzie King, W.L., 22–3, 25
Makabe, T., 3, 7, 18, 24, 27, 28, 75, 90,
    113, 119, 143, 164, 181, 187
Marpole (Vancouver), 81
Mass, A.I., 80
mass deportation of JCs, 24, 30
math/computer wizards, 104
Meiji era, 151
Metropolitan Toronto, 10, 17–18,
    26, 54, 61, 64, 76, 80, 81, 82, 108,
    149, 152, 153, 155, 160, 169, 170,
    181
Mexican Americans, 103
middle class, 38–9, 58, 181
Miki, A., 139, 204
Miki, R., 35, 146, 150, 160
military interest, 21
minority feelings and sentiments of
    Nisei, 71, 165

minority groups: Canadian, 22; defini-
    tion of, 164; middleman, 42;
    respectable, 92, 110, 167; urban-
    ethnic, 41; visible, 4, 137, 176, 193;
    white-invisible, 136
minority values, 96
Mission, BC, 28
Mississauga, Ontario, 44, 81, 107
mobility: geographic, 8; inter-gen-
    erational, 47–8; occupational-
    economic, 47
mochi, 66
model minority, 15, 56, 181
Modell, J., 42, 187
Momiji Health Care Society, 194
Montreal, 10, 28, 29, 61, 63, 77, 79,
    108, 116, 136, 137, 152, 153, 156
Moritsugu, F., 35
multiculturalism, 140
Mura, D., 60, 69

Nagata, D.K., 75, 76, 78, 80, 81, 83,
    154, 204
Nagel, J., 103, 104, 107, 127, 202
name calling, 50–1, 63
National Association of Japanese
    Canadians, 35–6, 114, 143, 146, 147,
    150, 151, 152, 156, 178, 192, 204
National Nikkei Heritage Centre, 36
national security, 21, 25
nativism, 193
needs-assessment study of JCs, 181
New Canadian, 24–5, 32
Nikkei, 197
Nisei, 12–13, 25; American, 25; defini-
    tion of, 201; of Montreal, 32; per-
    sonality traits of, 97; of Toronto, 4,
    28, 90, 183–93
Nisei community of Calgary, 118
Nisei club, 74

nominal members, 133, 134, 135, 159,
  175
non-British origin of Canadians in
  Metro Toronto, 185
non-communication: and concealment, 154; and silence, 165
non-members (ex-members), 131–2,
  134, 159, 160, 175; eligible, 175; stereotyped, 132
Novak, M., 91, 135

O'Brien, D.J., 123, 130, 142, 173, 174,
  175, 178
O'Bryan, G., 89
occupation: of Nisei, 47–8; of Sansei,
  45–8
occupational careers: perception of by
  Sansei, 48–9, 54–5
odori, 116
Oikawa, M., 26, 31, 203
Oiwa, K., 29
Omatsu, M., 153, 159, 160, 163, 168
Omura, S., 67, 85
Ontario College of Art, 65
organizational momentum, 179
Oriental group, 93, 109, 139
other-definition of ethnicity, 101,
  102–10, 166, 167
Ottawa, 10, 40, 99
outmarriage, 122, 124; rate of, 127

participatory norms, 143
Pearl Harbor, 21
per cent self-selection of friends, 189
peripheral members, 131–3, 134
Petersen, W., 125, 182
political avoidance, 139, 144, 146
political participation: of Sansei, 15,
  142–5; of Japanese Americans, 143,
  144; of Toronto Nisei, 192
Ponting, J.A., 177

Powell Street Festival, 33, 66, 112
Price Waterhouse, 147
prisoners' camps, 78, 79
Public Archives of Canada, 203
Public Archives of Ontario, 203

Quebec, 11, 39, 46
qualitative, in-depth research, 58

randomness, 12
Raymond, Alberta, 74
reawakening and rethinking, 146
racism, 28, 41, 56, 61, 141–2, 151,
  165, 176; cultural, 193; everyday, 50,
  104; and human rights, 54, 141;
  legacy of, 70; Sansei perception of,
  51; victims of, 84; victimization of,
  165
racist, 96
redress, 9, 10, 14, 15, 34–5; Issei view
  of, 151; Sansei response to, 15
Redress Agreement, 147
Redress Bill HR442 (U.S.), 147
redress movement, 116, 165; American Sansei view and involvement in,
  154, 200; campaign for, 35; Nisei
  attitude and involvement in, 152–3;
  Sansei view and involvement in,
  154–60
Reitz, J.G., 131, 132, 134, 135, 140,
  141, 169, 176, 179
repatriation of JCs, 24, 78
representativeness of sample, 12
restrictions of wartime, 22, 30
Revelstoke, BC, 77
Rexdale, Ontario, 64, 68
Rhodes, C., 187
Richmond, A., 185
Rose, P., 193

St Catharines, Ontario, 10, 106–7

sampling: snowballing method of, 11, 12

sampling group, 12–13, 38, 40

Sansei: American surveyed, 75, 80, 83; definition of, 11, 201

Sansei Club, 42, 68

Scarborough, Ontario, 42, 68

self-definition of ethnicity, 88, 101, 131, 166

self-employment, 46, 186

self-supporting projects, 22

Shamai, S., 41

*shikataganai*, 81

single-ancestry rates, 127, 128, 130; for Asian groups, 204; for white ethnic groups, 204

size of population, 126–7, 130; of Japanese Canadians, 126

Slocan, BC, 79

social distance, 193

social exclusion, 56; of Japanese, 51

social interaction, 131

socialization: ethnic, defined, 60; of Nisei, 71, 130–1, 172–3; of Sansei, 8, 14, 61–75, 88, 112, 165–6

social mobility of Toronto Nisei, 15, 182–8

socio-ethnic status of Sansei, 6

Sowell, T., 142

Statistics Canada, 17, 57

stereotypes, 54, 55, 94, 105, 166

Steveston, BC, 19, 77, 153

stigma, 94

study of economic loss resulting from internment, 147

success, 47, 49, 181

success story of Japanese Americans, 182

Sunahara, A.G., 23, 24, 203

Suzuki, B., 56, 57

Suzuki, D., 134, 176

symbol of ethnicity, 8, 136, 180

symbolic ethnicity, 97, 134, 180

symmetrical relations, 166

Takasaki, E., 106, 107

Tanaka, J., 29

Tang, J., 203

Thacker, C., 88

Thunder Bay, Ontario, 10, 34, 39, 78, 99, 116, 149

Tomaskovic-Devey, B., 127, 130

Tomaskovic-Devey, D., 127, 130

*Tonari-gumi*, 33

Torontonians, 11, 99

Ukrainian Canadians, 126, 204

underemployment of Asian Americans, 57

United Church of Canada Archives, 203

Uno, E., 158

upward mobility: of Asian Americands, 56; occupational, 48; of Toronto Nisei, 185, 187

Vancouver, BC, 10, 17–18, 19, 61, 65, 73, 77, 109, 169, 203

Vancouver Island, 22

Vernon, BC, 109

vertical mosaic, 189

victimization of JCs: legacy of, 61, 83

Vietnamese Canadians, 109, 110

visible-minority groups, 23, 53, 54, 71; assimilation and integration of, 6; of the U.S., 57

voluntarism, 115

voluntary organizations, 113, 190, 191

War Measures Act, 22, 148

Ward, W.P., 20

Watada, T., 82, 179

Waterloo, Ontario, 10
Waters, M., 57, 97, 103, 134, 136
West Coast, 3, 5, 22, 30, 44, 75, 105, 130, 192
white-collar jobs, 47
white ethnics of European ancestry in the U.S., 103
Winnipeg, Manitoba, 10, 39, 42, 84, 152, 204

Wong, M.G., 41
Wright, G.T., 203

yellow peril, 19
Yinger, J.M., 132, 134, 180
Young, E., 20

Ziegler, S., 129